THE LANGUAGE OF POLITICAL LEADERSHIP
IN CONTEMPORARY BRITAIN

Also by John Gaffney

FRANCE AND MODERNISATION (*editor*)
THE FRENCH LEFT AND THE FIFTH REPUBLIC: The
  Discourses of Communism and Socialism in Contemporary France
THE FRENCH PRESIDENTIAL ELECTIONS OF 1988 (*editor*)
INTERPRETATIONS OF VIOLENCE: The Handsworth Riots of 1985
  in the UK
POLITICAL CULTURE IN FRANCE AND WEST GERMANY
  (*editor with E. Kolinsky*)

Also published by Macmillan

The Language of Political Leadership in Contemporary Britain

John Gaffney

Senior Lecturer in Modern Languages
Aston University

St. Martin's Press   New York

DA
589.7
.G34
1991

First published in the United States of America in 1991

Printed in Hong Kong

ISBN 0-312-04638-3

Library of Congress Cataloging-in-Publication Data
Gaffney, John, 1950–
The language of political leadership in contemporary Britain/John Gaffney.
    p.   cm.
Includes bibliographical references.
ISBN 0-312-04638-3
1. Great Britain—Politics and government—1979–   2. English
language—Political aspects—Great Britain—History—20th century.
3. Politicians—Great Britain—Language.   4. Political oratory—
Great Britain.   I. Title.
DA589.7.G34   1991
324.2′2′092241—dc20   90–32848
                                                           CIP

For Deborah

'You don't have to do that to me, my dear – I'm only in politics.'

Margaret Thatcher to a curtseying shop assistant.

Contents

Foreword

The origins of this book lie in my research in French politics. While researching for my book, *The French Left and the Fifth Republic: the Discourses of Communism and Socialism in Contemporary France* (Macmillan, 1989), it became clear to me that the presidentialism of the regime and the media's preoccupation with personalities were insufficient explanations for the strong personalisation of contemporary politics; both the institutions and the media are influential, but the personalisation of politics is a highly complex phenomenon, and is in a subtle relationship with political tradition, and many of the ideas and myths underpinning a society. In the present study, I have analysed four leadership speeches in Britain in order to show how politics is depicted by leaders (and vice versa) in a non-presidential polity where the cult of the heroic individual is not strong, and where, until the 1980s, collective leadership, whether in the Cabinet, in Parliament or in the political parties, was the norm. The party conference is the moment of political life when leaders face their party and the public simultaneously. The leader's conference speech is, therefore, revealing of both the constraints upon and possibilities for the national presentation of personalised political leadership in Britain.

Acknowledgements

I am indebted to the following people for their helpfulness: Micky Gibberd of the Liberal Party, Andy MacSmith of the Labour Party, Robin Nelder of the Conservative Party, and Shirley Wheatley of the Social Democratic Party.

I want also to thank David Bell, Pamela Gaffney, Bruce Graham and Peter Morris for their helpful comments on various chapters, and Wendy Firmin for providing essential video material. I should like to extend thanks to the Department of Modern Languages, Aston University, for its support while I was doing the research for the book, and I shall be forever indebted to Catherine Bate who typed and corrected the manuscript.

John Gaffney

1 Introduction

POLITICAL LEADERSHIP AND BRITISH POLITICAL CULTURE

It is a generally-held belief that politics and politicians are afforded a low measure of public esteem.[1] Opinion polls suggest that a majority of the population take the view that there is too much television airtime devoted to politics, especially at election or party conference times, with party political broadcasts often registering (since they now no longer go out simultaneously on all networks) a change of TV channel. The letter columns of the newspapers frequently contain criticism (and almost never praise) of political leaders, criticism which ranges from the morally indignant in the serious press to the venomous in the tabloids. Even more apparently unpopular than politicians are political parties themselves. In the late 1960s, the unpopularity of Harold Wilson and, to a lesser extent, Ted Heath, was caricatural. In the early 1980s, Michael Foot, as Labour Party leader, bore the brunt of public hostility and, on occasions, ridicule. Margaret Thatcher, one of the most successful leaders in the political history of the United Kingdom, has suffered the label 'the most unpopular British Prime Minister ever'. Mrs Thatcher, however, like Harold Wilson before her, has been variously, and at times simultaneously, not only the least liked of politicians but also the most admired. And it is unquestionable that the political success of British Conservatism in the 1980s owes much to this 'most unpopular Prime Minister', and, arguably, something to that very unpopularity. Moreover, in conjunction with their apparent unpopularity, all British political leaders and many second-rank figures such as Edwina Currie, Ken Livingstone, Norman Tebbit, and Arthur Scargill are nationally very well-known, and the pronouncements and lives (especially private lives) of politicians have often elevated their status and fame to that enjoyed by non-political national media personalities. Many politicians are household names along with pop-singers, soap opera characters, and members of the royal family.

1

We come close here to paradox. Politics is disdained, but politicians, though apparently disliked, are well-known to the public, and their personal and political fortunes followed by large sections of the population. TV impressionists rarely need to preface their portrayal of British politicians with explanations of whom they are impersonating, and the puppets of Central Television's 'Spitting Image' are nationally and instantly recognised. It is the case, moreover, as our above remark concerning Margaret Thatcher suggested, that national politicians have often inspired admiration in public opinion, even affection, and sometimes great allegiance, and this latter not only within their political party but in the wider electorate as well.[2]

There is a further paradox here; in spite of the fact that Britain is often regarded as the cradle of modern political democracy, by the standards of interest in politics and popular political debate in other representative democracies such as Australia, India, France, Italy, Spain, Sweden, the idea of the British as a politically sophisticated nation is not a strong one, a generalised apoliticism, if not political ignorance, being far more readily assumed.

We should note, however, that the exercise of the suffrage is consistently high in Britain, especially at the national level, compared with many other representative democracies, in spite of the perceived pervasive dislike of politics and politicians. We should also note in this context the assumed sanctity of democracy and the democratic process in Britain. It is, in fact, arguable that the quasi-totality of democracy's tenets are held as self-evident truths in British political culture: the desirability of the freedom of the press, the right to organise, free speech, democratic elections, universal suffrage, the separation of powers, an impartial judiciary, an accountable police force, as well as the essential characteristic of Western democracy, namely, party government itself, and the right of, and necessity for, parties to organise, publicise themselves, and compete for power in democratic contests and with legislative programmes elaborated and presented to the electorate.[3] The reality of these 'truths' is debatable, of course; how free is the press, how ideologically conditioned is the electorate's responses to the media, how socially conditioned are British judges, for example? The principles, however, are not disputed. Indeed, in the case of certain of these elements (party government, for example), alternatives have scarcely any currency at all. Given, therefore, an apparent public ignorance of or cynicism towards politics and politicians on the one hand, and an apparently entrenched respect for democracy on the other, political personalities themselves stand in a dual, if not multiple, relationship to the two phenomena. They are mistrusted and disliked, while being capable of inspiring affection, admiration and allegiance; and they operate within a system whose fundamental rectitude is never questioned.

These several paradoxes raise politico-cultural questions of the first importance, and imply that the wide range of attitudes to political personalities within a representative democracy are in a crucial relationship to one another and to the way in which British democracy functions. Before situating the role of political leadership, let us establish what some of the characteristics of such a political culture might be.

There is a series of cultures in British society related to class, to region, locality, to confessional religion, ethnic group, profession, and leisure. Related to these, however, through shared experience, a common language, a national media, the generalised acceptance of a single sovereign parliament and so on, there are also, arguably, shared attitudes and perceptions, and beliefs held in common which create a wider political culture which co-exists with and informs the various sub-cultures. The varying perceptions of national politics cannot be properly understood without taking this common culture into account. We have already mentioned prevailing myths concerning fair play, the rectitude of democracy and so on. We can add to this the idea of a shared view as to how life itself is or should be, and what the relationship of this view to politics is. From these givens we can extrapolate some of the perceptual conditions in relation to which national political leadership itself operates, and explain the paradox of why politics and politicians are disapproved of, even suspected, and yet well-known, often admired and sometimes followed.

We can characterise the perception of life and the relationship of politics to it as a finite area or centre, the edges of which threaten stability and well-being. Irrespective of the shared culture, differing circumstances, histories, life experiences and social milieux will make the centre and the periphery different for different individuals and groups. Nevertheless for most people the centre involves the family, the local community, workplace and leisure, and interpersonal relations, and will include ideas concerning the maintenance or the incremental improvement of the conditions of life in the centre.[4]

In politico-cultural terms we can say that the 'edge' or periphery itself defines the centre to a significant extent, and can have a geographical reality as well as a metaphorical or psychological form. It defines and constrains the centre, however, as a psychological phenomenon involving fear or the sense of threat. Geographically, Northern Ireland has come to play this 'peripheral' role since 1969. This is doubtless the case also for the inhabitants of the province itself, although those held responsible for the threat to individuals, to family or to community stability are often not the same characters as they are on much of the mainland. Another geographical 'edge' in contemporary Britain is represented by inner cities: since 1980, places where stability and community security have broken down.[5] It is worthy of note here how, in both of these cases, evil is readily ascribed to some actors, fortitude to others, and how very strong political passions are involved in the population's reactions in this apparently apolitical society.[6] Other examples of the geographical edge (and we should stress here that the accuracy of perception concerning these sites is of no significance) are Liverpool under Derek Hatton, exclusive London clubs where decisions are made and unjust interests defended in unrepresentative groups of the Tory rich, or the masonic lodges throughout the country where estate agents, magistrates, local businesspeople, police officers and second-hand car dealers conspire to maintain an unjust status quo and impede local judicial and democratic procedures. In terms of the myths of democracy underpinning British culture, it is also worth noting how these several geographical sites all involve a threat to an imagined and cherished democratic process, which, if left to itself, would irrigate and improve the lives of everyone.

The edge can also be social, that is, a threat symbolically

represented by certain peripheral groups who presage chaos, deform the aspirations of communities, or block the proper development of a just, quietist centre: political demonstrators, the Stonehenge hippies, Black rioters, football hooligans, ex-public school cliques, royal hangers-on, are all examples of groups perceived as alien to an imagined or desired centre. We should also note, once again, the passion and dislike such groups engender in large sections of the British public, a public which is itself represented by the media as a unity encompassing the vast majority of the population.[7] We can observe here, however, that the centre and the edge, the heroes and the villains, vary greatly *within* the various sub-cultures. What is significant to our analysis of the way in which political leaders appeal for support is that, however divergent the views of what constitutes the centre, or the edge, however divergent the objects of the desire for stability or improvement, however varied the designation of heroes and villains, and of what should be done to maintain or change a situation, the vast majority of these basic beliefs are shared by most individuals and groups.

The centre is perceived as stable, family and community-orientated, its inhabitants sharing aspirations and lifestyles or desired lifestyles. And though it is 'imagined' and varying, it has a reality as well, or rather is informed by realities. Most people enjoy the same television programmes, and the same kind of holidays, want 'the best' for their children, share a similar range of tastes in music, fashion, and humour, and are tolerant of differences of opinion which do not threaten the centre, and so on. There is also a widely-shared belief that the centre is to a large extent self-regulating: remove impediments to proper expression and allow people to go about their daily lives and all will be for the best in the best of all possible worlds.[8] It is here that politics comes in. However sceptical the majority view of politics, few people believe that politics and government do not have considerable power to maintain, improve or threaten the stability of their situation. And it is from this that many of the attitudes towards politics spring. Politics (local and national) are perceived as necessary in the regulation of or changes to the centre/edge equilibrium. This explains to a certain degree the passion, the usual cynicism, the occasional loathing, and the even rarer admiration and allegiance, generated by politics and politicians in the public's mind. Over and above this, it explains the *moral* aspect of politics, because politics is linked necessarily to notions of sacredness concerning democracy, decency, the conduct of government and so on, and to the safeguarding of the centre from the threats to it. Attitudes to politics involve ethical issues concerning community and individual rights just as much as they do practical issues related to economic efficiency or self-interest.[9] We can say, therefore, that political *personalities* stand in a highly complex, practical, emotional, and moral relation to a psychological topography in the political culture. Paradoxically, an added reason for the focus of attention upon the political personality is that the political parties which they belong to and speak for are often themselves perceived as being 'edge' rather than 'centre' actors, and, like government and the faceless mandarins of Whitehall, extremely powerful ones at that.

Politicians stand in a morally ambiguous relation to the public because they stand in an ambiguous and extraordinary relation to the centre and the edge. They necessarily inhabit a kind of no man's land between the two, because, like witch-doctors, sages, soothsayers, or wise old owls, they are of the community and yet not of it.[10] Over and above this, they possess, like military leaders, power; power to act wisely and valiantly or foolishly and irresponsibly, morally or immorally, power to protect, save or threaten the well-being of a local or national community.

In the context of modern culture, with the inordinate ability of television to focus attention upon individuals, the *character* or perceived character of personalities in these circumstances takes on great significance.[11] And in such circumstances, the perceived personality traits of politicians link up with or else summon up views held in the wider society concerning the character traits necessary to or harmful to leadership. Given the wisdom/power duality, leaders, if they are to be successful, need to convince the public that they draw upon both of these resources, wisdom and power, and that, in their hands, the two are in a proper relationship. The *wrong* combination of that relation creates unpopular archetypes: at one extreme, the bad landlord or boss, or the power-mad or insensitive leader cut off from reality, and at the other, the wise and kind but ineffectual leader incapable of taking necessary decisions.

For leadership to be perceived as successful, the leader must be able to move back and forth across the line between the centre and the periphery while retaining his or her morality, as well as the strength to act for the well-being of the community, and the ability to see the proper and necessary relation between the centre and the edge (this last often involving a 'vision' not possessed by most people). At the level of the perception of national leadership, this raises the question of allegiance to political figures.

Churchill is, or has become, perhaps the most outstanding example of this perceived relationship between wisdom and the power to act; but with more restricted audiences either within political movements or organisations, or local communities or groups, other personalities (for example, Ian Macleod, and Nye Bevan, and, in the present period, Ian Paisley, David Blunkett, Brenda Dean, Arthur Scargill, and the late David Penhaligon) have enjoyed an influence based upon a restricted loyalty and affection, and upon the assumption of an ability to act effectively, an ability which exceeds their official status or position. For local politicians, this popularity and affection can be widespread in a small community. Within organisations themselves many leaders of 'currents of thought' enjoy a popularity, affection and allegiance which goes well beyond their function. In the recent and contemporary period: Tony Benn, Michael Heseltine, David Owen, and Ken Livingstone, have inspired and enjoyed such an affection which combines with an assumption of their political effectiveness and extraordinary abilities. The most successful of these, like Churchill, apparently combine the paradoxical elements described above, that is, a morality which is never overwhelmed by naivety, and an ability to strike, if necessary, brutally, and to do so in a manner unknown to 'ordinary people'.[12] This brings us to the question of how personalities are related both to politics as activity and to politics as organisation.

It is arguable that, in the public's perception, there is little awareness of the technical aspects of politics, such as the canvassing of internal support, Cabinet committees, relations between government and the bureaucracy and so on.[13]

These are relatively obscure phenomena, although they sometimes attract intense interest, as when select committees involve issues of great national interest, or there is a particularly vociferous Prime Minister's Question Time in the House of Commons, or when crises such as strikes or Cabinet conflicts reveal the relative strengths and capacities of personalities within government. All such events, on certain occasions, bring the workings of politics to the national consciousness. Mainly, however, perceptions of politics are restricted to general elections, by-elections, leadership contests, and party conferences, and perceptions of politicians restricted to news interviews, media reporting, and radio and television programmes such as 'Any Questions', 'Panorama', and 'Question Time'.

In terms of our discussion of leadership and its relation to politics, the party conferences offer a very good illustration of the complexities involved. They incorporate internal factional struggles in smoke-filled rooms, ritual demonstrations of political community and celebration, and the presentation of wider visions of an ideal national community, and, of course, extensive media coverage. In such a paradoxical situation, political leaders must demonstrate that they dominate each of these three worlds (the back-room negotiations, the public celebrations, the media reporting), while offering a wider vision and appeal to the national community.[14]

Political leaders, moreover, enjoy a dual relationship to political organisation itself: first, in terms of the leader's power within the organisation; second, in terms of the party members' perception of the leader's relation to the 'outside' (the public and the media). We shall deal with the significance of this dual phenomenon in the body of our analysis but can make two preliminary points here. The first is that media exposure of (and media 'attacks' upon) leaders and second-rank leaders can enhance significantly the internal support and loyalty offered to them by an organisation or section of organisation.[15] The second is that the public perception of both leadership and organisation at party conference time is very intense, and the relation of leaders to their organisations is seen starkly. The relation is thrown into higher relief given that, as we have said, political parties, often because their internal functioning is little understood (or only too well understood), are themselves seen as part of the 'periphery' inhabited by zealots.[16] All Labour leaders, because of the publicly-displayed dependence of leadership upon organisation on the one hand, and, paradoxically, the procedural democracy of conference on the other, are potential victims of this hostile perception. In such circumstances, leaders can often be suspected of either being the tools of darker forces, manipulated puppets whose strings are pulled by undemocratic powers too afraid or too wily to come out into the open, or else of being simply incapable of asserting their leadership upon a strong party organisation.[17]

The irony here is that the more public are the internal workings of an organisation, the more leadership dependence upon organisation can be witnessed and derided by outsiders. A converse irony is that organisations perceived as disorganised or unsophisticated, or in no relation at all to darker forces (the Liberal Party at times, for example, or any party in a period of organisational flux, doctrinal reorientation, or leadership struggle), can be mocked for their lack of institutional coherence or political seriousness given their claims to the leadership and government of the nation. Leaders who are perceived as being too far away from their organisation's wishes (Thatcher in 1986, Owen in 1987, Steel in 1988) can equally arouse suspicion and disapproval, and can create the potentially dramatic situation of a party's popularity overtaking that of its leader.[18] Political leadership, therefore, is in a series of complex relationships both to party and to 'opinion'. And, in the final analysis, leaders are utterly dependent upon their organisations; and those leaders, or potential leaders (Enoch Powell, George Brown, and David Owen are cases in point), who attempt to use extra-organisational opinion exclusively to coerce party opinion, rarely succeed, in British politics at least.[19] However, the use of 'opinion' as a political resource within organisation is a major phenomenon of underestimated value,[20] and in the contemporary period it is arguable that, notwithstanding the greater political sophistication of party members and activists, they, too, are affected by and respond to precisely the same dispositions and prejudices concerning the centre, edge, community, aspirations, and models of leadership which exist within the population as a whole. And of course all political organisations are extremely sensitive to the opinion poll ratings of their parties and leaders.

In terms of leadership 'types' there is a whole series of possibilities, though we should remember, given what we said earlier concerning the ambivalence or polyvalence of public perceptions of leadership, that most leaders incarnate composits of types. The strongest is the visionary, the person who sees, before others, how to maintain and protect and enhance the centre. Other types we could mention are the workhorses, the incorruptibles, the deliverers of the goods, the affable, the listeners, the entertainers, the sexy, the organisers, the compromisers, the fixers, the rogues who have become great leaders,[21] the reconcilers and so on. The important point here is that because of the very real influence of 'opinion' upon party, these qualities or types of leadership are relatively autonomous from party. They are not free of it, nor totally dependent on it, and they trigger responses both in the party and in the electorate, and between these two. If we call this political phenomenon or resource 'personalism' (a leadership focus which has effects upon attitudes, orientation, motivation, mobilisation and thereby upon organisational and ultimately (potential) political power), we can see that personalism has, in fact, *always* affected *all* political organisations and wider constituencies, irrespective of both the doctrinal underpinnings and organisational frameworks of organisations on the one hand, and the contemporary media treatment of 'personality politics' on the other.

Democratic theory has always been characterised, and especially since the European experience of Nazism, by what we might call an impersonalism: in a true democracy no single person is indispensable. In practice, however, individuals have always figured significantly both within organisations and in terms of their relation to the outside world. We should also stress here that demagoguery or 'charisma' are not indispensable characteristics of such leadership focus; Clement Attlee – who is now entering into the pantheon of great leaders and whose quietism was the hallmark of his leadership – being a case in point. This being the case, we should underline the point that personalism is not simply a creation of the media, but that the media has highlighted and amplified this aspect of political life and probably had a qualitative effect upon it in terms of how leaders or personalities are perceived both by their restricted following and by the electorate. Similarly, while the media does not 'create' political figures, as we have argued – the quasi-totality of them originating of necessity as leaders of a certain status and in possession of a certain power base within organisation itself – it can enable certain individuals to become national figures and thereby influence further their own political organisations and the political process generally. David Owen, Bryan Gould, Paddy Ashdown, Edwina Currie are examples of personalities who, partly through the media, have gone on to be perceived by their own organisations as one of the essential links between itself and the wider electorate.

In the light of the above, let us offer two hypotheses which we shall then examine by looking at a specific moment in recent British political life.

1. Political personalism is a complex and influential phenomenon in British political life which affects both the electorate and party organisation but which, possibly because of the near-taboo placed on the discussion of leadership because of the European experience of Fascism in the twentieth century, has been little considered outside analyses of totalitarianism on the one hand or 'personality politics' on the other, which associates the projection of political leadership with the selling of soap powder.[22]

2. The most appropriate way of understanding the relationship of political leadership to, first, organisation and, second, the electorate is through an analysis of the public discourse of political leadership because it is here that leadership is exposed simultaneously to both.[23]

In order to test these hypotheses, we shall examine the language of leadership on the highly publicised political occasion of the party conference. This occasion contains many of the elements germane to British political life: the public projection of party image, party business, the role of leadership, the scrutiny of the media, internal debates, press conferences and interviews, appeals to the electorate, reference to the myths underpinning British society and culture, appeals to party ideologies and to ideas and beliefs held by the wider national constituency, the presentation of policies and, of course, the reliance upon ritual and upon language. And unlike election campaigns themselves where everything is subordinated to 'winning', the party conferences demonstrate the complexity of the relations between the constituent elements of this organised political activity. In the years 1983–92 moreover (the latter the scheduled date of the next general election), the year 1986 reveals the subtlety of the relationships in the triad leadership/party/electorate. 1986 saw the parties poised for a national electoral contest. The conference season of that year involved them, therefore, within the context of the major organisational moment of party life, in a drive to 'sell' their image, ideology and leadership to the wider electorate. By the mid-1980s, it was also the case that all the parties, most of whom were opposed in principle to the idea of exalted leadership, had recognised personalised leadership as being one of the dominant, if not the dominant, factors in British political life. From the methodological point of view, the analysis of the language of political leadership in contemporary Britain in the context of the main organisational and doctrinal moment of party life is apposite for many reasons. Let us schematise the main ones here.

1. The party conference season offers a range of discourses and events (the conferences themselves, fringe meetings, topics and personalities singled out and given prominence by the media), all of which take place within the same overall political environment. Leadership discourse must take this profusion of activity, the sentiment it generates, and the media coverage it receives, into account. The discourses of leaders, therefore, offer the basis for comparative analysis, in terms of one another, in terms of their reception by the wider electorate and the media, and in terms of their relation to organisation.

2. As we have said, the party conferences are the site of the simultaneous presentation of the leaders' relation to organisation on the one hand and to the electorate on the other. Leadership, therefore, as both a discursive representation of the party to itself and to the wider public, and as the

personification of organisation and of ideology, takes place within this general context.

3. The conference is the highest point of cyclical party activity outside elections. It is worth noting here, moreover, the great status attached to attendance at conference by all parties (as demonstrated, in part, by the difficult process of gaining entry to some of them, and by the gravitas displayed by many conference delegates, irrespective of the presence of the television cameras). This means that the significance of leadership will itself be enhanced by the strong ritual significance which accompanies the conference.

4. Conferences offer good illustrations of policy presentation or policy-in-the-making, and, therefore, of the relationship of these to leadership. And in the pre-election year, many conference speeches, especially the leadership speech, contain significant electoral policy pledges to the wider public.

5. Conferences offer insights into party ideology at the moment when its readjustments to external pressures from opponents and potential supporters, its need to resolve internal conflict, and its need to express a sense of community are at their most obvious and calculated, and of course they throw into relief the relationship of party ideology to leadership. Given the public nature of the conference occasion, and all we have said regarding the requirement for leadership to respond to both its relation to and its freedom from organisation, this intra- and extra-organisational relationship makes of the leadership speech a crucial test of the leaders' competence.

6. In a certain sense, conferences witness not only the ritual celebration of political commitment, but also political activity or politics itself. This of course is enhanced, or aggravated, by the presence of the media. Conference is not only the place where politics takes place symbolically, as necessary celebration, ritual renewal and so on, but is often the site of political change itself. For example, many political initiatives of the subsequent 1987 Conservative government were first made public at the 1986 conference. In the case of the 1985 Labour Party conference, it was here, in public, and not in smoke-filled rooms or at branch meetings, that the Militant Tendency was definitively broken, and broken by the

leader's speech. In the case of the Liberals, in 1986 their potential governmental credibility on defence was shattered by the defence vote at their conference because it was opposed to an Alliance policy which was supported by the Liberal leader; it was not defence as an issue (most opinion polls suggest that unemployment and the social services are much more important factors in voting attitudes) but the notion of a break between organisation and leadership which was crucial to the undermining of the leader's position. In the case of the 1988 Liberal and SDP special conferences on the merger issue, the potential effectiveness of a third major force in British politics was founded (and foundered) partly on the media treatment of these events, and especially upon the media's treatment of political leadership.

7. Although party conferences affect leadership in a positive sense, allowing it and the party to publicise their apparent relationship to one another, they are also, because of the dual publicising and functioning of both leadership and organisation, fraught with danger, for, as we have seen, they are not only 'internal' events but also closely observed national events (through television especially), and are scrutinised by oppositions and by journalists who enjoy asking the questions that party activists do not dare to ask for fear of a public display of disunity.[24] Although party conferences are highly controlled and ritualised occasions, they still offer unpredictability and (usually through the power of individual rhetoric) can become sites of major challenges to leadership. The highly stage-managed quality of the 1986 Labour Party conference was an example of leadership recognition of this unpredictability (and attempts by the Labour leadership to 'control' conference through the conference organising committee are further evidence of this); the debate over unilateralism at the 1986 Liberal Party conference, an example of this unpredictability realised. Leadership, moreover, can be *publicly* humiliated or diminished, or even contested directly, although this is rare, and normally only the province of the Labour Party. Because of the procedural democracy of the Labour Party, Neil Kinnock's leadership can be affected, and has often been so, essentially through the defeat of conference motions with which he is strongly associated, or else by direct attacks upon

his leadership, as in the case of the 1988 conference. Conversely, in the case of the SDP, the defeat of several leadership-backed motions between 1981 and 1986 enhanced the status of David Owen by publicly demonstrating that his leadership was not, contrary to received opinion, authoritarian.

8. Given the general mythology surrounding leadership and the attention of the media, conferences allow rival leaders, or potentially rival leaders in certain circumstances, the opportunity to claim moral superiority over the established leadership. Simon Hughes' morally-charged speech on disarmament at the 1986 Liberal Party conference is a good individual example; any of Tony Benn's speeches at Labour conferences quintessential illustrations of the rhetorical undermining of incumbent leaders.

9. Party conferences, originally the sites of the expression of party identity and organisation to itself, have become, as we have said, in large part, public party occasions. Both leaders and those who attempt to contest, downgrade, upgrade, or defend them are very aware of this. The tension between these two rationales (the internal and the external) is now the party conference's dominant feature, and is at its most critical in the leadership speech.

10. On the question of the symbolic status of leadership, leaders themselves have to respond, in different ways, especially through developments in their rhetoric, to the *expectation* of leadership status. For Neil Kinnock, for example, because of the highly ambiguous and ambivalent attitude within the left towards heightened leadership status itself, a very particular rhetoric must be developed which, while avoiding self-aggrandisement and the insulting of significant groups within the Labour movement, must, nevertheless, inspire. The Conservatives too, however, in spite of their more unequivocal affection for 'strong' leaders, present leadership with considerable constraints, given the high premium placed upon it. In 1986, for example, Margaret Thatcher had to guard against or respond to several potential threats: the brutality of the pragmatic readiness of the Conservative Party to dispense with leaders who come to be perceived as an electoral liability; the uncertainty at that time surrounding her own popularity as a national leader; the

need to dominate a conference and a party with a rightist radical leadership, a strong centrist following, and a weaker, even more radical-right following (which is, however, far less embedded in British political culture, and which is, therefore, less threatening); and the expectation generated by the image of 'Maggie', or the 'Iron Lady', beloved of the tabloids. The more equivocal attitudes of the Liberals and the SDP to both the entrenched organisational procedures of the Labour Party and the more unfettered leadership of the Conservatives create their own particular set of constraints, as we shall see.

11. In the context of our earlier discussion, leaders must show that they are not threatened by the stridency of some of their more hotheaded companions, whose own major rhetorical opportunity is provided by the conference, while themselves maintaining the intensity of moral rhetoric expected at the party conference.[25]

These points raise the question of the cultural relation of political leadership to the political party and to the electorate, and to moral self-depiction in the context of its claim to pragmatic competence. In a word, leadership discourse must both express and direct the party in relation to the wider electorate; the projected image of leadership must demonstrate to the party that it can lead the way to national victory; it must also demonstrate to the electorate that it can lead the nation (thus simultaneously controlling and enhancing the party's pretensions to government).

The leadership speech at the party conference is but one moment of a long discursive process which we cannot pretend to recapture in the present study. It is, however, its most important moment. It is usually, though not invariably, the culminating point of the conference; significantly, in terms of the according of overt leadership status, the Labour leader's speech is the only one 'surrounded' by the conference, rather than symbolically presented as its culminating point. We should remember also the physical presence of all the leaders at the conferences (and also the significant absences suggesting disapproval, indifference, or a leader otherwise engaged 'doing more important things'), the perpetual references to the leadership by other speakers, and, of course, the inordinate focusing of the media upon leadership (in terms of both the interviewing of the leader during the conference period, and the relating of all issues to the status of the leader, both of which lend to leadership a significance which enhances, or undermines, the effective status of the leadership speech in the conference).

This brings us on to perhaps the most obvious, and therefore most under-researched, but, in ways we shall show, most crucial aspect of the leadership/party/electorate relation: the nature of the relationship of leadership to party in terms of the presentation of the two in combination as a 'rally of the people' in microcosm. Journalists address many issues, and interviewers attempt to expose many papered-over cracks. What is rarely addressed, however, by observers and journalists, or by leaders themselves, or even by party members critical of leadership, is the nature – the true nature if we can put it like that – of the relationship of leadership to party itself given, on the one hand, leadership's personalised presentation of the party to the electorate in terms of leadership response to prevailing myths and beliefs in the wider culture and, on the other, its personalised ideological presentation of the party to itself.

In the light of our discussion, and in these two contexts of the parties' and the media-vehicled electorate's relation to leadership, we can make here a series of points informing each of the four speeches to be examined, before going on to analyse the speeches themselves and their contexts.

In the case of the Labour Party, Neil Kinnock's speech will be shaped by the strong doctrinal anti-personalist tradition within leftism, and by the left's general opposition to Thatcherism as a personality cult. These two constraints will greatly increase the need for leadership to draw upon other forms of rhetoric from within leftism itself. David Owen's speech will be significantly informed by the need to present the Social Democratic Party publicly, in spite of the partially tacit, partially overt, personality cult around him himself, as being in possession of an ideology which, though remaining in some way related to him, goes beyond whatever he might be saying at any particular time. David Steel's style will be influenced by the exigency of presenting his party (or, in the absence of agreement between himself and his party, himself and some form of Liberalism) as governmental in essence.

Margaret Thatcher's style will be informed by the ambivalence surrounding the continuing political viability of her strong political persona and by the apparent unpopularity (in 1986) of dyed-in-the-wool Thatcherism and, therefore, by the need to modify this view, to repel the 'two nations' thesis attributed to her, and to do this without destroying the strong leadership persona itself.

All four leadership discourses must also deploy, normally without overt declaration (though in the 1986 context we have two interesting and extremely unusual examples of leadership discourse which must also *personally* either supply (David Owen) or else refute (David Steel) an ideology), the idea of the original (supra-party) legitimacy of leadership which: appropriates, expresses, and transcends the party's ideology; goes beyond the functional role and delegated legitimacy of party leadership status; and offers an image of national leadership to an electorate which did not elect it (this is, of course, less of an issue for Margaret Thatcher as Prime Minister, the only one in the four in 1986 to have held such office (irrespective of the fact that Britain enjoys a non-presidential system which does not directly elect the leader of the country)). The problem for the Labour Party here is not as great as it might at first seem – given its doctrinal tradition of non-personalist democracy – because a leftist leader can draw upon a tradition of leftism which has within it a whole series of myths, a millenarianism, and a romanticism, all of which aid such a leader rhetorically, perhaps even more than a rightist one, on condition that he or she *personifies* leftism. For the Alliance leaders, this problem is more difficult: first, because of the 'short' tradition of the Social Democratic Party and the 'thin' tradition of contemporary Liberalism; second, because of the problems posed by the leadership position of the Alliance itself – two leaders instead of one; third, because the Alliance must employ a rhetoric which is the opposite of that of the two 'demagogic' parties; and fourth (in the case of the Liberals), because David Steel was catapulted into this situation by the wider context of the developing personalism of the 1980s, not least the developing personalised image of the leadership of the SDP partner to the Alliance.

We shall see in the individual analyses how the several claims to an original personal legitimacy are exploited. We can stress here once again, however, that the rhetoric of leadership has little to do with the oratory of certain European leaders of the 1930s. The rhetoric of leadership – partly as a result of the continuing collective memory and lessons of Fascism – is far more subtle, is related to the specific myths and orientation of British political culture which we discussed above, and operates under many new informing factors and constraints than when employed by leaders in the past (not least the 'small screen' exigency, irrespective of the size of the conference-hall audience).[26] One of those constraints worth mentioning here is that it is imperative, given the doctrinal traditions of the political parties – and this is equally true of British Conservatism under Margaret Thatcher –, that the non-personal or the impersonal be brought into leadership rhetoric in a significant way; all political leaders must present themselves as representatives both of the shared political culture which we discussed above, and of the political traditions which they are articulating, however personally inspired the 'vision' they might portray. The creation in leadership discourse of a particular relationship between a leader and a wider legitimating source is necessary for several reasons: first, in order that leaders protect themselves from both their doctrinally-informed party activists and the media (who will expose both 'empty rhetoric' and unbridled personalism to the full); second, in order to offer the notion of a programme of government, which, if personalism is to be accepted by the party, must come *from* the leader but be *part of* the party; third, in order to mitigate the effects of a 'charisma' which would suggest an unfettered leadership, that is to say, a party, a polity, and, by extension, a country, which could not function without one single leader (the antithesis of democracy); and fourth, and more prosaically, in order to 'offer the goods' to an electorate often considered as voting with its wallet (although one should not underestimate the *mythical* quality of a political programme which presents itself as offering the public a consumerist promised land).

It is difficult to integrate references to practical or technical subjects into rhetoric without appearing prosaic, and yet leaders must be seen to do so in order to demonstrate that they understand the day-to-day world, while envisaging the ideal future. At the same time they must show that their vision is not distorted by the mundane and the practical, and that they are not dominated by Whitehall or other experts. There are standard devices for coping with this problem: thus, a practical measure (say, the privatisation of the gas industry) is presented as part of a wider scheme; conversely, an ideal society (say, a belief in a just society, or in pacifism, or the overthrow of tyranny) is depicted as a logical, practical measure. The need to balance these competing demands arises, in part, from the nature of the party conference itself, as both an occasion for communion and an occasion for setting a programme of policies. Hence, the peculiar characteristic of British political leadership; one of its most intense expressions occurs within the high point of the organisational cycle, and cannot be dissociated from it.[27]

Leadership discourse, therefore, must satisfy many, often contradictory, requirements: it must be different from party, part of party, reflecting of the party while transcending it, persuasive at two levels of allegiance (party and electorate), respectful of party procedure while elevating party to a non- or trans-organisational status. Leadership must also offer to the electorate (but also to the party and on its own doctrinal and mythical terms) the notion of individualised national leadership, must recommend the party to the wider electorate and be seen as having done so, must 'interpret' tradition to the moral satisfaction of the party and to the practical and moral satisfaction of the electorate, and must present itself as inspired by the party and by and for the people. Further, it must impose leadership persona itself as transcendent of organisational constraints, as individual, as attractive (even irresistible), while remaining the personal expression of a particular interpretation of society at a given moment of the party's history. And, of course, it must present itself, and the party from which it springs, as being in a perfect relationship to the exigencies of the political culture or cultures of which it is a part.

Let us look then, by analysing the leadership speeches of David Owen, David Steel, Neil Kinnock and Margaret Thatcher,[28] at how four British political leaders have coped with these multiple constraints and enhanced their leadership status within organisation in their attempts to project themselves towards a wider source of allegiance.

2 David Owen and Social Democracy

THE CONTEXT

In the first six years of its existence, the SDP perceived itself and was often perceived by outsiders (and new supporters) as being an 'anti-party party' (an expression used by Roy Jenkins at the 1986 conference). Before analysing David Owen's speech, I wish to discuss what lies behind this notion, what the claim to be an anti-party party signifies, and what significance such a claim has for leadership discourse.

The SDP was created in March 1981 by four senior Labour Party politicians who came to be known as the 'gang of four': Roy Jenkins, Shirley Williams, David Owen and Bill Rodgers.[1] The *raison d'être* of the Social Democratic Party was based upon opposition not only to the Labour Party's policies on Europe and defence, but also to its existence as a cumbersome machine which had in some way become dissociated both from 'real life' and from Labour's political mission. And it was the accusation that the Labour Party was an 'old' party as much as its leftward radicalisation which offered the gang of four their justification for forming a dynamic new party. From its creation, the Social Democratic Party attracted to its ranks, not only ex-Labour Party members and others who had been actively involved in politics, but, more importantly, non-party people, people who in many cases had previously been uninterested in organised politics, or else dissuaded from political activity by their view of established politics.

This combination of intention on the part of its creators and inexperience on the part of its membership meant that the Social Democratic Party was anti-party in the sense of being almost anti-politics. This has major implications for the party's stylistic presentation of itself in discourse. It would mean that the party should be seen as 'straight-talking', as the antithesis of the tradition of politicking and of secret back-room negotiations. While representing 'corridor politics' as a

21

dishonest, rather than as, say, a necessary element in the political process, the Social Democratic Party had to present itself as operating in a different mode, one which transcended that of its adversaries. This meant that Social Democratic rhetoric possessed the potential for a discourse which was transcendent of political organisation itself. However, it was the case that the established parties also presented themselves as transcendent of themselves through the use of high rhetoric, especially in their leadership discourse. SDP discourse, and particularly its leadership discourse, had, therefore, to be anti-party in this sense also, that is to say, as disdainful of high rhetoric as it was of backroom political discourse.

The Social Democratic Party portrayed itself from its inception as a party of ordinary (educated) Britons who rejected both (high and low) manifestations of political discourse. This, however, creates a fundamental problem for leadership discourse in terms of its establishing an ideology-through-discourse which was itself necessary if the wider electorate was to identify the party over a period of time. This, as we shall see, was its main endeavour in the mid-1980s (1985–88). We can say, therefore, that its attempt to establish a recognised ideology and discourse had as one of its formative conditions the rejection of established political ideology and discourse. One of the ways of counteracting the potentially stultifying effect of the Social Democratic Party's self-confessed rejection of the old ideologies and their accompanying rhetoric was to exploit the notion of glamour, newness and contemporaneity, as well as the physical, arguably sexual, attraction of its leader, David Owen. Such an undertaking, however, has a fragile quality which links the party's fortunes to a significant and precarious degree with the media's treatment of it and its leader.

In these circumstances of the need to reflect the image of a new, almost anti-political, movement, and, perhaps paradoxically, of a potentially governmental team (containing, of course, a potential Prime Minister), leadership discourse becomes crucial to the idea both of a new 'ideology' and of an alternative form of political leadership. Let us examine briefly three factors which frame SDP leadership discourse, before examining the immediate context of the speech, namely, the conference itself: the status of the audience of Social Democratic Party discourse; the Social Democratic Party as part of an alliance with another political party; and the problems surrounding the presentation of Social Democratic Party leadership itself.

1. The audience

The question of how Social Democratic Party leadership treats its actual (conference) and ideal (wider) audiences is important, given that, in the first case, activism must be maintained and, in the second, sympathy and allegiance generated. The Social Democratic Party audience, both real and imagined, is a 'reasonable' one. It is true that certain key issues (South Africa in the 1986 context), as well as areas of cultural and moral concern such as the arts and 'Sport for all', which are given great emphasis by the SDP, can be treated with a high moral rhetoric, but, essentially, a Social Democratic Party audience has to be presented as reasonable and, therefore, unemotional. This means that outside certain issues – and the moral dimension of the South African question was indeed taken up by all the other parties – the range within the rhetorical register of Social Democratic Party leadership discourse is severely limited by the need to present Social Democracy as rational, reflective and mature.

This exigency would have been less problematic if the 'mould-breaking' of British politics desired by the SDP had taken place at the 1983 election, that is to say, if there had been a national electoral response to a quietist rhetoric. This, however, did not happen except at certain sensational by-elections between 1981 and 1987, and the SDP itself became, because it had to sustain itself and survive like all political parties over time, 'a political party', but one endowed with an essentially reasonable rhetorical style.

2. The Alliance

A second defining and constraining characteristic of Social Democratic Party leadership discourse (which is not present in the two main parties) is that the Social Democratic Party leader needed to present himself as prime ministerial without usurping such a role from the other Alliance leader, and, therefore, without presenting Social Democracy as the sole source of doctrinal authenticity. The association with the Liberals offered other constraints too. First, it meant that older parties could not be derided to the point where the Liberals (older than the Labour Party and – arguably – the Conservative Party) became the inadvertent target; stemming from this the notion of political tradition itself could not be attacked by the SDP. This created a significant rhetorical handicap in that the SDP's major claim to legitimacy, its newness, could not be exploited to the full.

The association with the Liberals does not, however, simply impinge upon Social Democratic Party discourse; it shapes it significantly. The Alliance as a political ideal transcended the Social Democratic Party just as the Social Democratic Party transcended the established political parties. This will involve leadership discourse in emphasising the similarities and differences between the two undertakings (the SDP and the Alliance) without ever being able to address each properly (in the first case for fear of making the Social Democratic Party seem redundant, in the second, for that of making the Alliance seem false). After the 1987 general election the perceived need for the merger of the two parties was defined partly by the fact that the discourse of the two parties (and the question of the national representation of leadership) could not be developed while the Alliance lasted: a party cannot define itself as transcendental (that is, as an ideal community) if it is only a part of something else. Such reconciliation was effected, in part, by silence or dissimulation – one of the essential characteristics of established political parties. In this way, the existence of the Alliance forced the SDP to adopt certain of the party characteristics it had hoped to challenge.

3. Leadership

The third defining characteristic of SDP leadership discourse was that the party was created from above. It is true that it represented itself as responding to a groundswell 'call'. Nevertheless the leadership was still symbolically set apart from its base, its legitimation predating the party and calling it into existence and organised expression. The mythical status of David Owen's leadership was modified somewhat by the intial leadership of another leader (Roy Jenkins, 1980–83), but Owen's persona was based – until merger became critical in 1987 – upon an implicit claim to his 'natural' leadership. And in the absence of a high-profile ideology and perceived set of policies (although the latter had been developed since 1981 and were impressively presented in 1986) it was leadership discourse which to a great extent supplied the party with its self-identity after 1983. Irrespective of the actual ideological and policy input of activists, the Social Democratic Party, therefore, because of the discursive incoherence of a young party, had to be presented nationally as *his* (Owen's) party. Paradoxically, David Owen's projection of himself in discourse is, in fact, constrained by this reality rather than enhanced by it, as we shall see below.

This practical necessity for firm guidance from the top confers a particular status upon Social Democratic Party leadership, and we can apprehend both of these elements – guidance and enhanced leadership status – in the leader's discourse. The exceptional status of leadership is thrown into high relief at a conference, given that many activists, although articulate, had little public (discursive) experience. To a certain extent this idea of unusedness to public speaking was necessary to Social Democratic Party rhetoric and self-projection, and – paradoxically – many conference speakers exploited this rhetorically. It is also the case that the experience that existed (essentially ex-Labour Party) had to be mitigated in order to ensure that the Social Democratic Party did not resemble discursively a Labour Party MK II. As regards 'guidance', this almost deliberate vacating of discursive expertise and prescription by most speakers enhances leadership persona still further.

Leadership status, therefore, was privileged because the SDP had to present itself as inexperienced, whether or not this reflected reality. One of the main rhetorical effects of this upon leadership discourse is that it accentuates what we might call the rhetoric of certainty, that is, a leadership style which distinguishes itself from a necessarily uncertain membership (and which, in fact, found itself in very uncertain political circumstances). This element of certainty will be complemented and strengthened by the need to present SDP leadership as a counter to bad leadership. The need to represent actual leadership as better than other leadership is present in all political parties. In the SDP, however, this imperative is increased because the SDP (and its leadership) must be justified as a party *called into existence* as a response to bad leadership.

The need to enhance leadership status is increased by the obvious need to present David Owen as a potential Prime Minister. This places him in a very privileged position *vis-à-vis* the party (a position shared, in part, by the others in the gang of four, but whose national status, in fact, increased only as that of the leader increased). The origin of this status, which allowed him, and them, to form the party, was based not upon his previous membership of and status within the Labour Party, nor even upon his exercise of parliamentary membership, but upon significant experience of government, something which distinguished him and the other creators of the party from *all* other SDP members. And, in the case of David Owen, his position as ex-Foreign Secretary, which allowed him to suggest his global vision of reality, enhanced his standing still further. (Roy Jenkins was remembered as Chancellor and as EEC President, and, although the former post had greater status than that of Foreign Secretary within the governmental hierarchy, it did not equal Owen's claim to visionary leadership. This was still more true of Shirley Williams (previously Education Secretary) and Bill Rodgers (previously Transport Minister), both of whom deliberately diminished their own significance *vis-à-vis* David Owen (even though Williams had once been tipped as Britain's first woman Prime Minister).) As we shall see, the governmental and international status enjoyed by David Owen is exploited in his discourse, distinguishing him still more from the mass of the party. A further feature which set David Owen apart from his only two possible rivals, Roy Jenkins and Shirley Williams, was his apparent youth. The exploitation of youth (informed by similar phenomena in other countries, cf. Felipe Gonzalez, Gary Hart, Pierre

Trudeau, and all dating back to and evoking J. F. Kennedy) was an essential symbolic strategy of the Social Democratic Party, and distinguished it from the two main parties (although 1983 also saw the replacement of Michael Foot by Neil Kinnock).

We can add to this the fact that, apart from the other members of the gang of four, the other Social Democratic MPs, and one or two other party officers such as Polly Toynbee, the journalist, and Sue Slipman, Director of the Council for One-Parent Families, David Owen was the only nationally known figure, even to many Social Democratic Party members themselves. This would increase the idea of Owen's discourse as being the undisputed univocal voice of the party.

Another factor influencing David Owen's leadership discourse, and this is now a feature of all party conferences, given that all parties have internal conflicts, is that of the leader having to be seen to carry the conference, either effortlessly or because of 'strength' (although some leadership-backed motions were defeated, thus indicating the 'democratic' aspect of the party). In the case of the Social Democratic Party, with its reasonableness as a doctrinal prerequisite and its desire to prevent its democratic practice from becoming a process which necessarily involves conflict (as it does in the Labour Party), leadership status will be enhanced by a style of delivery which suggests a quiet, assured, self-confidence.

The significance of leadership, therefore, given the organisational and doctrinal circumstances of the Social Democratic Party, will be enormous. Leadership discourse will need to provide an image of natural leadership, as well as activist reassurance, guidance, a synthesis of intra-party differences, party difference, governmental status, the youthfulness (of both leader and party), a media personality, and the notion of an original justification for the SDP, that is to say, an ideology or vision of the world (as a prerequisite to changing the world). This focus upon leadership also means that the Social Democratic Party will be highly dependent upon the idea of leadership as an expression of Social Democracy itself. The leadership speech, therefore, is a potentially critical moment of the party's cyclical activity. A 'wrong' leadership speech or a contested one, therefore, could have an inordinately damaging effect upon the status of the leader and of the party as a non-conflictual political movement. In these circumstances, the need for Social Democratic Party members to echo the leadership will be increased, thus constraining further the development of a contestatory voice within the party. The ideology of the party, therefore, will be contained in the speech, not only because the leader's discourse reflects party discourse, but also because it shapes, to a significant extent constitutes, party identity.

Before examining the speech itself, therefore, let us look briefly at how the conference frames and encourages leadership status and its relation to organisation and ideology.

The 'ideological' requirement of the SDP conference was partially fulfilled by the series of impressive policy documents, many of them independently costed, and by the central *Partnership for Progress* document which was the printed evidence of Social Democracy's claim to government: policy, ideology, and serious-mindedness. This 'party' legitimacy was stated, in particular, by Shirley Williams on the Tuesday of the conference, when she identified the difference between the SDP and the Labour Party as being that of a difference between a party which had policies and one which had none (an earlier criticism of the SDP being that it had no policies and that it was unclear what it stood for). The overall effect of this, as far as leadership is concerned, is that SDP leadership is able to present itself as leading a movement sophisticated enough to organise a series of governmental policies. David Owen is not just, therefore, a 'leader' but a leader of 'something'. This *relationship* to party will in fact increase his credibility as a national leader.

Throughout the conference, there were numerous references by speakers to David Owen, many of which picked up humorously the media representation of his arrogance or its portrayal of the Social Democratic Party as 'his' party; conference facilitates the demonstration of the idea that such dependence upon leadership is exaggerated. Paradoxically, in the SDP context, such displays only increase the suggestion that leadership pre-eminence is organisationally acceptable. The conference discussions are quintessentially the voicing of a party as community, rather than as a leadership-dependent party. This 'freedom' and maturity of the party enhances the status of a leader who is depicted as enabling such a young party to flourish as a mature organisation while remaining a leader of extraordinary status. Bearing in mind the fact that David Owen's speech takes place in relation to this 'independent' rendering of party voices over the previous days of the conference, when every aspect of (potentially) governmental activity was dealt with, let us now examine the speech itself.

THE TEXT

David Owen's measured, self-confident, by turns serious and ironic, apparently somewhat arrogant manner of speaking (both during the 1983–87 period when he was the unquestioned leader of the party and after) is the opposite of what we might call the 'high' rhetoric of traditional political discourse. David Owen is, in fact, the least rhetorical (in the dramatic sense of the word) of the four leaders we are studying. This restrained, assured manner conveyed the impression, reflected in opinion polls, that David Owen was the most 'ministerial', if not 'prime ministerial', of the three opposition leaders. It is clear that he consciously chose such a style, advocating a controlled, undramatic form of political exchange, and it is this style, in conjunction with his unquestioned leadership of the party, which informs the manner in which Owen's political persona is discursively conveyed. This has certain implications concerning the projection of the SDP itself. Theoretically, a 'mature' party in a representative democracy is one which needs no single leader (except at moments of acute national crisis). This tension between a particular treatment of leadership (underpinned by the media treatment of David Owen) and the need to project the party in a certain way will be reflected in the leadership speech itself, which we shall analyse below. We can say here that the tension involves a relationship between the 'personalised' projection of the SDP (the party as the organisational expression of David Owen's personal vision) and an 'impersonalised' one (the party as the organisational expression of a wider ideology or social vision, shared by many but *conveyed by the leader*). This tension was to declare itself overtly in 1987 when David Owen resigned from the leadership in a demonstration of his opposition to the proposed merger with the Liberals. This event did not establish one of these projections as more 'real' than the other but, rather, illustrated the existence of such a relationship, the origins of and doctrinal reasons for which we have stated. In 1986 this relationship of tension was concealed because official party discourse and leadership discourse were coincident.

Two qualities related to David Owen's tempered style can be noted here, and which will affect rhetorically the presentation of the leader's persona: first, there is very little deviation from the written text in front of him (interestingly, the few deviations that occurred involved a focus upon Owen himself which we shall note in our analysis); second, the speaker is able to use humour, a kind of comic relief (precluded from a speech such as Neil Kinnock's, in which a dramatic style makes such interventions inappropriate) through which the personality of the speaker is further revealed. Let us then analyse the text from three perspectives which, taken together, construct and contextualise the 'persona-in-discourse' of David Owen: the relationship of the speaker to the audience/s; the depiction by the speaker of (political) society; the form of consequent political action encouraged by the speech and its relation to the idea of moral vision.

1. Relationship of speaker to audience

We have already mentioned the understated style of speaking which betrays David Owen's personal wish that political exchange be conducted in a 'reasonable' manner. One of the effects of this is the ascription to him of the personal qualities suggested by such a form of exchange: he is reasonable, serious-minded, statespersonlike and so on. It is worth noting that when Owen wishes to continue speaking and bring an end to applause, he merely repeats quietly the first word of the following sentence, in marked contrast to David Steel, Neil Kinnock and Margaret Thatcher who all counter applause by much louder repetition. It is on the basis of this projected style that the relationship between the speaker and the audience is established. The relationship depends upon the construction of a series of 'characters' in the speech and the speaker's relationship to each of them. The multiplicity of these characters is often implied rather than stated, thus allowing for the imperceptible transformation of one character into another. This is why we refer to the speech's audience/s rather than audience. There are, of course, actual audiences: the delegates, the TV viewers, the journalists. As well as these, however, there are other, more notional, interlocutors: the electorate, the SDP as an organised whole, as a movement of opinion, as a policy-making body, as a group of specialised MPs, as party to an alliance, and as a potential government.

The use of the pronoun 'we' often refers to one or several of these entities. The wider public is referred to as 'the voters' (sometimes referred to as a unity, 'the electorate'), 'the people of this country', 'the nation', 'our country', or 'the British people'. Many of these would appear ultimately to be one character (the public) but in fact are not, or rather they are overlapping characters who are depicted, as the speech progresses, as possessing not only the reasonable, serious-minded status of the speaker, but also a more mythical status. Some of the characters form composites: the most telling of these is a composite made up of the people and the SDP itself, that is to say, the representation of the actual delegate audience as a symbol or microcosm of a future ideal society. All of these characters are addressed directly by the speaker, and the relationship between speaker and characters is established, maintained and developed essentially by the use and play of personal pronouns. There are other characters, however, who are created in the discourse but who are spoken *about* rather than *to*. We shall come on to the significance of the different relations between the speaker and the other characters in the next section of this chapter when we examine how the speaker 'populates' and represents society. Here we can say that these referred-to but unaddressed characters frame the relation of the speaker to the addressed characters. The unaddressed characters are: the enemy in the form of other political parties (and the actors within them), the poor (and the old and the sick), and foreign countries who are observing Britain. Let us, here, examine the speech and identify and comment upon the interplay between the addressed audience/s and the speaker.

Near the beginning of his speech (unscripted) the speaker declares:

I want to talk beyond this hall to the people of this country (2)

What is interesting about this statement is that it has the declared quality of transforming the whole of the ensuing speech into a kind of address to the nation, thus enhancing the status of the speaker and that of the occasion itself. It is not, however, an accurate statement. As we have suggested, the audience/s addressed are multiple, and this multiplicity functional to the speaker's relationship to them. One of the effects of such a bald declaration is to endow the actual delegate audience with the status of national representatives (they are the lieutenants of someone who can address the people of Britain). By the same token, it also *distinguishes* speaker from audience (only he can make a claim to speak to the people as a whole). The claim, therefore, has an enhancing effect (while being a false claim) in that it creates the illusion that David Owen's speech is the discursive expression of an unmediated relationship between the speaker and the people.

The speech opens as a classical conference acknowledgement of the speaker's recognition of the sense of occasion. David Owen had been formally introduced by the party's President, Shirley Williams, who eulogised the leader by referring to him, in the closing sentence of her introduction, as 'one of the most remarkable, if not the most remarkable, politicians in contemporary British politics'. David Owen begins his speech by apparently countering this recognition of his elevated status:

Shirley, to whom we, and I, owe so much (1)

The two personal pronouns here indicate both speaker recognition of the audience and the special status of the speaker himself. The opening sentence is followed by a humorous comment about the weather (we shall analyse the role of humour below) and then, after a long pause, comes the declaration of intent, already quoted, to address 'the people of this country'. We can see in these opening lines that the essential elements of the speech are already assembled: the acknowledgement of 'we' (the party) by 'I'; the difference between them; the closeness between them; the personality of the speaker (prepared to express gratitude, able to joke, yet possessing a sense of gravity); and the apparent reaching out beyond the actual audience, after having acknowledged it, to an ideal one, that is to say, the establishing before the audience in the hall of an unmediated relationship between speaker and ideal audience. It is worth noting here the form of address to the people of the country: the 'I want to talk to' phrase is repeated, thus reinforcing the presence of 'I'. Another quality of this phrase is that it is not an impassioned form of address (that is, not 'I want to appeal to' or 'reach out to' but simply 'I want to talk to'). This suggests both ease of communication and privilege, thus further emphasising the status of the speaker. He continues:

> Let us hope for all of our sakes that the Election is not postponed ... We are already in the midst of a cynical pre-election consumer boom (3–4)

Given the declared intention of addressing the people, the 'us', 'our' and 'we' of these two lines refer to the people as a whole. What is also implied, however, along with the ability of the speaker to look into the future and thus towards the desirability of an early election (this clairvoyance recurs many times, as we shall see), and the ability to see through others' deviousness, is the preparedness of the SDP for the impending confrontation (and, by extension, for government). And, given that it is the election that the speaker is referring to, the 'our sakes' further implies both the speaker's and the party's readiness to play a national role. The reason given for the desirability of an early election is not tactical but moral: 'for our national well-being' (3) (and the 'our' here links 'us', the party, with the wider 'people'). In terms of the speaker's relation to the preceding statement ('I want to talk'), the unquestioned desirability of an early election implies the visionary certainty of the speaker while offering (personal) reassurance to an audience clearly *uncertain* until the speaker's manifestation of his own (now their) certainty. And to express certainty on uncertain issues is one of the hallmarks of leadership discourse.

The next paragraph begins 'Will voters fall for it again? I doubt it.' As well as the suggestion that the speaker can see into the future and into the minds of the voters, we can see here a clear shift of addressed character away from 'the people' to the audience. This shift offers to the actual audience/the party the opportunity to share the insightful certainty of the speaker. A further implication here is the conveyed *difference* between the audience and the voters, the latter possessing the attribute of dupes who 'fell for it' before, not an insight the speaker could address *directly* to the 'people of this country' without risking disfavour. Interestingly, in the same paragraph, the speaker distinguishes the forthcoming (1987) election from previous ones, thus conferring historic significance upon the event:

> For this is going to be a very different Election from any that we have known since 1929 (5)

The 'we' here suggests Britain as a whole. The effect, however, is to extend this significance to the party itself as (a) participating in British electoral history and (b) possessing (via the historical knowledge of the speaker) a historical memory (we shall come back below to the notion of the SDP's/David Owen's possession of historical knowledge).

The addressing *of* the audience *about* the electorate is continued:

> Repeated polls ... show a ... three-way split in the minds of the electorate (6)

This slight movement in characterisation, moreover, from 'the voters' to 'the electorate', is itself significant. In the first place it moves from a liberal individualistic depiction to a corporate idea of a single entity, here, the electorate. In one sense, the terminological change is minor. One could say, with more or less the same meaning, 'the minds of the voters'. The actual phrase used, however, implies a division within one entity, a disruption of an imagined harmonious totality and, therefore, a three-way split in the mind rather than a three-way split in the distribution of minds. What is depicted is not a set of voters who should be won over but an undecided and confused entity which must be restored to harmonious equilibrium. The implication, of course, is that all the voters will vote Alliance. This implication, barely credible, but nevertheless given an airing, is modified immediately by the speaker's stressing (7) that, in spite of his desire to claim 'outright victory', there will be no 'obvious winner'. The audience is addressed as being aware of this ('you know'), and thus as possessing an honesty and clear-sightedness lacking in the other parties ('even the other parties know in their heart of hearts'). The audience, then, knows that a 'balanced Parliament' is probable. This paragraph has the effect of showing the pragmatic reasoning which informs the SDP, as well as the hypocritical attitudes of the other parties. Both of these themes dominate the speech from this point onwards: the depiction of the party's adversaries on the one hand, and the pragmatism of the SDP on the other. We shall return to these themes in the next two sections of this chapter.

The attack upon the two main parties continues over the next four paragraphs. The direct relationship of speaker to audience is maintained by the derisory treatment of those parties and by the metaphors used which provoke laughter and applause (see below), and by the second, very short, paragraph of the four which offers the SDP as the healer of the disunity created by the 'old entertainers':

> Our new politics is about partnership, about sharing power, about cooperation ... and above all about national unity (9)

It is worth noting that the stressed words, those which follow 'about', are 'partnership', 'sharing power', 'cooperation', and 'national unity'. The four 'abouts', however, refer silently back each time to 'Our new politics', contrasting 'new' (the Alliance) with 'old' (the 'old entertainers'). Interestingly, David Owen substituted 'Our new politics' for the less personal 'The new politics' (published version).

After the comparatively long initial criticism of the Labour and Conservative parties, the speaker returns to the interplay of speaker/audience/s with a disdainful 'Now let's leave them [the other parties] alone'. This is followed by the very pronounced intrusion of the speaker's persona into the speech:

> All over the country the thing that people ask me most is 'What is the real truth, David, about the state of the British economy?' I tell you, the situation is neither as bad as Labour pretends nor as good as the Conservatives claim. Let's be objective (12)

This passage contains several significant features. First, it follows on logically from the preceding attack on the two main parties because the attack implies the need for an analysis of the present socially damaging political situation. Second, the image evoked is of the speaker in 'the country' (not at Westminster or in his constituency, for example) listening to people and clearly in possession of and ready to offer 'the real truth'. Third, there is an implication that 'people' ask David Owen many other questions, like a confused community (of children?) coming for counsel ('the thing that people ask me *most*' [my emphasis]), and that they know him by his first name (this, interestingly, was unscripted). Fourth, the 'I tell you', which prefaces the assertion of the Labour Party's pretence and the Conservative Party's (false) claims (both dissimulations of 'the real truth'), conflates the people 'all over the country' and the SDP audience, for a moment not only conferring the status of 'the people' on the party, but also highlighting its need, like that of those other 'people', to seek 'David's' advice and guidance. Finally, the 'Let's be objective' in this context means not only that the speaker is removed from bias, but also that he can enlighten both the people and the party because he possesses exclusive knowledge.

There then follows detailed critical appraisal of the national economic situation, which, because of the way it is introduced (cf. 'the real truth', 'Let's be objective'), takes the form of personal revelation. The objective appraisal mentions jobs, over-manning, trade union power, manufacturing, and competitivity (13–19). From paragraph 18 onwards, however, (18–21) it is informed by a plethora of first person plural pronouns, and gradually becomes, as we shall see, not a consideration of the prevailing *situation* but a demonstration of the speaker's insight into the potential qualities of the *people* who will bring about change. Let us concentrate then on the use of pronouns in this part of the speech (18–19).

Our underlying economic weakness
We are still in economic decline
Our balance of payments
Our share of world exports
We won't continue to compete
We have now sunk
We were the third
Italy overtook us
Spain will have overtaken us
Why is this happening to us?

It is clear from these examples that 'we', 'our', and 'us' refer to 'the nation'. After this (20–25) the identity of 'we' and so on remains the same, but the qualities ascribed to 'we' are transformed (and are offered as personal insights in the form of answers to the question 'Why is this happening to us?', that is to say, a question to which the speaker knows the answer, while giving 'voice' to an imaginary questioner who does not know the answer). Let us list the relevant phrases in order to see how the quality of 'we' is modified:

We are not an idle nation
There is great inventiveness . . . amongst our people
The talent we know lies within our nation
Why do we go on allowing Conservative and Labour . . . to impose . . . ? [implied: 'we shall no longer']
Are we afraid of change? [implied: 'no longer']
The tiny minority . . . risk making our country
We've got to stop this
We have damaged ourselves
The chopping and changing . . . prevents us
We have got to stop being afraid
Of course we can and should temper market effects
It is our persistent lack
Can we not learn?
Can we not adjust?
Let us remind ourselves that most of our partners
Let us remind ourselves

We can see, throughout these paragraphs, that the pronoun 'we' (and 'us' and 'our'), though still linked unequivocally to 'the nation', has introduced the notion of admonition by the speaker of 'we' for its failure to recognise the greatness which it possesses and which the speaker can see. It is as if he is showing the people how fooled they have been and how courageous they must become. This part of the speech, therefore, implies the rousing call of the speaker/party to a slumbering, duped and fearful people (cf. 'Can we not learn?', 'Can we not adjust?') In this way, without distinguishing nominally the shifting identities of 'we', part of that 'we' (the speaker) can speak *for* the people, the expressed policies and intentions being assumed to be those desired by the imminently-to-be-aroused people. Once this unity is discursively established, 'we' becomes once again the speaker/Alliance.

> Yet to us it is obvious . . . but we have to persuade others
> Persuade them
> National unity will certainly be frustrated if we allow
> We, for our part, are ready
> Our programme
> We will take into account
> We will have made it clear
> We will vote on your behalf
> We might not have the largest number of seats
> We have a duty
> We can risk a second election
> The Alliance . . . is determined
> Our determination
> Our task
> It will take time, but we know it can and it must be done

It is in this third phase of change in the nature of 'we' (26–36) that the 'we' (the people) is talked *about*. It is here that the significance of these subtle, barely perceptible changes becomes apparent: the speaker must reconcile in his discourse the discrepancy between the idea of the party/Alliance as representing the wishes of the people on the one hand and the fact that it enjoys only small support from the people on the other. The first point, the Alliance as representing the wishes of the people, must be maintained if the party is to perceive itself as a microcosm of a future ideal society. The second point must be stressed as a means of mobilising party activists (henceforth inspired *by* their status as microcosm) to go out and persuade others. This is why, in the third phase ('we' as the Alliance/the speaker), the other central character is not so much the other parties (though these are named as the apparent factor inhibiting change), but the electorate itself. If we go through these last paragraphs once more (26–36) we can see that 'we' is juxtaposed less with a 'they' (the government) than with a 'they' (the electorate) [the emphases are mine]:

We have to persuade *others*
Persuade *them*
We will vote on your behalf, the behalf of *the voters*
We have a duty not to allow *the voters'* wishes to be ignored
The voters are not stupid
They will know
Those politicians who refuse to listen to *their* views, the views of *the voters*
We will trust *the voters* and *they* will trust us
You know it's time *people* throughout the country ought to start asking them [the Conservatives], and doing it now
The Alliance . . . is determined to listen to *the voters*
Determined to convince *the voters*

We shall come back in the last part of this section to the interventions and significance of the first person singular pronoun in these paragraphs and in the rest of the speech. The bulk of the paragraphs 37–60 (the greater part of the speech) is devoted to the elaboration of the SDP's policy on tax reform. There is some continuing interplay of speaker and audience identity, but for the most part this section of the speech involves the speaker's direct elaboration of SDP intention. We shall examine the underlying significance of this in section 3 of this chapter.

In the closing paragraphs of the speech (61–74), the use of the first person plural pronoun 'we' returns. 'We are right' begins the first eight of the fourteen short final paragraphs (61–68). This repeated certainty acts in a classical rhetorical manner as a crescendo at the end of the speech. What is significant here is that the certainty proceeds from the assumed correctness of the preceding long argument (essentially, about tax reform), and projects the total self-assurance of a speaker offering concluding certainties as proven by the argument.

In the final paragraphs (69–74) the notion of 'we' juxtaposed with the people (the link between the two being trust) returns:

> Our attitudes are far closer to the true heartbeat of the British people. The nation can trust our Alliance, trust us to tell the truth, trust us to negotiate in good faith, trust us to defend our freedoms. Above all, we are determined to forge again a new sense of unity within this nation (69)

We shall return to this notion of trust in section 3 of this chapter. Here we can say that its essential basis is evidenced not only by the sureness of judgement of the speaker but by the *moral* relationship being posited between David Owen/the Alliance and the people.

The final utterance of the speech returns unequivocally to the declared audience, 'the people of this country':

> Trust us and we will not fail you (74)

There is a certain irony in the fact that this character (here, 'you'/the people) is only unambiguously addressed in the closing line of a speech the declared intention of which was 'to talk to the people of this country'. We have, however, elicited in part the functional role of the speaker's direct addressing of several audiences. Let us now, before describing the speaker's representation of society, examine how the speech (essentially through the use of the personal pronoun in relation to the audience) defines the particular persona and character of the speaker.

We have already highlighted certain traits: the humility and proper sense of obligation in the opening lines ('Shirley, to whom we, and I, owe so much'); the privileged relations established between the speaker and audience/s; the quiet, self-assured, somewhat grave manner. A counterweight to these is David Owen's use of humour which establishes a direct rapport with the audience, suggests the approachable, friendly quality of the speaker, and provides, as I have said, a function equivalent to comic relief, allowing distraction in a dense, political speech.

The first example comes at the very beginning:

> I don't think any of us thought we could get as much sun as we have here in Harrogate. Someone up there seems to love us (1)

This kind of humour not only punctuates the gravity of the speech, it also frames it. The above remark, for example, comes just before the 'I want to talk beyond this hall to the people of this country', thus throwing the second remark into higher relief. All four examples of humour are set within very 'serious' passages.

The second joke comes a quarter of the way through the speech, when David Owen, after saying that he, David Owen, refuses to condemn all that Neil Kinnock and Margaret Thatcher say, adds (unscripted):

> Even David Steel is right . . . sometimes (21)

Such a remark, capitalising upon the media treatment of 'the two Davids', and allowing the speaker to make a joke about his own apparent arrogance, nevertheless still maintains the media image, keeping also the disproportionate focus upon party leaders rather than upon party policies.

The third example comes just over halfway through the speech:

> Our tax system has multiplied and mutated like a virus – you'll be glad to know that I checked with doctors that viruses still do mutate (43)

This example puts the focus once more upon David Owen specifically, in this case, upon his former, socially charismatic, profession of medical practitioner.

The fourth example comes nearly three-quarters of the way through the speech, this time using the media as the foil:

> I repeat, not to raise taxes. Do you journalists want that in code? I can offer you morse code or semaphore (50)

All four asides are unscripted and lend spontaneity to the speech. They come, however, as we have seen, at regular intervals, thus breaking up the high seriousness of the text, and allowing collusion between the speaker and the audience while holding the focus of the speech upon the speaker.

The other main humorous effect is achieved through the use of irony, used in descriptions of the Conservative and Labour parties. We shall examine this in section 2 of this chapter. Also in section 2, we shall look at the notion of the expertise and knowledgeability of the speaker which is displayed throughout the speech, though especially in the main passage where David Owen talks of the tax system and its reform. Here we can note that linked to this notion of knowledgeability is another personal quality of the speaker: his sense of history. There are several examples of David Owen's knowledge of recent political history (especially the previous 10 years). More important, perhaps, is his displayed knowledge of the significance of more distant historical events. In this context we can mention, in their order within the speech, 1955, 1959, 1929, the 1960s, 35 years ago, the post-war period, the Boer War, and 1924. Few of these dates are fully explained, in this way constraining the listeners to agree rather than manifest ignorance, or else to imagine themselves as sharing such knowledge. Moreover this assumption by the speaker of knowledge on the part of the listener also confers upon the party the speaker's own sense of history, itself a prerequisite to the party's ability to lay claim to the speaker's possession of a moral vision. We shall examine the context of this vision in section 3 of this chapter.

In fact, all of the qualities displayed by the persona of the speaker: truth-telling, prediction, knowledge, expertise, moral rectitude, a sense of history and, as we shall see, justice, efficiency and drive, offer an 'ideological' basis to a young party in search of an identity. We can see also that these qualities are mediated through the persona of the speaker so that in a certain sense he is both the vehicle of the ideology (he expresses its ideas) and the personification of it (he possesses these qualities).

The speaker's status as both vehicle for, and personification of, ideas is reinforced by several interventions of the first person singular pronoun and the focusing of attention upon the persona of the speaker. We have examined many of these examples. There are several others worth mentioning, all of which have the same function of displaying either the personal qualities or else the importance of the speaker. We can list them and what each indicates:

Will voters fall for it again? I doubt it (5) [knowledge and prediction]
There is not now, and I suspect there will not be (7) [certainty]
I would be, of course, preferring to be able to claim [but will not] (7) [honesty]
I am convinced (20) [certainty]
I am convinced, now (21) [certainty]
I will believe that if and when I see it (27) [certainty]
When a Cabinet Minister, Kenneth Clarke, said recently on 'Any Questions' to me (35) [centrality of speaker]
I predict . . . and I relish the prospect (47) [prediction]
Its architects in our party have our full support (52) [ambiguous use of first person plural]

We can see that the imposition of David Owen's persona is complex but that its underlying rationale is the projection of the visionary certainty of the speaker. This certainty is the condition of his interpretation of *how* society functions and, by extension, how it can and should be changed. Let us look next, therefore, at how British society is represented in the speech, before examining how this is related to the appeal by the speaker to the people.

2. The representation of society

The representation of society in the speech also comprises a series of characters, and it is worth pointing out, once again, that the society described and the remedy which proceeds from the description are offered as the personal analysis of the speaker to the 'country' (cf. 'I want to talk beyond this hall to the people of this country. I want to talk about achieving prosperity and ending poverty' (2)).

British society is represented as a rich, potentially enthusiastic, positive entity, which is held down and strait-jacketed by a repressive, alien system, which itself is maintained by the two adversarial characters, the Conservative government and the Labour Party, and their leaders, Margaret Thatcher in particular. The essential characteristics *shared* by the adversaries are self-interest, shallowness, hypocrisy and cunning:

A cynical pre-election consumer boom (4)
Vote now and pay later
They act half the time in cahoots (8)
It [the Labour Party] pretends (10)
Behind the red rose is a clenched fist
Dangerous [the Labour Party]
Labour pretends . . . the Conservatives claim (12)
No honest Conservative can claim (19)
The farmyard noises of the House of Commons (20)
They will be betraying their own supporters (27)
If Labour or the Conservatives want to do a shabby deal (30)
Contempt for the voters' wishes (34)
They want to ignore the voters (35)
She wants you to forget (38)
The Labour Party dares not talk straight (46)
Mrs Thatcher hopes to bribe (47)
She believes the British people can be blindfolded and bought
The Government boasts (55)
Labour stir up envy (72)
The Conservatives glorify meanness

In conjunction with the exposition of their shared moral shallowness and deviousness, one of the striking features of David Owen's depiction is the *collusion* between these villains. The prevailing metaphor for this sham alliance is the music hall, which lends further derision to the description, adding the quality of mediocrity to the adversary:

Yet what a spectacle . . . old entertainers trying to keep alive music hall routines in seaside halls (8)
[The Conservatives] can neither sing nor dance to a new tune, even if one was capable of being written for them (11)
Political play-acting (21)

These risible characters possess other characteristics: they 'scoff', are 'bitter', are 'petulant', are 'puerile'. What they have created, however, in order to maintain their positions within a whole political and social structure which bears down upon the people is an 'old-fashioned, rigid, unrepresentative parliamentary system', a 'suffocatingly centralised nation' whose 'dead hand' kills 'energy, enterprise and innovation' (20). Two points are worth stressing here. The first is that many of the references to the hypocrisy of the adversaries are immediately preceded or followed by evidence of the *speaker's* honesty. The 'spectacle' passage is immediately preceded by David Owen's admission that the Alliance cannot win an outright victory (7), the Conservatives proclaiming falsehoods followed by the 'people's' question ('What is the real truth, David?' (12)), the reference to 'play-acting' immediately followed by 'I refuse to say that everything that either Neil Kinnock says or Margaret Thatcher does is always wrong' (21).

The objective result of this depiction of the people and those who control the political system is that the nation is seen as being wasted and as if slipping downwards, past other nations, into decadence and impotence. The word 'decline' abounds. Britain has 'sunk' from third to nineteenth place in 35 years. It is arguable, moreover, that the illustrations used by the speaker appeal, not to the fair-mindedness, but to the nationalist prejudice in British political culture. The two comparisons made (the first has overtaken, the second about to) are with, respectively, Italy and Spain, two nations long regarded in British culture as inefficient, backward, lazy and 'Latin' in the nordic, arguably racist, sense of the term.

Beneath the repressive structure lie 'the people of this country'. What is significant about this is, first, their great (and repressed) qualities (although, as we have seen, the negative quality of being capable of being duped is necessary to the speech), and, second, the personalised quality of the observations concerning the people. The following are not simply remarks, but insights:

Not an idle nation (20)
There is great inventiveness and imagination amongst our people
The talent we know lies within our nation
The voters are not stupid (31)

Our country is capable of developing the inner strength (36)
In all conscience – and this is still a country of good conscience (43)
We believe they . . . will respond generously (47)
There is nothing that our nation cannot together achieve (71)

Just as great qualities must be tempered in the speech by the rhetorically necessary idea of the gullibility of the British people, so must the enumeration of these qualities be tempered, as we have seen, by admonition:

We have got to stop being afraid of competition (22)
It is our persistent lack of competitiveness (23)
Can we not learn? Can we not adjust and adapt to modern experience? (24)
Let us remind ourselves

Arguably, these failings can be interpreted as being caused by the government, and the banding together around inspired leadership as the way of overcoming failings or inadequacies. The didactic, admonitory tone, however, remains, and is justified in the speech by the display of the speaker's knowledge, this last, however, more than a simple enunciation of facts, being rather the means of revealing his *insightfulness* in terms of his perception of the qualities of the people. This is a prerequisite to his projecting some kind of special relationship with them which, in turn, legitimates the subsequent call to action. He confers mythical status upon them and transforms them into an inspired community ready to follow an inspired leader ('Given unity, there is nothing that our nation cannot together achieve' (71)). Before this, however, he must indicate the breadth and depth of his *knowledge* in order to justify his possession of insight concerning the British people.

Indications of the speaker's knowledge abound and are (paradoxically) reinforced often by the absence of personalisation, that is to say, of a prefixing 'I believe' or 'I would like to make the observation' and so on. David Owen's knowledge and insights are normally enunciated with an impersonal directness which indicates the assumed truth of the observations (one of the qualities of the visionary). We have seen examples of the stated 'truths' and of the speaker's historical knowledge, and his 'seeing through' the adversary. Other examples are his understanding of the economy (12–19), his suggested knowledge of how to negotiate to advantage after the election (28–31), and finally his knowledge of defence issues and world affairs. Paragraphs 19, 20, 22, 24, 25, 48, 49, 60, 67, and 68 all indicate the speaker's grasp of international affairs and of Britain's place within them. It is here that the speaker's former role as Foreign Secretary enhances his overall image of having 'global' knowledge. The main display of the speaker's knowledge, however, is coextensive with the main topic of the speech, the proposed Alliance reform of the tax system (37–57). Let us examine this in some detail.

The long passage on the reform begins with the identifying of the inequalities, inefficiencies, injustices and damaging effects of the present system. The passage bristles with figures and comparisons, and detailed knowledge of both the present and the proposed system. From paragraphs 53–57, the form and effects of the proposed system are given and, once again, detailed costing and figures provided, all of which underline the thoroughness of the proposal. We can make two initial points here: first, this long passage is the only one where detailed SDP policy is elaborated (as we have already mentioned, the conference as a whole demonstrated a whole range of new policy initiatives); second, the listener is led through the detailed programme by means of certain key words and phrases which link the stages of the elaboration like a reasoned, and complex, argument which re-appropriates to the speaker what is ostensibly, and presumably, SDP policy, rather than exclusively personal beliefs and intentions:

Now we cannot do this
Also
But not satisfied with that
Now, before
But it is also
Now reform of the tax system and benefit structure
The result is

Yet, not only . . . it is also
Yet because of
I predict
I might add
They forget that
We want
But the difference
Whereas
Therefore
That means
Let me remind you
By merging
By restructuring
Now to pay for this
We restructure
We keep
By comparison
As a result
Beyond these measures

We can see that arguments in the passage are linked
logically as in, say, an academic lecture, thus enhancing the
pedagogical aspect of the speaker's persona as well as the
serious-mindedness both of the speaker and of party policy.
We still need to ask, however, why, in a rallying speech, only
one policy proposal is elaborated (unusual in a leadership
speech), why it is so detailed (and in fact suggests a higher tax
bill for many potential Alliance voters), and why it is the
longest single passage of the speech, and yet is, in content,
arguably rather arid. The clue to the answer lies in its
national application and its apparent symmetry, a symmetry
which reflects the functioning of an efficient, and just, society
in the manner of 'from each according to his abilities, to each
according to his needs'.[2] The passage is not only a demonstration of the speaker's knowledge and the leader's exposition of one element of party policy; it is an elaborate
counter-metaphor to the image of the repressive total political structure maintained by the adversary, and which we
identified above. It is a metaphorical image informing both
the means of attainment and the realisation of an ideal
society. It is both a release mechanism from constraining

structures and an analogy of future society. The balanced manner of exposition fulfils the expectation of the SDP as a practical, reasonable party, while the metaphor itself fulfils the expectation (necessary for both activists and electorate) of *utopianism*. This is one of the major rhetorical innovations of contemporary political discourse which accompanies the 'new realism' of the 1980s: the presentation of the utopian as rational, and in apparent non-utopian form (and, we might add here, the depiction of the adversaries' cold 'realism' as immoral). The passage on tax reform in fact recapitulates the: repressed society; vehicle of release; free society movement of the rest of the speech. And such coded utopianism, just like declared utopianism, is based upon a moral vision. Let us, therefore, go back over the speech in order to demonstrate how this moral vision is achieved.

3. The call to action and moral vision

In the earlier part of the speech, the moral undertones concerning the hypocrisy of the powerful, the waste of talent, the danger to the security of the nation, are apparent. It is also worth noting that the long passage on tax reform is prefaced by a passage of high moral tone which refers to the wider national question, as if the tax reform passage were a response to it:

> Our task is to offer a way forward. Forward to a more self-confident and united Britain. Our country is capable of developing the inner strength and unity to fight back and revitalise our fortunes. It will take time, but we know it can and it must be done (36)

Moreover, in the early part of the long passage itself, where the speaker details the existing system, he uses a reference akin to the earlier music hall metaphor concerning the government's deviousness: 'Mrs Thatcher is trying, by a conjuror's trick, to focus your attention only on income tax' (38). The deviousness is, therefore, akin to subterfuge of a moral kind. This is reinforced by certain key phrases:

> She wants you to forget (38)
> By a supreme irony
> Telling the electorate that she had no intention of doing so
> Every penny they have taken off . . . they have put back . . .
> through the back door

The speaker goes on to say that, with the intended community charge, the government is moving from its Victorianism (that is, its uncaring attitude to the poor) to a medieval (that is to say inhumanly brutal) position. The subterfuge is compounded by the government's procuring others (the public utilities and services) to collect their taxes for them. The speaker then develops his argument using the *other* supposed aspect of Victorian morality (the middle-class conscience, and concern for the poor), a morality which goes hand in hand with the historic industriousness of that class:

> The poverty trap is perhaps the most cruel of all the anomalies in our taxation system. But it is also economically damaging to this country (40)

In spite of the image thus projected of the SDP being perhaps more 'tough' than 'tender' (a slogan coined in the previous year), more concerned with economics than with human tragedies, the tax argument remains a moral one, the 'efficiency' argument being a justification for the moral rather than an added advantage to it. In the paragraph following the 'economically damaging' remark, for example, the word 'damaging', which refers in the previous paragraph to the economy, refers here to 'damage' in a moral sense: 'the damaging effect of relatively high taxes on the low paid' (41). And the paragraph ends with two moral references, only one 'efficiency' reference:

> It destroys dignity. It damages family life. It defies all logic (41)

In the contexts of both the total social transformation aspect and the moral aspect of the speech, the following sentence is the clue to the whole passage, and to the speech as a whole:

> Now reform of the tax and benefit structure is part of economic revival. Reform would help to release the energy

and the vitality of those in work, and to restore the self-respect and freedom of choice of not only those who are out of work but of the handicapped, the pensioner and the one-parent family, as well as the low paid (42)

The tax reform is a mechanism or element to be inserted by a new government into social life, and one which will trigger a releasing action within the social totality. It will also be a moral action. We have already seen how the utopian can be presented as practical. This inversion also applies to the 'efficiency' thesis as being an inversion of a moral one. We mentioned above how the notion of 'efficiency' within Social Democracy is as much a cover for the moral thesis as vice versa. Here, the moral change that Social Democracy will trigger follows on from the fact that its 'efficiency' will bring self-respect to the disadvantaged in society (and, therefore, by extension, to everyone). This intertwining of the illogicality, inefficiency and immorality of the present system (plus the perception and mastery of detail and figures of the speaker) runs throughout the tax reform passage. Here, bearing in mind that this is one complementary aspect of a morality/efficiency duality, let us list the accumulated moral references in this section of the speech (37–56), all of which amount to the speaker's perception of the moral state of the nation (for which the taxation system is the metaphor):

Harsh, uncaring society which ignores the needs of those who cannot compete (37)
Notoriously unfair (39)
The poverty trap ... the most cruel of all the anomalies (40)
The damaging effect (41)
The damaging effects
Unfair
Let alone think it fair
It destroys dignity. It damages family life
The handicapped, the pensioner and the one-parent family (42)
Poverty line (43)
Poverty line
In all conscience – and this is still a country of good conscience – we must act to end that injustice

The duty to end poverty
A depth of poverty in Britain which should be seen as a national disgrace
The poverty line
Nearly one-third of the population, many of them young children . . . struggling to feed, clothe and decently house
We must not pass by on the other side
Genuinely in need (44)
Complexity which denies so many their rights
The inefficiencies and injustices of our taxation and social security systems can only be solved by a radical structural reform
Restructure the whole system
Many of the poor actually grew poorer under Labour Governments (46)
Poor (48)
The poor
It [the SDP reform] is fairer and simpler. And it will not be easily evaded by the accountants for the rich (52)
Those who need help (53)
A tax that bears hard on the lowest paid
[With the SDP reform] the poverty trap is abolished (55)
Families in poverty
Families . . . poverty
The disabled and handicapped will receive at last proper help (56)
Poverty

Later in the speech, this combination of separateness from and sympathy with the oppressed is reinforced further:

Far too many of our neighbours have their pride crushed by unemployment. Too many of our neighbours have their dignity violated by racist attacks. Too many live in constant fear of crime and violence. Too many families see their children's future diminished by lack of money, lack of support, and crumbling schools and medical services. It's time for all our people – North as well as South – Scots, Welsh and Irish – women as well as men, whatever their class, creed or colour – to enjoy their fair share in the fruits of Britain's success (70)

In terms of our analysis, there are two essential points to make here. The first is the creation-in-discourse of the character, 'the poor'. It is worth noting from all of the references here, and throughout the speech, that this character (plus the disabled, the handicapped, the pensioner, and the one-parent family) is never addressed directly. Although the speaker talks 'to the people of this country', he only ever talks *about* the poor. The poor are an entity which exists (is repeatedly given existence within the discourse), but which is a mass, a totality and is 'other'. This is functional, and brings us on to the second point. The morally-charged creation-in-discourse of the 'other' entity, the poor, has a significant defining effect upon: the SDP audience, the 'people of this country', and the speaker. All are depicted as a 'middle class' that is, not part of the category 'poor'. Hence we can see that the SDP was a middle-class party, not essentially through the socio-economic background of its members and so on, but through the way it *described* itself in discourse.

This discursive description is of a particular kind, and here we can see the depth attributed to the SDP's status as middle-class. First, it is a middle class which incorporates everyone between the 'rich' and the 'poor', that is to say, the quasi-totality of the nation. We can see that the SDP, therefore, is not trying to present itself as being representative of an *actual* middle class, but is endeavouring to transform the nation (and the party members' perception of themselves) into a middle class of a particular kind. Second, we can say that not only are the many references to poverty and the poor (and 'the handicapped, the pensioner, and the one-parent family' (42), 'women as well as men, whatever their class, creed or colour' (70)) essentially clichés, but that the references to the implied (never named) middle class and its qualities are equally so:

> In all conscience – and this is still a country of good conscience – we must act to end that injustice (43)
> The Tory Party underestimates the conscience of the British people (45)

and the Samaritan:

> We must not pass by on the other side (43)

These three references are not only indicative of the existence and distinctiveness of this caring entity (there are 'sides', and 'we' are on one side, 'the poor' on the other), but also – through cliché – *defining* of it. The cliché here has a rhetorical justification: it conjures instantly a *type* of middle class, that is, an assured, self-confident, caring, moral and generous class, precisely the (mythical) *other* middle class of the Victorian period. There are two reasons for this: first, David Owen is creating discursively a counterweight to the notion of Thatcherism as a return to the Victorian period; second, outside (European) Socialism and British trade unionism, the only elaborate set of ethico-political values in British political culture are those of the reformist Victorian or post-Victorian middle class. And, practically speaking, the great bulk of social reforms in the 20th century were the result of the political intervention of that class, or a fraction of it, whether Labour, Liberal or Conservative reformist. This particular middle-class identity in the speech is further underlined by continual references to the damaging effects of the present system and the enhancing effects of SDP reforms upon the family, whose *sentimental* reality was the creation of the 19th century middle class, and which still arouses strong cultural sentiment in British society. The notion of threat to the family informs the speech to a significant degree. We have seen several examples of references to the family. Another striking example is the speaker's (up-to-date) reference to drugs: 'Violent crime, drug addiction, and vandalism are plaguing this country, the rich as well as the poor. The latest menace is the drug "crack", poised to sweep into this country' (24). Unlike, say, vandalism, burglary, or football violence and so on (essentially working-class issues), the problem of drug addiction has, since the 1960s, always been perceived as a trans-class, occasionally essentially middle-class, problem, and therefore one to which an SDP audience would be especially sensitive.

This is not to say that the use of cliché and the depiction of a mythical, caring middle class point to a false sentiment or an unreality in the issues described, only that, rhetorically, cliché is a widely used political resource which, here, is used to connote effortlessly and instantaneously a deeper moral view. This moral sentiment runs throughout the speech. We have already seen the many examples given of the moral shallowness of the government and the Labour Party. And it is worth underlining once again here that it is this, rather than their inefficiency, which is given the greatest stress in the speech. And on the question of inefficiency, it is the waste, in both a practical and a moral sense, that is constantly emphasised in the speech, a waste not only of money but of a generation, and, beyond that, of a nation.

One of the most telling illustrations of the moral theme is the speaker's reference to South Africa. The contemporaneous, widely-reported repression of dissidence in South Africa, and the generalised hostility of the international political and business community, allowed David Owen to accuse Margaret Thatcher of making Britain 'the moral leper of the world over Apartheid' (67). Over and above its highly-charged moral condemnation, this reference indicates the speaker's awareness of both topical and international issues. More than this, however, it confers upon the SDP a morally-charged 'we shall not be moved' quality, which was enhanced by the fact that South African embassy staff/agents had infiltrated the conference itself and distributed letters to the conference delegates, seeking their support for South African government policy. (And in terms of what we said earlier concerning families, it is perhaps worth pointing out that much of the indignation generated in Britain over the South African issue in 1986 was the result, as in Soweto in 1976, of the South African government's brutality towards children.)

The first eight of the final fourteen paragraphs, which follow on directly from the long passage on tax reform, begin with the phrase 'We are right' (the paragraphs concern productivity, inflation, the trade unions, profit-sharing, industrial revival, social policy, internationalism, and defence). These eight short declarations follow on, as if logically, from the tax reform proposals, and like them they connote release mechanisms within the social structure, making them all further effects of the radical structural reform. The tone of the declarations, however, brings us back to the role of the speaker. The eight-times repeated sentence 'We are right' not only underlines rhetorically the certainty of the speaker but also emphasises his *rightness*, both in terms of correct interpretation and, given what we have indicated, in terms of his being morally right (and we have already seen how the 'truth-telling' quality of the speaker indicates factual truth *and* moral truth, that is, a truth which unmasks falsehoods). It is interesting to note, moreover, that seven of the eight declarations are followed immediately by very 'active', positive verb infinitives which generate the notion of action, as if the crusading Alliance were *already* in government. This is not merely wishful thinking but a device which creates, in the discourse, the impression of the SDP as governmental:

We are right to introduce
We are right to hold
We are right to keep
We are right to promote
We are right to put
We are right to stress
We are right to be
We are right to insist

This rhetorical series ends on an assertion of rightness which is, in fact, a statement about the status of the speech as a whole:

Our attitudes are far closer to the true heartbeat of the British people (69)

This is, moreover, a claim both to accurate analysis and to moral affinity. The logical consequence of such a declared belief is (political) allegiance through total trust:

Our attitudes are far closer to the true heartbeat of the British people. The nation can trust our Alliance, trust us to tell the truth, trust us to negotiate in good faith, trust us to defend our freedoms. Above all, we are determined to forge again a new sense of unity within this nation (69)

The requesting of trust in these matters comes in the form, not just of straightforward appeals, but of appeals based upon the demonstration of their legitimacy, given the topics dealt with, that is to say, upon the moral legitimacy of the speech itself. Trust, truth, good faith, the defence of freedoms and the forging of a (lost) unity are the promise of a

national, industrial, and moral revival, and the attainment of
an ideal society:

> Given unity, there is nothing that our nation cannot
> together achieve. We will best help the aspirations of the
> British people: a happy home life, rising living standards
> for their families, a pleasant environment and a thriving
> economy around them, if we are seen to stand for indi-
> vidual success and harmonious communities (71)

The promise is stressed again immediately:

> To give voice to the ambitions and hopes of the British
> people (72)

and again:

> To enable those hopes, those ambitions, to be fulfilled (73)

The speech ends:

> Trust us and we will not fail you (74)

From our analysis, we can see that the tone of the speech,
which mirrors the quiet, reasonable persona of the speaker,
is, nevertheless, essentially, a highly moral speech, full of the
rhetoric of moralism. This morality, linked to the assumed
efficiency-orientated endeavour of the SDP itself, allows the
SDP to present publicly, and allows the speaker to present
publicly to the SDP, the basis of an ideology, mediated
through the inspired vision of the leader and involving the
'universalist' vision of the British nineteenth-century social
reformers. And the crusading spirit of the 'new' vision is
reinforced by the complete certainty of the speaker in what
was, in fact, an extremely uncertain political situation. This
certainty-within-uncertainty would lend David Owen significant authority in the aftermath of the 1987 general election
when he purported to carry with, or indeed within, him the
vision of Social Democracy itself, which legitimated, over and
above party constitutional right, his refusal to bow to the
democratic procedures of the party as it moved into merger
with the Liberal Party. It was not his leadership of the party
alone which enabled him to do this but the *nature* of that
leadership which allowed him to take his (true) followers into

the political wilderness in a Gaullian *'qui m'aime, me suive'* manner. The SDP encouraged this element within itself in the aftermath of the 1983 general election by accepting David Owen as its undisputed leader and by accepting and encouraging his particular style of leadership as a response to the highly personalised leadership of Margaret Thatcher. The SDP, as we shall see, was not the only British political party to do this, but, in 1987, after the general election and the decision to merge, the rejection of David Owen's thesis (the symbolic rejection of his vision) was not simply a 'democratic decision' within the SDP, but the rejection of its own undeclared strategy, that is to say, the strategy of allegiance to an inspired leader, which had been allowed to flourish between 1983 and 1987, and which saw its climax in 1986. This does not mean that the SDP or a merged Alliance would henceforth reject this form of leadership, but that it recognised that such a form was incompatible with a two-party alliance (or with the organisational process necessary to merger), and would have to be re-created, if at all, only after merger, when the process, the provision of a 'new' ideology by an inspired leader, might be repeated.

3 David Steel and Liberalism

THE CONTEXT

The television journalist, Vincent Hanna, reporting the Liberal conference for BBC2's 'Newsnight' on 22 September 1986, captured the essence of what had been the Liberals' dilemma throughout the 1980s when he described the party as one traditionally perceived as being made up largely of the well-meaning 'busybodies' of local communities, but wanting to project itself as a credible, hard-nosed party capable of government. From an analysis of the conference as a whole, we can say that the Liberals hoped to resolve this dilemma not by the wholesale replacement of the traditional image by one which was more appropriate to the responsibilities of government but rather by a reconciliation between valued traditional perceptions (essentially, morally-inspired activism) and a new image (essentially, leadership-inspired realism). This was to involve the development of the moral register within Liberalism and its presentation as informing and endorsing a practical, governmental orientation, and its leader's governmental status. One of the problems in any such reconciliation was that the Liberals have been viewed traditionally not only as a moral community but as one of a very particular kind, that is, individualistic and, by extension, both anti-organisation and anti-leadership (indeed, David Steel's original leadership of the party was seen to a certain extent as a change from the developing élitist leadership style of the Grimond and Thorpe years). Nevertheless, at the level of discourse and self-presentation, and with the added governmental credibility of the alliance with the SDP, such a reconciliation was possible and, to a certain extent, had been taking place over the previous five years.

The role of the 1986 conference was to reaffirm and develop an interpretation of society, and of power within that society, which was based upon a guiding moral view which would be collectively stated and then *restated* by the leader of the party. However, this ritual demonstration of doctrinal and organisational reconciliation was arrested by disagreement over what was perceived as the most moral of all issues, and which was to have far-reaching consequences for the practical political claims of the Liberals, the Liberal leadership and the Alliance, namely, the defence issue. The defence policy disagreement, and the resulting inability of the party to publicly reconcile the activist and leadership drives within itself, when the conference voted against the direct wishes of the leader, was an unexpected event to which leadership had immediately to address itself, thus transforming dramatically its own symbolic function. For this reason the Liberal conference of 1986 was an exceptional and intriguing moment in the political life of Britain.

The notion of the crusading impetus of the 1986 Liberal conference was given by the President-elect of the party, Des Wilson, a figure of national standing since his campaigning days, particularly in the pressure group for the homeless, Shelter. His presidency at this moment of the party's governmental reorientation underlined its continuing campaigning image, as well as the continuing moral orientation within the Liberal movement. His speech at the opening session of the conference was passionate, populist, anti-Westminster, anti-corruption, sometimes almost sentimental, and it set the tone for one of the dominant themes of the week, namely, a crusading moralism which was given extremely enthusiastic endorsement by the conference audience. One of the interesting aspects of Wilson's speech in this context was that he spoke in the manner described above but with a projected conviction that the Alliance was on the threshold of power.

The speech which followed Des Wilson's was the SDP leader, David Owen's, address to the Liberals. This took place in an atmosphere of clear Liberal suspicion of him, caused, not only by his policy differences with the Liberals, especially over the defence issue, but, more importantly, by his ambivalent attitude to the notion of the equal status of the two party leaders. Not only the policy-orientated content of Owen's speech (which, nevertheless, contained certain references to political ideals) but also his very presence at the conference acted as reminders of the political realities in which the Liberals now found themselves involved. The typically measured tone and practical orientation of Owen's speech contrasted strongly with Des Wilson's passionate address. David Owen, of necessity, referred to the defence issue. The references in his speech, however, were ambiguous, thus implying, paradoxically, the SDP's intransigence on the issue. The applause at the end of his speech was polite.

We can see already that the defence issue was not simply a matter of policy, but loomed very large, given that it was the point at which many issues crossed: the moralism in the party, its pragmatism, the viability and integrity of the Alliance, the nature of the Liberal leader's relation to the leader of the other party in the Alliance and, by extension, the nature of his relationship to his own party, and the question of the Liberals' need to modify their 30-year opposition to Britain's nuclear deterrent if they were to enter an election, and, potentially, government with the same policy as the SDP.

The contentiousness of the defence issue and its crucial relation to leadership meant that, in the circumstances of the defence vote on the day after David Owen's speech (which threw the conference into turmoil), it became an imposed test of the moral and practical legitimacy of the Liberal leadership itself. David Steel's speech which closed the conference should be seen in that context. In certain respects, moreover, the defence issue had come to be perceived as a Steel/Owen issue, and was linked to the idea that the SDP was imposing (essentially through the attitude of its leader, particularly his public scepticism concerning the Alliance defence commission's proposals published in June of the same year) the SDP/Owen's defence policy as a precondition of imagined government. This controversy over leadership-related policy differences, and the fact that it was, in large part, Owen's persona which was forcing the Liberal leader to present an equally personalised image of his party (and of his control of it) in order to confirm his equal status with Owen, make Steel's speech the most problematic of the four speeches we are studying.

The projection of David Steel's leadership persona had to respond to the question of leadership in two ways: he had to project a form of leadership acceptable to the party, that is to say, a leadership image compatible with Liberalism (however sensitive the Liberals might be to the exigencies of the Alliance and the media more generally); and he had to enhance his leadership status outside the party (the creation of what appeared to be a governmental vocation being partly dependent upon David Steel's attainment of a governmental status in the eyes of the voting public). This double constraint does, of course, apply to all the leaders. In Steel's case, however, the second exigency was further influenced by the generally assumed conviction of his secondary status to David Owen. The defence vote, therefore, threw into question David Steel's leadership status *vis-à-vis* his party, not only at the level of Liberal ideology, but also at a more personal level, given that his status *vis-à-vis* David Owen was already under scrutiny.

We can say, therefore, that the interrelating of the moral, practical and leadership aspects of the defence issue at the conference meant that this was not just another case of a leader 'losing' a conference vote – this has happened regularly at party conferences of the Liberal, Labour and, more recently, Social Democratic parties. Nor was it even a setback such as that suffered by Gaitskell on the same issue in 1960 at the Labour Party conference; in the case of the 1986 Liberal conference, we have an example of a leader being forced to demonstrate through discourse, not only that he represents the 'true' ideological tradition of the party through a claim to personal legitimacy, but that his opposition to the party was not the direct result of his subservience to *another* leader (David Owen). And we can add that David Steel had to assert such ascendancy in the context of a party which had followed, since the 1920s, a strong anti-authoritarian tradition with little recourse to strong leadership as a rally focus. Finally, given the implicit assumption that David Steel's personalised leadership had been, in part, imposed from without (by the existence of a personalised leadership in the other party to the Alliance), the imposition of his leadership authority would be highly problematic; its reimposition in the context of the defence vote even more so. We can see, therefore, that the problem of what *kind* of personalised leadership style David Steel should adopt was a constant one within 1980s Liberalism, and was thrown into even greater relief at the point where he was demonstrably, or arguably, not representative of the party at all, and therefore unable to present himself as the personification of it.

The question of personification is made even more difficult within Liberalism, even when the leader is in harmony with the party, because of the difficulty of identifying an ideal-type Liberal. The 'types' within Liberalism are generally represented by the local activists, as we have seen, very often with a commitment to grassroots community politics and not seriously interested in national power (sometimes appearing, indeed, apolitical when contrasted with the tough figures in other parties), or else by the few Liberals who have achieved national prominence, the MPs, who themselves comprise a very diverse group. It is far easier for the other three leaders to claim representation or even personification of their party, especially in the case of David Owen and Margaret Thatcher (although the Labour leader too can show himself to be above sectional interests and representative types where necessary, presenting himself as distanced from party activists *in order to* transcend differences, given that it is accepted that a Labour leader cannot be a personification of, say, both traditional unionism and Lambeth council activism). The Liberal leader, however, in the 1986 speech, cannot even pretend to generalise an ideal-type, but must *accentuate* the notion of the grassroots Liberal activist as myopic in order to lay claim to his own greater legitimacy. This makes his speech of vital interest, for it was through this channel that he attempted, from a position of extreme weakness, to reassert his leadership status and at the same time enhance it in order to lay claim to an authority which would sustain his leadership after the conference was over.

Within the party itself, even though Steel could not personify an ideal-type of party member or activist, he possessed the advantage that no other second-rank leader within the party (with the possible exception of Paddy Ashdown) was in a position to challenge him at this level of symbolic personification of Liberalism. Steel's own image was more statesmanlike than, say, the late David Penhaligon's and he appeared more ordinary than, say, Lord Mayhew or Jo Grimond at one extreme, Cyril Smith at the other, more experienced and mature than, say, Simon Hughes. It is not that these figures would have contested the leader's leadership status itself, but that their existence might suggest symbolically a potential alternative form of leadership. We should add to this that, given the increasing focus upon leadership, the idea of threatening one of the few national Liberal figures who possessed possible governmental status would have represented a threat to the party itself. This explains, in part, why the conference was willing to respond to David Steel's speech so enthusiastically, in spite of the defence vote, thereby facilitating his task. Nevertheless, the 'rally' quality, which exists within Liberalism without reference to leadership but to which David Steel had been able to lay claim, was now in danger. And before harmony could be restored, the leader had no choice, in terms of the need to reimpose his own symbolic authority for the reasons we have given, but to oppose the conference as a totality (given that a majority vote becomes symbolically the decision of the totality).

This meant that David Steel was forced to strip the conference of its legitimacy and derive his own directly from another source, thus shattering the collusion which is normally established between leader and audience in a leadership speech, and which normally *masks* the leader's claim to a legitimacy outside organisation and outside the restricted ideology and traditions of which it is the declared expression. This, none of the other leaders was faced with (Steel's speech was, in fact, the only one of the four speeches we are studying which involved any heckling). Even the new, balanced juxtaposition of the moral and practical orientations of the party, begun by the opening speeches of Des Wilson and David Owen, and which interacted developmentally through the quasi-totality of the interventions throughout the week (straight party business speeches and the defence debate itself do not fall into this category), had to be implicitly refuted by the leadership's denial of the conference's legitimacy in order that the leader's speech establish a new, morally-based pragmatism borne (now explicitly) of the personal judgement of and reinterpretation of Liberalism by the speaker. The fundamental problem, therefore, was one of legitimacy. David Steel had to reach for his legitimacy over the conference audience and those it claimed to represent and draw directly upon another legitimacy, thereby denying the conference audience the status of ideal audience or microcosm of a future ideal society, and thus denying himself all the benefits to leadership status that normally accrue from such conferring of ideal status.

What David Steel's speech does do, however, and it is this which makes it such an unusual, indeed practically unique, illustration of leadership discourse in contemporary British politics, is to demonstrate the full impact of personalism upon organised politics in present-day British political culture, for one could argue that, given the importance ascribed to the defence issue and its effect upon the Alliance, an importance acknowledged by the Liberal leader himself, this was a resigning issue. Such necessary isolation from the symbolic harmony of leadership and party was to diminish David Steel's claim to inspired leadership in the ensuing period, and, although this aspect is not part of our analysis here, doubtless contributed to his ultimately untenable position when the next major contesting of his claim to leadership surfaced in the course of 1987. Before going on to our analysis of the text, let us summarise our discussion.

The prevailing view of the Liberal Party was one of a political community united by principle (essentially the defence of the individual and concern for local communities), but which had not possessed a national 'calling' or credibility since the heyday of Liberalism which came to an end after the First World War. Its national political standing was, in fact, based, in part, upon the perceived value of a political organisation little interested in the power politics of the two main parties. Its influence, however, was significant in certain areas of the country; it had a long experience of local politics and, nationally, could still lay claim to lineage from figures such as Gladstone and Lloyd George and from the nineteenth-century tradition of Liberalism. It also had or had had one or two nationally known and respected figures in its ranks, such as Jo Grimond and (before a personal scandal ruined his career) Jeremy Thorpe, and several politically active peers and MPs. The party had, moreover, enjoyed some national political power in the 1970s, deriving, under David Steel's leadership, some of the status of national responsibility through the period of the Lib-Lab pact with the Labour government in 1977.

In the 1980s, with the formation of the Alliance, the Liberal Party had been thrust into a potential governmental role which placed considerable emphasis upon the status of the party leader, David Steel, in terms of both his standing as a national figure and potential Prime Minister, and his own position *vis-à-vis* the highly personalised leadership of the Liberals' Alliance partner. David Steel's problem, irrespective of the defence issue, was therefore one of endowing an identifiably idealistic political community (which possessed, nevertheless, a certain claim to governmental credibility) with the status of a party of potential government. The leadership's losing of the defence debate questioned Liberalism's capacity to become, with the SDP, such a force, but the defence issue also raised the question of whether the moralism underpinning the Liberal Party was too strong to allow its leader the scope to undertake negotiations on behalf of the party, and to effect adjustments to Liberal policy in order to facilitate its assumption of power.

In these circumstances, the leadership speech would involve the projection of a leadership persona which would fulfil three requirements if Steel were to continue his attempt to take the party towards national power: first, that of demonstrating, in the context of the reopening of the defence controversy, the resolute character of the leader in the face of adversity, and this in such a way as to avoid the accusation of his discourse being illegitimate in terms of Liberal ideology; second, that of reimposing his authority to speak in a particular way, both as a Liberal and as a leader, by, in the first case, drawing upon a legitimacy from within Liberalism, and, in the second, demonstrating his equal status *vis-à-vis* the other Alliance leader and other national leaders; and third, that of offering a way out of the impasse and a solution to the internal conflict, and after this, of course, the prospect of government. In order to do this, David Steel was obliged, because of the defence vote, to place unusual stress upon his own persona as the focus of these three discursive requirements. Let us, therefore, examine the speech as a totality in order to see how these requirements are dealt with, and then identify the several discursive strategies which enhance the status of the projected persona of the speaker in his effort to deal with them.

THE TEXT

1. The argument

The speech begins with the very deliberate fracturing of the collusion speaker/audience:

> Well, Mr President and fellow Liberals, one of the traditional sports of party conferences is guessing the length of the Leader's ovation. And I don't advise anyone to take a bet on that this afternoon (1)

This opening utterance, projecting the courage of the speaker, as well as his refusal to win over the conference from the outset with some collusive remark, marks the difference between this speech and most other forms of leadership address. Not only is the persona of the speaker defined *vis-à-vis* the party (isolated and courageous, and not looking for approbation) but the notion of the conference itself as a ritual celebration is undermined. It is replaced here by the suspending of conferred or self-conferred status, status which may or may not be re-conferred by the end of the speech. In this way, the whole speech is underpinned unequivocally by the relationship of leadership to party.

The exceptional nature of this occasion is underlined in the following paragraph when the speaker says 'I had planned to address my speech to a wider public . . . , but that part will now have to be shorter, because I want to address some very particular words to the Liberal Party and our allies in the SDP' (2). The contrast here with, for example, David Owen's 'I want to talk beyond this hall to the people of this country' is striking. An inversion has taken place which is presented as having been imposed upon the speaker from within (by the conference). The above quotations explicitly represent the audience as having denied the leader the opportunity to make a 'call' to the people. The 'some very particular words' utterance underlines the notion of controlled admonition and is followed by 'People outside under-

stand that applause is no substitute for getting our programme right' (2). In this way, the 'people outside' have conferred
upon *them* a status that the audience inside the hall lack,
underlining further the insight of the speaker and his own
understanding of the people. By the same token, the projected idea of the leader's isolation from the conference is
paralleled by the projection of his positive relation to the
'outside'. This is, therefore, an implied claim to an alternative
form of legitimacy which will recur within the speech and act
as a replacement for conference-conferred legitimacy.

The first main part of the speech (paragraphs 3–50, over
half of the speech) is an appraisal of the national situation
which, in the context of the opening paragraphs, enacts
discursively the speaker's relationship to the outside, reminds the audience of a reality they are depicted as having
forgotten, and displays the knowledge of the speaker.
Moreover, as the speaker has already indicated, it is the (now
necessarily shortened) address to the 'wider public'. Rhetorically, however, there is no distinction between this part of
the speech and the subsequent address to the party; the
national overview is the demonstration in discourse of what
the conference is throwing away, namely, the ability to act
upon the polity at a national level. It is significant in this
context that the sentence which links the prefacing admonitory remarks (paragraphs 1 and 2) to the first main part of
the speech (paragraphs 3–50) is 'There has been a special
urgency to our deliberations this week, because an election
cannot be far away' (3). This evocation of an election is not
only a reminder of the seriousness of the national situation
and a portal to the long passage of appraisal of this, but
implies that the 'special urgency' itself has resulted in mistakes. Thus there is revealed here a certain leadership
'understanding' of conference: the mistakes which resulted
from the urgency reflect the well-meaning nature of the
conference (at worst it panicked itself into unilateralism for
fear that in government the party would have its hands tied).
Leadership 'understanding', however, not only enhances the
speaker's position in that he, as more 'governmental', knows
it was the wrong conclusion, but further suggests that his
view will be not only an *accurate* version of the practical
moralism that triggered the urgency and the practical judge-

ment taken in response to it, but also an exemplary demonstration of clear leadership vision which – unlike conference – does not fall into error.

The speech proper begins with the notion of the party and the country poised on the threshold of a change of historical significance:

> The destructive years of Thatcherism are drawing to a close (3)

This utterance, with its connotation of a long night of suffering breaking upon a day of deliverance, projects directly upon the audience the idea of the need to be prepared, in order to assume its historic role. Reflecting David Owen's defiant welcoming of an early election, Steel announces:

> We will be ready for that election just as soon as the Prime Minister nerves herself to call it (3)

This fearless declaration, which reinforces the speaker's courage, is based upon the observation that, for his party, campaigning is a way of life (3), while their opponents are 'frightened' (4) of the Liberals' strengths 'on the ground', and that the Labour and Tory parties have had the 'fright of their lives' (4) (in recent by-elections). The speaker declares that, in contrast to the other parties, 'we are ready to join battle'. In this paragraph (4), personal pronouns, rather than 'the Liberal Party', are used: 'our opponents', 'our strengths', 'we have been', 'We've polled more', 'we have achieved', 'we gave the Tory and Labour parties', 'we have shown', 'we are ready'. It is true that the earlier remarks ('campaigning as a way of life', 'our strengths on the ground') refer to the Liberals rather than to the Alliance, and are, moreover, a reminder of the speaker's awareness of the Liberal tradition. Nevertheless the only named entity in paragraph 4 is the Alliance itself: 'There is no such thing as a safe Tory or Labour seat against the challenge of the Alliance' (4). In this way the speaker, conflating the party with the Alliance itself, implies that the success or proper expression of the one is dependent upon the reality of the other (even though the information is given as a simple attack upon the government itself). The use of the first person plural pronouns 'we', 'us', 'our', plus 'the Alliance' of 'Liberals and Social Democrats' is reiterated through the next long paragraph (5) as the speaker extends his analysis (although there is a tantalising reference to 'Liberal government' (at local level)), and reminds the audience of what the alliance of the Liberals and the SDP has *already* achieved: 250 local government by-election victories, an influx of young people and of women into the town halls. The military metaphor of 'advancing' (us) and 'retreating' (them) is also evoked here. Together, these assertions construct for the audience a clear microcosmic (local rather than national) picture of what they are throwing away.

This, of course, given the discord between leader and conference, raises the implicit counter to the speaker – government at what cost? This implication is dealt with immediately as he goes on:

> Now let us be clear about what the general election will be about. It will of course be about who will form the next government. But it will also be about the sort of government that the country needs. As well as the choice between Tory, Alliance and Labour, Britain will also be choosing between good government and bad government (5)

This is an excellent illustration of how the speaker conflates the moral with the practical, for, as we shall see, 'good' government will be depicted as just as much moral as efficient, 'bad' government as much immoral as inefficient. Interestingly, the linking of the practical and the moral enhances the speaker's moral credibility as well as his (superior) knowledge of what government itself is (cf. 'Now let us be clear'). The depiction of bad government is prefaced with 'I hardly need to explain to you what bad government is' (5). This not only allows the audience, for the first time in the speech, to 'know' something, and momentarily to collude with the speaker, but also permits the speaker to go on to tell the audience what good government is. Moreover, the conflation of the moral with the practical takes the conference back past the defence debate and vote to what was to be the discursive undertaking of the conference, namely, a reconciliation of moralism and pragmatism suggestive of a morally-informed governmentalism. Taken together these comments on Alliance successes and government failures are in themselves indirect criticisms of the audience who are threatening the possibilities of future good government.

The following paragraphs, then (7–14), involve speaker elaboration of what 'good' government entails (and the expression 'good government' is repeated at the beginning of each paragraph). Although the elements of this exposition involve traditional Liberal tenets (electoral reform, constructive government, decentralised government, open government, government in the public interest, government enabling people to govern themselves), they are, nevertheless, given the leadership portrayal of an irresponsible renegade conference, illustrations of the speaker's own personal insight. Moreover the elaboration of each of these Liberal tenets also involves the combination of moralism and pragmatism which we have identified: electoral reform is justified partly as the need for 'consent, not ... domination' (7) (moral), partly as 'the way to get the majority behind the government' (practical); on decentralisation 'central government is trying to do too much' (10) (practical) and 'a very great deal ... should be done at local level, at regional level, and in Scotland and Wales by their own elected governments (moral); on open government, 'The point of a Freedom of Information Act ... not to punish' (11) (moral), 'We have to learn from experience, see what works and what doesn't work, and avoid making the same errors again and again' (practical); on government in the public interest 'as long as the Tory and Labour parties are bound hand and foot' (12) (practical), 'As long as Mrs Thatcher and Mr Kinnock continue to refer patronisingly to "our" people' (moral); on government as facilitative, 'enabling ... people to run their own lives' (moral) (13), 'we are never happier than when ... we can move on to help others towards self-reliance' (practical).

Along with the personal mastery of the moral/practical interrelation (an interrelation the conference is presented as having abandoned), we have in these several paragraphs devoted to what constitutes 'good government' the notion of the speaker's quiet vision of a harmoniously governed country. This vision, presented, moreover, as we have seen, in the form of traditional Liberal tenets, not only implies the speaker's proximity to a true Liberalism but is significantly personalised by the sentence which closes this part of the discussion and sets the scene for major persona intervention:

> So just ask yourself whether the sort of government I have described, far-sighted and constructive, open and decentralised, enabling people rather than controlling them and governing in the public interest, is possible in Britain today. Well, I tell you this much (14–15)

With this abrupt personalised remark there is created audience expectation of the speaker's admonishing 'second part' of the speech, that is to say, of an implied 'Well, I tell you this much, not if you vote at conference the way you do'. He does not, however, say this: the 'this much' turns out to be a strong criticism of the pendulum politics of British government (we should also note here the use of alliteration and hard consonant sounds in the following quotation, underlining the speaker's strength). It is as if the speaker is preoccupied with greater things than the admonition of wrong-doers. And it is this personal *preoccupation* with wider issues which leads into the 'second part' of the speech:

> And the result for the country has been decade after decade of decline and degeneration. If you want good government only our Alliance can provide it. But we aren't going to get an Alliance government unless the Alliance is credible. And that brings me to Tuesday's debate (15)

This lead into 'Tuesday's debate' is, therefore, dramatic. Not only is Tuesday's debate (the defence debate) presented as that which will make the 'vision' unattainable (cf. 'unless the Alliance is credible'), but the reference to it also swings the audience, *direct* reference to which had been minimal, back into the speech. The long-anticipated threat of 'I want to address some very particular words to the Liberal Party' (2) now comes into its own. This sudden reappearance of the audience is extremely unusual in contemporary political discourse, given the predominance of the conflation audience/wider public/ideal community. It is, therefore, all the more striking. The schoolmasterish tone ('And that brings me to Tuesday's debate') is immediately reinforced by the equally reproving:

And before I turn to the subject of defence and disarmament itself, I must tell you bluntly that two characteristics of our debate on Tuesday disturbed me (15)

Such a parenthesis further diminishes the audience in that it suggests that the substance of 'Tuesday's debate' cannot be addressed until the speaker has dealt with two even more irritatingly peripheral issues of party irresponsibility. What is interesting about these apparently prefacing points is that, although the phrase 'Before I turn' suggests that the speaker is obliged to waste his time in admonition before getting down to 'real' issues, the two 'characteristics' discussed are not, in fact, merely preliminaries but are, as we shall see, integral to the defence debate itself. We can see, therefore, that the discussion of the defence issue has been framed within repeated examples of both explicit and implicit reproach. The first 'characteristic' combines the moral/practical issue with admonition:

The sight of the Liberal Party reverting to a habit which I thought we had kicked ten years ago ... rather than dealing with the real harsh world ... our goal of ridding our country, our continent, our world of nuclear weapons. That we must assert with all the passionate intensity at our command (15)

Before going on to the second characteristic, the speaker opens out the debate to the need for a programme, 'the painful steps we must take to reach that non-nuclear goal' (16), makes direct reference to Chernobyl, refers to Jo Grimond's support for multilateralism, and directly insults the audience by describing the conference vote as the equivalent to (Labour) Lambeth lamp-post signs declaring Lambeth a nuclear-free zone. The suggestion here is that the dissidents (that is, the majority vote) are in the wrong party. The speaker follows this insult by the evocation of 'a genuinely nuclear-free world', thus implying that the conference vote is a fine example of misguided, myopic, self-indulgent utopianism. In his closing remarks on the first 'characteristic', the speaker rounds on the conference while asserting his own passion, his understanding, his leadership and his humility:

Well by God after seven years of this benighted govern-

ment the country needs a party with a lot of heart, and I
am proud to lead it. But it needs its head as well (17)

The logic of the outburst is subtle. The 'by God' is directed
clearly at the party conference, but the possible accusation of
leadership betrayal is deflected because what follows is anger
at the *government* not the conference ('this benighted government'). It is, therefore, a demonstration of 'head and heart'
working in perfect rhetorical equilibrium.

Substantial applause followed this critical assessment. This
contrasts well with the low-key introduction. It is the discussion of the second characteristic which builds up, this time
very rapidly, to a high rhetorical tone:

And the second point which troubled me (18)

This is immediately followed by a withering reference to the
'well-intentioned but completely misguided belief that in
some way this Assembly's task was to accentuate the few
remaining points of difference with the SDP in order [pro-
testing voices], in order to, in order to, in order, in order to
"strengthen my hand" in manifesto negotiations with David
Owen' (18).

David Steel is tackling here, head on, the strongly implied
notion of the conference's decision as being a kind of
collective comment on his personal credibility *vis-à-vis* David
Owen. Rhetorically, this is very effective. The speaker, by
emphasising one aspect of the vote (its possible implication
concerning Steel versus Owen), diminishes the other (its
being a doctrinally-inspired decision of conference). In this
way, the speaker need only, in the first instance, disprove the
doubts raised by the first aspect in order to enhance his
position *vis-à-vis* the second. What is implied here is that the
conference did what it did *not* out of morality, but because it
considered David Steel as inadequate to combat David
Owen's strong personality. The repeated references to and
implications of the speaker's strength of personality have
already created the conditions for his ability to refute this
view (we shall examine these below). Here, by twisting the
conference vote into a question of personal judgement of the
leader, he is able to destroy its credibility:

That is a breathtaking misjudgement (19)

The notion of the misguided judgement of the conference is reinforced here by the physical description of the leader's response (it is clearly *his* breath which was taken away by the absurdity of the conference's assumption). This is a particularly good illustration of the speaker manipulating the potentially damaging defence vote to his own advantage. Whatever the intention of the vote, the speaker chooses to portray it here in such a way as to enhance his own combative image. Paradoxically, this dramatic personalisation is immediately transposed on to a party/Alliance level. The leadership personalisation remains, but the impression given is that the speaker, as leader of part of the Alliance, knows exactly what he is doing in terms of the Alliance. What is also suggested, however, is that the leader is, in fact, the sole true interpreter of the Liberal input to Alliance policy, not because he wants to be, but because irresponsible elements in the party have made this inevitable, and that the conference has displayed the most immoral of characteristics, namely, betrayal of trust. The next remark is a reminder to the audience of the necessity for loyalty to an agreement entered upon at an earlier stage, as if this earlier agreement implied consequences which the party has forgotten:

> We are either in alliance or we're not. We must live and breathe the Alliance. It's unthinkable that we enter the election with two defence and disarmament policies. But neither David Owen nor I are prepared to arrive at any election policy as a result of some botched-up bargaining, haggling process (19)

Logically, this is no reconciliation of the leader's responsibility *vis-à-vis* the conference, but *is* an answer to the depicted 'real reason' for the vote: lack of faith in the leader who has remained true by those who have not. The self-justification continues on the personalised level, legitimating without discussion the bone of contention itself, namely, the Alliance decision-making process:

> We [the two leaders] wouldn't convince the country. We wouldn't convince you. We wouldn't even convince ourselves (19)

This is followed by the speaker's bald assertion of what the

Alliance (that is, its leaders) will do, and here the distinction Alliance/Liberals is even greater, and is strengthened, not only by the concept of 'judgement' itself (which the conference lacks), but by the fact that it is 'our judgement' (that is, the two leaders'):

> We will arrive at our election policy by applying our common judgement to the problems which will face the next government on taking office (19)

This passage concludes the accumulated invective of the speaker. It is clear from our analysis that anger, some controlled, some apparently not, has been one of the major resources of the speech so far, here directed essentially at the audience (later it will reappear as a more 'just' anger, directed towards a wider enemy). The display of personal anger, however, though rhetorically effective in one sense, as we have seen, can also be a dangerous device for a leader to deploy. The speaker, therefore, now transforms it into a more magnanimous emotion which, furthermore, re-establishes a relationship of solidarity with the audience:

> I am reported as being angry with this Assembly. My emotion is not one of anger but of profound frustration that what you hope for and what I hope for, namely electoral victory for Liberalism and the Alliance, may have been temporarily and unnecessarily put at risk (20)

This reconstructing of a relationship, an implicit form of forgiveness, is given credibility by the speaker's immediate extension of value to the audience:

> But I say 'temporarily' because yesterday two events took place which sent a clear signal to the public that we are on our way again (21)

This remark also suggests that the speaker can, through all the confusion, 'see' the valuable beneath the superfluous, distinguish the historically relevant from the unimportant, and, in fact, maintain his judgement in the context of his own strong emotions, a quality the audience lacks. The first of the two 'events' is the conference's 'overwhelming' (that is, more than the defence vote) endorsement of the Alliance's *Partnership for Progress* document, and of the procedures governing the elaboration of the manifesto. The 'forgiveness' and collusion, therefore, further legitimate leadership authority, in that the two endorsements offer scope to leadership action:

> Both David Owen and I are well able to move forward now on all policy issues including defence on the basis of that document, and that is a clear message I give to you, the SDP and the electorate (21)

We can see, therefore, that the speaker deals with opposition mainly by combating only the implied criticism of his leadership weakness *vis-à-vis* David Owen. We have, moreover, in the above quotation, an indication that the speaker is, in fact, accepting, in a certain respect, the legitimacy of the conference (contrary to the view expressed by many observers that he was rejecting conference's legitimacy because it was not delegatory). This acceptance (of the conference's endorsement of his views) is not simply a convenient one (he accepts what he wants, rejects what he does not) but is functional to his status. At certain points, the conference and the leadership will be in agreement, sometimes not. The leader and the conference are *both* in a relation to another legitimacy which the leader *always* corresponds to, the conference *sometimes*. And the source of difference lies in the fact that the conference's emotionalism sometimes loses sight of the party's mission, whereas the leader's does not.

We have already seen the leader's claim to legitimacy via the 'wider public' (which Liberals subscribe to, given that they want to represent the people in government (potentially) and locally (in fact)). Leadership legitimacy, therefore, is not based upon a claim to solely personal vision, but will draw upon other forms of legitimacy (which we shall discuss in the next section of this chapter), of which this is but one. The irony here is that the speaker's conferring of legitimacy upon the conference, as depicted in this part of the speech, is used to legitimate personalised leadership's authority to act independently of a momentarily (re)valorised party legitimacy ('Both David Owen and I are well able to move forward now').

The treatment of the 'other event' takes the conference out of itself, and the speech out of what has been up to this point practically a solely hostile relationship to the conference.

David Steel is here referring to the talks he had with David Owen concerning the Tuesday vote (talks which had taken place the previous day). Humour is used twice here to counter the possible accusation of arbitrary leadership: 'What the *Sun* would call secret talks – watched by about 7 million people' (22), and 'Neither of us subscribes to the doctrine of infallibility of party leaders – at least I don't [Laughter], but nor does he' (22). Nevertheless, both the reference to 'the other event' and the humorous illustrations maintain the personal focus of the discussion, and further enhance the notion of the leadership as the only site where real decisions are taken. It is at this point that the speaker declares:

> But turning now to defence and disarmament policy itself, let me reiterate the fundamentals on which we are agreed (23)

Interestingly, this and other 'on which we are agreed' phrases (repeated four times, and strangely reminiscent of Gaitskell's famous 1960 speech to the Labour conference) are both a recognition of the conference (what we, the Alliance, (and conference) are all agreed upon), and an authorial analysis of the confusion that the conference has occasioned (what we (the speaker and the audience) are all agreed upon even though the conference betrays its own confusion). This will lead on to further *leadership* evaluation of the whole issue itself (cf. 'But turning now to defence and disarmament policy itself'), this making up the second, and longest, single passage of the whole speech (paragraphs 23–39). Referring to the defence issue in this explanatory way allows the speaker to reaffirm not only the party's but, more importantly, his own position on defence and disarmament. The 'We are agreed' passages involve: NATO ('We are firm in our support for the NATO Alliance') (24); a moratorium on further deployment of cruise missiles (25); the inclusion of Polaris in missile reduction talks (26), this passage including the speaker's giving to the party a small lesson on how to negotiate (27) (and here there are two references to the Labour Party, further suggesting that the Liberal dissidents are fellow-travellers of an unrealistic Labour Party (cf. the earlier remark concerning Lambeth

lamp-posts)); and opposition to Trident. A further reference
to European co-operation, moreover, is personalised ('And I
believe we can achieve ... through collaboration with our
European neighbours') (29) and focuses attention upon the
Alliance leaders' high profile visit to Paris earlier in the year.
The patient re-statement of agreements ('That's agreed'
concluding each aspect discussed) ends with an ideological
encompassing by the speaker of both Europeanism and
Liberalism when he remarks that the policy is 'wholly in tune
with the European ideals of the party, that we have proclaimed consistently since the 1950s'. This is a subtle reminder
of the *speaker's* awareness of the Liberal Party's traditional
opposition to the nuclear deterrent, and of his own historical
sensitivity.

The discussion of the disarmament issue continues for
another ten paragraphs, but from here on is further personalised by two methods, the first, straightforward speaker
intervention (essentially the use of the first person singular
pronoun), the second, the use of statements portraying
either the speaker's knowledge or his certainty. This part of
the discussion is prefaced by a reference to the two Liberal
MPs who spoke in favour of the defence amendment.
Rhetorically, this presents a thorny problem for the speaker
because he must distance these two from the accused audience, especially the extremely popular Simon Hughes, whose
impassioned speech arguably swung the vote. This he does
by references to them which portray them as, in fact,
agreeing with him, and which are followed by a complete
separation of them from the conference itself, involving
flattery of them and the ridiculing of the conference:

> Now my two parliamentary colleagues who spoke against
> the policy resolution both said that a non-nuclear Europe
> was a final aim and that their amendment was not intended
> to frustrate the efforts we are making to find an effective
> European policy. Very well, we shall go on doing so. But
> how I wish that the texts approved by our assemblies would
> more often match the speeches made in their support (30)

This is immediately followed by further personalised certainties as the speaker widens the discussion to the international diplomatic context:

> The international context in which we have to make
> defence policy doesn't stand still. There are some hopeful
> signs ... I welcome ... And I hope ... But there are also
> less hopeful signs. Mr Gorbachev ... has not yet aban-
> doned ... And we have to accept ... And the American
> troops are not likely to be around in their present numbers
> ... And that means ... And we all know (31)

We can see from these illustrations that the speaker is here
reminding the audience of the complexity of the issues while
displaying his own certainty. The implication is that Liberal
defence policy must rest upon the superior judgement of the
speaker/party leader. The previous 14 paragraphs are depicted in this way as having *become* Liberal defence policy.
This idea is dramatically strengthened at the end of paragraph 31:

> And with Labour having nothing credible to offer, the
> choice will therefore fall between Conservative defence
> policy and the Alliance alternative. And let me spell out
> that choice (31)

This notion of there being only two choices increases the
status of Liberal leadership policy ('let me spell out'), giving it
an equal ranking alongside Conservative policy (while marginalising the defence policy of the UK's second political party
as laughably irrelevant, and also marginalising, in the same
instant, the dissident Liberal vote, by making it, like Labour's
policy, a non-issue, thus enhancing the authority of the
speaker as the only protagonist to Conservative policy). The
spelling out of 'the choice' involves five paragraphs which
weigh 'Conservative' policy against 'The Alliance'. Each of
these paragraphs begins with 'The Conservatives will ...'
which is countered each time with 'The Alliance will ...' The
legitimation of this particular Liberal/Alliance view is further
confirmed by the use of the future tense, the same tense used
for Conservative *and* Alliance, thus according Alliance policy
a reality both as a future governmental policy and as an
actual opposition policy. The discussion ends with the sentence: 'These are the differences between the two sets of
policies' (36). Never, here, is the opposing view within the
party itself voiced. Indeed, at no point in the speech is the

other argument within the party given discursive space and thus any credibility. The only two presented cases, and therefore the only two imaginable policies, are the 'Conservative' one and the speaker/Alliance's.

Towards the end of the long passage on defence, speaker persona intervenes again with the voicing of a personal appraisal of Mrs Thatcher which denounces her 'obsession with nuclear firepower' as 'a wholly distasteful, macho obsession' (37). (The implication is that the 'real man' here is the proponent of the Liberal leadership's view.) An emotive passage then follows and acts as a link to the next part of the speech, the discussion of social issues. Not only does this emotionalism allow the speaker to carry the tone used in the discussion of defence over into the domestic discussion, it also implies that the wider resolution of the (domestic, social) issues are part of the speaker's overall review of political reality (which includes defence and disarmament):

> The real power of Britain – the power of a nation at peace with itself, the power of a nation fully employed, the power of a country with civilised standards, caring for its old, investing in the education of its young, providing for proper housing and medical care (37)

And the link to the discussion of the 'nation at peace with itself' is made by use of a personal insight ('I don't doubt'), and an insightful historical analogy (with its implied reference to a heroic English role model, Francis Drake):

> I don't doubt that when the Spaniards of the 16th century planned their Armada there were many who discussed in the minutest detail the galleons and the guns that were to reduce England to servitude. And these preoccupations hid from them the truth of Spain's national weakness – the sterility of its social order, the bankruptcy of its economy (38)

Underlying the speech so far, therefore, are four interrelated themes, all of which define the relationship of the speaker to the audience: (1) a warning to the party not to expect a comforting speech; (2) a presentation of what the party is throwing away; (3) a scornful appraisal of the conference's views on defence and disarmament; and (4) the speaker's interpretation of the defence question.

The bulk of the remainder of the speech deals with four issues, all of which are ideally suited to the interrelating of the moral and the practical: education (40–42); housing (43–49); international issues (50–58); and racism in Britain (59–60). As with David Owen's speech, where pragmatism was a cover for moralism, these four discussions 'betray' the high moralism of the speaker, as well as his knowledge (and this, as in Owen's speech, via speaker enunciation of party policy). This prepares the discursive ground for the concerted projection of the speaker's persona at the end of the speech (61–67). Let us examine here, however, how the moral, the practical, and the personal are intertwined.

On the practical front, education is seen as *necessary*: 'Economic recovery and our future prosperity depend upon education' (40). The practical suggestions are, however, imbued with and outweighed by a highly moral tone:

A far-sighted government . . . could do nothing less (40)
We can't go on wasting the human talent of Britain
Our whole society that's impoverished (41)
In education, too, the Thatcher years have been the destructive years
The quality of the people who teach our children is vital too (42)

The explicit moral register here is striking (following the logic of the argument backwards to the analogy with sixteenth-century Spain's internal national weakness, the implication is that the nation's educators are capable of avoiding for the country a fate such as the Spanish Empire's). And at several points in the section of the speech on education, the word 'partnership' appears, thus surreptitiously legitimating the Alliance document itself, *Partnership for Progress*. There is also developed here the notion of the foundations of a *new* society. The first of these is education, portrayed as being in a necessary relation to other things, like the foundation stones of a building or the keystone of an archway:

We have got to invest in the future of education. And we've also got to invest in housing (43)

We can see from this that the issues discussed in the leader's

speech are being presented as a totality or mutually dependent series from which any deviation or opposition is tanta-
mount to an undermining of the whole.

In the passage on housing, the moral indignation of the
speaker increases further (and the juxtaposition of this
personal emotionalism is enhanced here by more frequent
reference, not to Conservative policies, but to Margaret
Thatcher herself). Let us list here the accumulation of
personalised and moral references concerning housing:

I can think of nothing more demoralising (44)
Nothing that makes people feel more degraded than to
have to eke out ... in conditions which, frankly, deny any
possibility of a good life
The facts are deeply disturbing (45)
What do these figures mean in human terms?
I don't know what effect statistics like this have on you, but
... they fill me with fury. Fury [applause], fury ... Fury ...
at this government whose policies have made the mess and
misery so much worse (46)
But what we've got to do is turn our fury into positive
action (47)
And I promise you
The people degraded
Human wretchedness which Mrs Thatcher in her tours of
the Tory luncheon clubs of Britain never even bothers to
see
She simply doesn't understand
This lethal cocktail

There then follows (48) a detailed list of what an Alliance
government will do, this a long passage which ends: 'it is not
only unacceptable in human terms, it is economic madness
not to build and renovate houses'. These references are
followed by a personal 'Commons' insight, and an expression
of the honesty of Alliance MPs, and the deviousness of
Labour MPs (and therefore an associative connotation with
any misguided Liberal who wants to be like the latter).

We can see from the above examples that exactly the same
format as that employed in the examination of defence and
disarmament is being used in the discussion of education and
of housing: pragmatism, moralism, moral appraisal of the

Labour Party, the notion of the Alliance as being the only
real opposition to the Tories, the giving of information to the
conference, a controlled emotionalism, and personal insights. And the end of the discussion of housing backs up the
idea of the speaker's warning those who might undermine
the effectiveness of a combative Liberalism:

> The Alliance is about to launch a great housing campaign.
> Let's all support it. We must act to end this national
> disgrace (50)

As if any Liberal could possibly oppose or even be only
lukewarm to such a proposal. The connotations, however,
are clear. It is not only the housing campaign that the
speaker is referring to, but leadership-inspired Liberal policy
itself in all domains, which is being reinforced rhetorically by
the implied interdependence of all the issues being discussed.

The third subject (international issues) is introduced and
involves a widening of the discussion from the domestic
(education and housing, subjects which Liberal activists are
highly informed about and involved in) to the international
(where leadership experience and authority prevail). The
discussion of international issues echoes, to a certain extent,
the leader's earlier international observations concerning
defence and disarmament; more interestingly, it is framed in
similarly moral terms. And we should note, once again, the
interdependence of these issues with the three domestic
ones:

> Now I've been talking about the internal condition of
> Britain. Abroad this government has chosen isolation and
> impotence (51)

Six of the eight paragraphs begin with the word 'isolation'
or 'isolationism': in Europe, in the Commonwealth, in
NATO, in the UN and UNESCO; isolation as a result of
narrow nationalism; and isolation 'from the instincts of the
people' (the reference here is to Live Aid and to UNICEF).
The speaker is drawing here upon the communitarian aspect
of Liberalism in order to criticise government policy. Viewed
from such a perspective, isolationism is evidence of the
adversary's poverty of spirit.

It is at this point that the speaker comes on to one of the most morally charged of international issues, the plight of Black South Africans. Apart from the moralism of the passage on South Africa, it is significant that it focuses specifically on Margaret Thatcher (rather than on governmental attitudes themselves), homing in sharply on her character and underlining her personal pettiness and own poverty of spirit:

> What a commentary on the real values of our Prime Minister (58)
> Mrs Thatcher . . . prefers . . . short term profits
> She talked gloatingly
> She prevaricated
> Sanctions – the only peaceful form of pressure on Pretoria – she described as 'immoral' (59)
> The infant mortality and the malnutrition
> A system which . . . condemns the . . . majority of the people to scratch a living
> Our Prime Minister . . . sympathy, not for the oppressed, but for the oppressor

These remarks link up with the overall tone of the speaker's discussion of international issues and, interestingly, the speaker *appropriates* here the moralism of the *left* (that is, of the party 'dissidents' close on certain issues to the Labour Party), using terms normally found in leftist discourse: 'fascism', 'reactionary terrorism', 'shackled and muzzled press', 'oppressed/oppressor'. Accompanying the moralism, moreover, is the notion of false, inadequate leadership, the personalisation of such leadership throwing into relief the moral leadership qualities of the speaker himself.

The South African discussion logically moves on to a concomitant 'racism at home' (60) (and we should note here also the general use of the term 'racism' (for example, 'her profound racism') rather than 'racialism', the former being a more left-wing term than the latter). The consideration of racism 'at home' concerns essentially a discussion of the visa system being imposed by government and the (mis-) treatment of, for the most part, New Commonwealth immigrants in their attempts at family reunification and visits. It is interesting to note here that the speaker confines his remarks on racism to those of a more 'domestic' nature and does not tackle the more politically volatile problem of riots (several of which had taken place in the previous year).

In all four discussions (education, housing, international issues, and domestic racism), the speaker has demonstrated an unequivocal sympathy for groups generally embraced by the left. The discussion, moreover, lends itself to a strongly 'moral' tone: education, concerning children and teachers; housing, the poor, families, and children; international issues, organisations such as UNESCO, the Black oppressed; domestic racism, New Commonwealth families (plus an attack upon racism within the police, see paragraph 61). The end of the discussion of the four topics, and the introduction of a brief humoristic passage which prefaces the major climactic intrusion of leadership persona into the speech, involves further reference to Mrs Thatcher herself:

> But Mrs Thatcher remains impervious to criticism and reality, cosseted in a Cabinet from which she has removed all independent minds (61)
> She is candidate for No 10 again. Or is she? (62)

This passage not only allows the speaker to pause, as it were, before the closing passage of the speech, and to allow momentary humour into the speech, but also allows a further 'Commons' insight, and an attempt to exorcise the problem (which was to dog the Alliance into the following year and the general election) of the politically debilitating dual leadership of the Alliance. The passage involves the speaker's analysis of 'a much under-noticed interview' which raised the question of how long the Prime Minister would remain in office after an election. The humour of the passage is created by the notion of 'coupling' which arises from this: the Conservative alternatives being, judging by the laughter of the audience, hilarious. Various partners are put forward for 'Thatcher', the most hilarity-provoking being 'Gummer', 'Cecil' and, most of all, 'Currie'. This comic relief allows the audience a certain respite before the most dramatic moment of the speech: the concerted imposition of speaker persona upon the audience, the appropriation and displaying of an alternative claim to leadership legitimacy, a call for audience acceptance and endorsement of such legitimacy in a practical attempt to wrest from the party the explicit right to negotiate in the Alliance, and a symbolic attempt to wrest legitimacy from the audience itself as the representative of Liberalism. And the increasing references to Margaret Thatcher also imply Liberalism's equivalent, David Steel, at precisely the point in the speech where the speaker makes his most dramatic appeal to the audience.

The closing paragraphs (63–68) begin with a phrase which echoes the initial warning (paragraph 2) of the speech, which stated baldly that the party was throwing everything away as a result of its irresponsible behaviour:

> Now, fellow Liberals, the country *hungers* for a change of government (63)

The conditions of this change (which, given the speech so far, will involve not only a change of government but a change of society) are put as a major historical development which is now under threat. The Liberal Party has advanced:

> From the fringes of politics to the very centre of the stage, to the heartlands of Britain, to the edge of power, thanks to you, the people in this hall, and to tens of thousands of people who are not here today (63)

The conference is thus offered a tempting image of how close the Liberals are to power. It is, moreover, flattered ('thanks to you'). This flattery, however, is qualified by the withdrawing from the conference audience of any idea that it might be considered symbolically (as it is in most leadership addresses) as the party itself, or the microcosm of a future society by the 'tens of thousands of people who are not here today'. These latter are further endowed with a quality which the conference, as we have seen, has earlier been denied: the ability to establish the proper relation between the ideal and the real (irrespective of whether, in reality, the conference audience represents the true or near-true core of those 'tens of thousands').

An illustration of the real achievements of the party (as opposed to the aberrant conference) then follows, and takes the form, once again, of the communicating of personal experience to the inexperienced audience. Examples are given of the leader's own experience of a housing scheme, of a tenants' co-operative, and of industrial partnerships (64) in different parts of the country. In the context of the speech these are not simply local examples of Liberalism but microcosms of a national Liberalism. The notion of 'real' Liberalism is, therefore, underlined, to the detriment of the pie-in-the-sky Liberalism of the conference itself. The brutal reality follows these examples of nascent national Liberalism:

> But Britain as a whole is not a Liberal country, and we cannot convert it into one until we achieve power (64)

In the context of its own (local) experience of power, this brings the conference back, at the end of the speech, to the indispensable nature of the leadership/party/electorate relation.

The closing lines of the speech focus exclusively upon the persona of the speaker (65–68) and involve a concerted legitimation of his leadership from outside the present audience. The concertedness and the restrained emotion imply the rectitude of his position and the illegitimacy of the conference's. He first projects both himself and his experience in a witty denunciation which is immediately transformed into a highly rhetorical and emotional appeal to Liberalism as a missionary force:

> Now I am not interested in power without principles. But equally, I am only faintly attracted to principles without power. [Applause.] Without power, all our resolutions, all our idealism, all our passion will remain mere intention, mere hope, mere dream. We have so much to do, so much to change, great tasks to achieve. But we will do nothing, change nothing, achieve nothing unless we can first gain power and then use it wisely (65)

He then moves on to make a claim to a source of legitimacy which reaches beyond the conference to an event which predates it and which negates the conference's authority to counter his personal will and personal sense of mission:

> Ten years ago I became Leader of this party, the first leader of any party to be directly elected by its members throughout the country. And when I became Leader there were a number of promises I did not make. I didn't

promise to be a new John Stuart Mill and re-write the party's philosophy. I didn't promise to be a new Lloyd George and raise the wealth and resources of our organisation. [Laughter.] I didn't promise to be a new Gladstone running four administrations to the age of 85. But what I did promise was to lead the party to the achievement of power for Liberalism in our generation (66)

I made that commitment to you. And I will keep it. But you made a commitment to me. And I require *you* to keep it. [Applause.] (67)

The final sentence of this quotation obliterates the legitimacy of the conference vote while simultaneously appealing to *another* Liberal legitimacy. In this way, the speaker, bypassing the conference-as-party, lays claim to a more fundamental, though organisationally justified, form of allegiance, namely, his original elective leadership legitimacy. This not only renders leadership more legitimate than conference, but goes further than this in its implication that the conference has somehow betrayed the leader.

The closing passage involves a further appeal to another source of legitimacy, an implicit suggestion of the conference's inability to see beyond the four walls of the conference hall, the assertion of the leader's ability to do just that, and an implicit appeal to the conference to see what the speaker can see. It begins:

Beyond this hall people are waiting and *willing* us to win (68)

Collusion between speaker and audience, therefore, is re-established conditionally but is presented as a prerequisite to the success of a complex and important undertaking, involving a collusion of the conference audience/party with other transcendent groups, all rhetorically united by the word 'together' (see below). The keystone of this complex rally is the speaker himself and his moral vision (here depicted as his commitment to the party) but also involves the notion of honour, that is to say, the requirement that the party honour or re-honour an ancient allegiance which the leader has never forgotten. The leader's unfailing vision is, therefore, the key to the reconciliation of the ideal/practical dichotomy, such reconciliation being itself the automatic prerequisite to victory (and all the social changes which flow from it):

> Willing us, you and I – together. The parliamentary party and the party in the country – together. Liberals and Social Democrats – together. The British people – together. My commitment is to turn hope into fact, intention into achievement, and dream into reality. I will honour that commitment (68)

The wisdom of the leader's speech, therefore, implies a teleology which has been interrupted by the conference defence vote. The speech implies, by the same token, the conditional *re-establishment* of the teleology. In this sense, the speech involves the *necessary* dismissal of the conference and a *modified* renewal of allegiance to the leader as a prerequisite to the re-establishing of the teleology. He is forced by the conference defence vote to portray the party as being *not* part of that teleology (which leadership speeches must normally do), thus displacing the whole teleology on to himself and on to the 'qualities' of his leadership persona. This he can only do if he talks, as we have seen, as he does. By the same token, he is constrained to augment even further his own original and exclusive status in order to create an alternative to party legitimacy. The speech is, therefore, apart from the personalised argument we have identified, informed by a series of enhancements of the leader's persona which act as illustrations of leadership's personality traits. Let us, then, examine these.

2. Personality traits

Over and above the highly personalised argument itself, the authority and the legitimacy of the speaker's persona in the argument are emphasised by five elements in the speech which, taken together, amount to a portrait of the speaker's personality: the use of 'truths' and maxims which, acting as lessons in politics to the audience, frame the general discussions and confer on the speaker the status of political philosopher; the use of humour which, while serving the same functions as humour in David Owen's speech, allows for significant speaker/audience collusion in an unusually tense moment of the relationship between the two; the representation of David Steel as being in complete control of his relationship with David Owen, and in a position of equal, if not (secretly) superior, status to him; illustrations of the speaker's passion which betray both his moral and his combative strength; and, finally, significant reference to other sources of legitimacy which both act as a new legitimacy for the speaker and further undermine that of the audience. Let us list and comment on these here.

(a) Maxims and truths

People outside understand that applause is no substitute for getting our programme right (2)

The destructive years of Thatcherism are drawing to a close (3)

Real strength in a parliamentary democracy doesn't consist of imposing a minority view on the majority, it consists of finding the policies and giving the leadership which can unite the nation (7)

Let me define what I mean by 'Good government'. First, it should be constructive ... Good government should be de-centralised ... Good government should be open, not secretive ... Good government should be in the general public interest, not in the vested interest of one section or class in our country ... good government should help people to help themselves (9–13)

Declaring the objective isn't enough because the objective is not a policy (16)

The country needs a party with a lot of heart ... but it needs its head as well (17)

A nation that doesn't house its citizens properly is not entitled to call itself a civilised nation (47)

The occasional racist taxi driver is a minor social irritant; any racist policeman is a major social menace (61)

Without power, all our resolutions, all our idealism, all our passion will remain mere intention, mere hope, mere dream (65)

Each of these examples illustrates the speaker's wisdom,

his political realism, his reflective character and his morality, and further demonstrates that the projection of the speaker's personality is not solely dependent on pronominal reference. In fact, speaker status is increased by the deliberate impersonalism and, therefore, the universality of these statements.

(b) Humour

Paradoxically perhaps, given our analysis, there is an abundance of humour in David Steel's speech. Much of it is related to references to David Owen, and we shall examine these in the next sub-section. Let us here list the other examples:

> One of the traditional sports of party conferences is guessing the length of the Leader's ovation. And I don't advise anyone to take a bet on that this afternoon (1)
> And we are ready to join battle in Knowlesley North, just as soon as the slogan 'Kilroy *was* here' becomes a reality (4) [a reference to the out-going Labour MP and media personality, Robert Kilroy-Silk]
> And Nigel Lawson, the Chancellor of the Exchequer, is the ringmaster of this election circus (9)
> In the 1970s there was a party leader in Denmark who achieved some limited success . . . by arguing that he would save costs and reduce taxes by withdrawing his country from NATO and installing a taped message in Russian at all his country's airports saying 'We surrender.' (28)
> 'The Prime Minister has many qualities but I can't say that over-enthusiasm for the aid programme is one of them' (58) [Quoting ex-minister Timothy Raison's resignation letter]

Like the maxims in the speech, these humoristic interventions allow for a certain collusion with the audience, the comic relief, apart from its usual function, facilitating a relative de-culpabilising of the audience.

(c) The Steel/Owen relationship

In the context of the references to David Owen, we should bear in mind the many references to the SDP and especially to the Alliance itself. The frequent mention of David Owen here not only further increases the (discursive) reality of the Alliance, but also exorcises, by naming, the ghost of what was widely held to be David Steel's innocence *vis-à-vis* David Owen's assumption of superiority to, and even scorn for, his Liberal counterpart:

> The ... well-intentioned but completely misguided belief that in some way this Assembly's task was to accentuate the few remaining points of difference with the SDP in order [protesting voices], in order to, in order to, in order, in order to 'strengthen my hand' in manifesto negotiations with David Owen (18)
>
> Neither David Owen nor I are prepared to arrive at any election policy as a result of some botched-up bargaining process (19)
>
> We [David Owen and David Steel] wouldn't convince the country. We wouldn't convince you. We wouldn't even convince ourselves. We will arrive at our election policy by applying our common judgement ... We have ... we will ... as we (19)
>
> Both David Owen and I are well able to move forward now (21)
>
> The other event of yesterday concerns David Owen. We had what the *Sun* would call secret talks in London – watched by about 7 million people ... [Laughter.] Neither of us subscribes to the doctrine of infallibility of party leaders – at least I don't [laughter], but nor does he. And in fact no one should be worried by differences in style, or even occasionally of opinion between David Owen and me (22)
>
> At least when they vote for us the electors know they're getting Steel and Owen for the full four or five years. But who will they be getting if they vote Conservative? Thatcher and Howe? Thatcher and Tebbit? Thatcher and Gummer? [Laughter.] Thatcher and Cecil? [Laughter.] Or a truly well-matched duo, Thatcher and Currie? [Laughter. Applause.] I'm not sure that's quite what John Biffen had in mind when he called for a balanced ticket (62)

Given that the Owen/Steel relationship was crucial to Liberal Party leadership status at this point, let us comment upon this aspect of the speech in some detail.

First, it is clear that David Steel is projecting himself as being not afraid to talk about a near-taboo subject, viz., does

David Steel not realise that everybody thinks he is dominated by David Owen? He is thus replying to an unvoiced belief and, by so doing, contributes to its refutation. Second, his readiness to talk in a lighthearted manner about such a topic implies a secret fundamental knowledge possessed by the speaker which all others have been (hitherto but now no longer) unaware of. Thirdly, and relatedly, the speaker implies that he understands David Owen (both his strengths and his weaknesses), and this better than anyone else. Fourthly, the quotations cited suggest that any Napoleonic tendencies David Owen might have are severely constrained by David Steel's moral commitment to a contract (cf. 'We are either in alliance or we are not' is as much a censorship of SDP deviation from such a commitment as it is of the conference's). Fifthly, the several humorous references indicate that the Liberal leader is unworried by the party's own tentatively addressed concern that he is or will be dominated by David Owen. The references to Owen display to the party that it does not share (and therefore cannot know, and therefore is wrong in its interpretation of) the realities of the David Steel/David Owen relationship. And the speaker's stress upon this relationship is a further demonstration of what he knows and the audience does not know. Sixthly, the many comments on David Owen, and on David Steel's relationship with him, enhance the reality of personal leadership generally, thus legitimating it further, to the further diminution of the legitimacy of those who do not accept it. Seventhly, the references suggest that the speaker is no one's fool, even that he alone is aware of the perceived problems to the extent that he knows them better than does even the other person involved, David Owen. Finally, the references imply one of the most deeply-held myths in the political culture of, probably, all polities, namely, that wily political figures will overcome their self-appointed superiors (cf. Stalin, Trotsky; de Gaulle, Leclerc; Steel, Owen) after having allowed them to assume an apparent superiority.

(d) Passion
We have already seen how anger is used by the speaker as a discursive resource both to dominate the conference itself in the context of the defence vote, and in certain cases to

display a restrained Christian 'just anger' *vis-à-vis* the government's immorality. Let us restate and comment on these and
the other examples of outbursts which, cumulatively, project
the speaker as profoundly passionate and carrying within
himself (in conjunction with an as if unleashed Old Testament fury) the humanistic outrage and moral indignation of
the New Testament:

When I look at the vast Tory majority in the House of
Commons, when I see those serried rows of smug faces (6)
Our commitment to a reformed electoral system is unqual-
ified and absolute. We shall use all our weight and power
(8)
The long term and the future of the next generation are
being mortgaged by this moral myopia (9)
But we aren't going to *get* an Alliance government unless
the Alliance is credible (15)
And before I turn to . . . I must tell you bluntly (15)
All the passionate intensity at our command (15)
Well by God (17)
That is a breathtaking misjudgement . . . We must live and
breathe the Alliance (19)
I am reported as being angry with this Assembly. My
emotion is not one of anger but of profound frustration
(20)
We will strain every sinew (27)
But how I wish that the texts approved by our assemblies
would more often match the speeches made in their
support (30)
Our burning concern (39)
And what an indictment it is of past governments (41)
I can think of nothing more demoralising than bleak
sub-standard housing, nothing that makes people feel
more degraded than to have to eke out their daily lives in
conditions which, frankly, deny any possibility of a good
life (44)
I don't know what effect statistics like this have on you, but,
twenty years after *Cathy Come Home* and twenty years after I
became more personally involved with the problem as
Chairman of Shelter in Scotland, they fill me with fury.
Fury. Fury at successive governments whose neglect has

created this mess. Fury above all at this government whose policies have made the mess and misery so much worse (46)

But what we've got to do is to turn our fury into positive action (47)

Levels of human wretchedness which Mrs Thatcher in her tours of the Tory luncheon clubs of Britain never even bothers to see (47)

It is not only unacceptable in human terms, but it is economic madness (48)

And don't let people tell you we can't afford it (49)

Our words and our actions match each other squarely and honestly. And theirs don't (49)

We must act to end this national disgrace (50)

A crude and senseless vendetta (55)

Britain ought to be leading the way in support for world development. But what chance is there of that? (57)

What a commentary on the real values of our Prime Minister (58)

The horrifying and violent realities of Apartheid (58)

The Dallas-style affluence of Cape Town or Johannesburg (59)

The failure to discipline and eradicate racists within their ranks (61)

We have so much to do, so much to change, great tasks to achieve (65)

The first point to note here is that there are many examples of this strain of moral indignation in the speech. The second is that, when taken together, these examples demonstrate that the speaker's anger is not directed solely or even primarily at the party. The personality of the leader presented here is that of a man who has not only pursued power in a realistic way but is passionate about the moral aspects of life itself. In this way, the moral outrage directed at other issues not only fills out the persona of the speaker but also legitimates the anger which he directs at the party itself. The anger which is justified by attitudes to issues which Liberals hold dear (housing, racism and so on) in its turn justifies the anger turned on the conference. And the fact that the speaker contains his anger (at one point denying that it is anger and calling it rather frustration (20)) only serves to imply an even greater anger which is not expressed, as well as suggesting that he is able to control his formidable emotions (because it is simply what better people do) in a way that the conference cannot (because of the way it voted on the defence issue). Given, however, that the things which infuriate the speaker are, in nearly all cases, those which infuriate any decent person, there is a collusion between speaker and audience which further constrains the audience to accept the legitimacy of the speaker's anger.

(e) Claims to an alternative legitimacy

We have seen how a series of indirect claims to legitimacy is made through insights, maxims, the use of the Commons illustrations (of the 'I know, I was there' kind), the demonstration of knowledge, and so on. Let us here indicate the more explicit claims to legitimacy which take the form of direct reference, and which enhance the status of the speaker while setting up an alternative legitimacy to that of the audience. These alternative sources can be classified as those of: 'outside' individuals; the party and the Alliance (and the conference when it votes in accord with the leader's views); the people; and the speaker himself (over and above the liberal use throughout of the first person singular).

(i) Other individuals

Tennyson: 'Their honour rooted in dishonour stood' (6)
Jo Grimond: 'As Jo Grimond wrote on Wednesday: "For Britain alone to abandon nuclear weapons would be to retreat from those doctrines of international collaboration and collective security which have been a main aim in Liberalism."' (16)
Gary Hart: 'I agree with Gary Hart in criticising . . .' [At the time Hart was the highly popular expected Democratic candidate for the 1988 US presidential elections] (54)
Gladstone: 'William Gladstone's famous phrase, "the negation of God erected into a system of government"' [on South Africa] (59)
Journalists: 'Even journalists of the right like John Junor, Bernard Levin, and Peregrine Worsthorne have been

scathing in their condemnation' (61)

J. S. Mill and Lloyd George: 'I didn't promise to be a new John Stuart Mill ... I didn't promise to be a new Lloyd George ... I didn't promise to be a new Gladstone' (66)

(ii) The Liberal Party/The Alliance

In every part of Britain we are advancing (5)

I am proud to lead it [The party] (17)

Your ... endorsement (21)

The European ideals of this party, that we have proclaimed consistently since the 1950s (29)

The Alliance is about to launch a great housing campaign. Let's all support it (50)

The Liberal Party has advanced ... to the edge of power ... thanks to you, the people in this hall, and to tens of thousands of people who are not here today (63)

Many Liberal ideas are no longer just in pamphlets (64)

(iii) The people

I had planned to address my speech to a wider public (2)

People outside understand (2)

We've polled more votes in parliamentary by-elections than the Tory and Labour parties (4)

We Europeans (30)

And this, as I have seen, can transform the quality of life for millions of people (47)

Now, fellow Liberals, the country hungers for a change of government (62)

(iv) The speaker

I must tell you bluntly (15)

I too want intellectual consistency and integrity (16)

I am proud to lead it (17)

And the second point which troubled me (18)

And I, and I believe we can achieve (29)

My two parliamentary colleagues (30)

How I wish (30)

Here in Eastbourne I opened ... I visited ... I've visited (64)

Now I am not interested in power without principles. But equally, I am only faintly attracted to principles without power (65)

Ten years ago I became Leader of this party, the first leader of any party to be directly elected by its members throughout the country. And when I became Leader ... what I did promise was to lead the party to the achievement of power for Liberalism in our generation. I made this commitment to you. And I will keep it. But you made a commitment to me. And I require *you* to keep it (66–67)

The last quotation, which is the near-final utterance of the speech, is, in terms of our analysis, perhaps the most important of the entire speech and demonstrates the nature of leadership address to the conference. In the first place, allegiance to the persona of the speaker is asserted as a prerequisite to the achievement of governmental power. More importantly, however, the claim to legitimacy imposes upon the audience the Durkheimian notion that all that is in the contract is not contractual, that is to say, that the audience has momentarily forgotten the true sense of the party's original commitment to the leader at the moment of his election. He, on the other hand, is represented as never having forgotten the bond which the audience has here undone, the sacred agreement inadvertently or irresponsibly broken. The audience is, therefore, endowed or re-endowed at the end of the speech with a legitimacy, the recognition of which will bring 'power for Liberalism in our generation' *on condition that* it (re)ties its initial, mythical bond with its leader:

My commitment is to turn hope into fact, intention into achievement and dream into reality. I will honour that commitment. Together we have made a commitment to the people of our country and they require us to keep it (68)

4 Neil Kinnock and Democratic Socialism

The two operating principles of a contemporary Labour Party conference are fundamentally opposed to one another. The first is that the conference is the major organisational expression of internal party life, the second, that the conference is now a major media event. These two principles exist for the other parties too but because of, on the one hand, their lesser sacralisation of the conference itself and, on the other, the lesser media focus upon the notion of division, the tension is less keenly felt. In the Labour Party, this tension has significant implications for the status of leadership, both within the party and outside it.

The Labour Party has a long doctrinal tradition based upon hostility to the notion of personalised leadership. Doctrinally, leftist parties are, or assume themselves to be, inoculated against overtly personalised leadership (it is an implicit tenet of leftism that no single person is indispensable). Such a tradition constitutes a severely constraining critical discursive resource which may be used against leaders who lay claim to personal vision (the most common example of this being the accusation of authoritarianism). Moreover, in the historical context of the left generally, and particularly in the context of the British Labour Party, the idea of leadership 'sell-out' has a strong pedigree. All Labour leaders have enjoyed this dubious reputation: that once they gain power, and especially governmental power, they become corrupted and lose their sense of direction and connection with their purer party and doctrinal base. A heightened leadership status, therefore (especially in the context of the acute personalisation of leadership in the 1980s), will inform this accepted view still further, which in turn will increase the leadership's claim both to a continuing connection to the roots and myths of British leftism, and a moral strength

100

which protects it from succumbing to the traditionally corrupting influence of power.

Despite its doctrinal mistrust of personalised leadership, however, the party has traditionally tolerated this phenomenon on condition that leaders 'say the right thing' as it were, that is, maintain their discourse within the parameters of party policies and doctrine, thus projecting themselves as spokespersons for these and as the voice of contemporary Labourism. Given, however, that the range of opinions within the party is so diverse (and the fact that most Labour leaders to date have led their party from the right, particularly after they have enjoyed governmental power) it is very difficult for a Labour leader to claim to represent the whole movement. The difficulty, moreover, is aggravated by the opportunities given to alternative and dissenting voices (both by internal party democracy and by a media eager to exploit such differences to the full) to refute the claims of leadership. While it may be argued that such discordancy is, to a certain extent, the hallmark of the democratic process, one of the characteristics of 'successful' leadership in 1980s Britain was its undisputed character. In such a situation, therefore, the undermining of the idea of undisputed leadership will have particular political effects.

Because of the traditional hostility to personalised leadership, the Labour Party leader is also constrained by organisational procedures and by the distribution of power within the party. Labour leaders have much less power *vis-à-vis* the party and its activity and official discursive expressions than do, for example, leaders of the Conservative Party. Hence, in part, the moves at national level to centralise certain aspects of party activity since Neil Kinnock's election to the leadership in 1983. This development was motivated as much by the perceived need for an image of unfettered Labour leadership and the deployment of an uncontradicted discourse, as by the obvious advantages to leadership of greater central control.

The relative organisational weakness of the Labour leadership position obviously has symbolic repercussions upon the image of the party's leadership, an image which can be questioned at the conference in particular. Many leadership-backed issues are regularly defeated at conference and the leader often attacked, directly or implicitly, by rostrum speakers – though only rarely, and usually only implicitly, by platform speakers. On this last point, however, it is common knowledge in the party that at any given time in the party's history certain National Executive Committee (NEC) platform figures are hostile to the leader. Hostility to the special according of status to leaders can be emphasised by those on the platform who make a moral or doctrinal point by remaining seated after the leader's speech during the standing ovation, now considered de rigueur at party conferences. (In 1986, however, only Joan Maynard and Dennis Skinner, applauding, and Eric Heffer, not applauding, remained seated. By the same token, Tony Benn's applauding and standing enhanced further the idea of the left's endorsement of the leader's status at this conference.)

With regard to attitudes towards leadership within the Labour Party, all conferences now take place within a particular *kind* of media scrutiny. The media searches for division within all parties. But in the case of the Labour Party it assumes this division to be a constant and exploits it relentlessly. Given its own appraisal of the traditional strain of hostility towards leadership on the left, the media will take full advantage of anything which resembles the undermining of leadership authority within the party. Linked to this, especially since the Conservative election victory of 1979, is the generalised exploitation by the media of the question of the Labour Party's credibility as a party of government, and, therefore, by extension, of its leader as a credible Prime Minister. Three of the six Labour leaders since the war have held prime ministerial office. Throughout the 1980s, Neil Kinnock could not claim ministerial, let alone prime ministerial, status. Apart from the obvious symbolic disadvantages of this, Kinnock's only scope for a display of authority was within his own party.

In terms of Kinnock's leadership status *vis-à-vis* the party, we can make several further observations. First, after four years of major conflict within the party which culminated in the electorally disastrous 1983 election, fought under the leadership of Michael Foot, Kinnock was portrayed as a leader who symbolised the party's return to the road to

power. Secondly, Neil Kinnock's leadership status was enhanced by what was known at the time as the 'dream ticket'
partnership of himself (centre-left) as leader, and Roy Hat-
tersley (centre-right) as deputy leader, a ticket which was
designed to symbolically portray and practically effect the
reunification of the party after the divided years of 1980–83.
Such a situation would enhance Kinnock's claim to a kind of
rally leadership. Thirdly, in 1986, Margaret Thatcher was no
longer, according to polls, such a popular figure as she had
been during the Falklands War of 1982, and there was even
speculation that she was regarded as an electoral liability by
many Conservatives, with all the consequences within the
Conservative Party which might ensue, and all the kudos a
united Labour Party and its leader might gain from these.
Fourthly, the Labour leader remained, in spite of his party's
political fortunes in the 1980s, the most likely alternative
Prime Minister to Margaret Thatcher. Fifthly, Neil Kinnock's
standing as a strong leader, within the party and among the
wider public, had been raised by his widely publicised action
against the Militant Tendency in the previous year, and by
his spectacular attack upon it at the 1985 conference (which,
interestingly, had taken the form, in the media and, in part,
also in reality, of a personalised duel between the leader of
the party and the deputy leader of Liverpool Council, Derek
Hatton). This notable event was a demonstration of how the
Labour Party leader had in effect used the party conference
as a media event, not only to improve his own personal,
national status, but also to weaken a perceived opposition,
and thus increase his authority in the party.

  Therefore, there was a generalised view inside the party,
because of the notion of post-1983 revival, and outside,
because of media treatment, that the Labour Party had
become 'Kinnock's' party to a certain extent (and, by extension, the conference 'his' conference). This view had been
strengthened by the fact that, by 1986, Neil Kinnock and his
style of leadership had gained the increasingly publicly
verbalised backing of the majority of the trade union leaders
within the party (whose organisations had a 40 per cent stake
in the election of the leader). The party, moreover, aware of
its electoral difficulties, was developing, at all levels, a generalised discourse of 'realism', and a recognition of the need to

be more sensitive, whatever the merits of such democratic processes, to the public effect of its internal struggles. Organisationally and doctrinally, therefore, the party was responding to the media-led assumption that political success was dependent upon demonstrations of party solidarity with leadership and that the image of unopposed 'strong' leadership was an electoral asset.

The 1986 Labour Party conference, moreover, in part as a result of this general response within the party, was qualitatively different in its self-presentation from all its predecessors. It was generally regarded as smooth, professional, slick. It was 1986 that saw the majority of male speakers on the platform dressed in smart lounge suits; the platform itself well designed with a subtle use of materials and colour – to the advantage of beige and grey and the detriment of 'revolutionary' red – and avoiding, with the TV camera in mind, the usual distraction to the eye of people moving around behind speakers; the introduction of the rose symbol to replace the red flag; well-run debates (speakers often selected in advance); the avoidance of interminable unscheduled arguments between protesters from the floor who knew conference procedures and officials who were less sure of them; the use of closed sessions to deal with internal disciplinary procedures; relaxed press conferences; a glossy party literature, and so on. The 1985 conference, moreover, had already seen a significant personalisation of the leader's speech, particularly as a rhetorical device in the attack upon Militant, and thus the legitimation of this style of discursive delivery through the creation of a developing tradition and consequent expectation of a personalised leadership discourse. By 1987 this now-legitimated personalisation would become a vital element in the Labour Party's election campaign, if not its most dominant feature.

On the questions of the internal and projected status of the Labour Party conference itself, we can make several observations. There is, for example, a great deal of real 'business' to get through (and, invariably, it is not completed); paradoxically, the 'dryness' of this aspect of the conference enhances its ritual sense of importance. Moreover the conference delegates themselves vote on policy, on internal procedures, on the topics selected for debate, and on the election of officers, each of these having a significant effect upon the distribution of power inside the party's decision-making bodies, and upon subsequent policy itself; the decisions taken at conference are therefore very much more important than those of, say, the Conservative or Liberal parties where conference decisions in practice have no statutory effect upon leadership decisions. This idea of the seriousness of the Labour conference is boosted by the Labour Party's own view that the other conferences, especially that of the Conservative Party, are merely charades where no real decisions are taken.

Therefore, because of its procedural correctness, its elaborate nature, its very real effects upon power relations within the party, its historical sense, and the status conferred upon its delegates, the Labour Party conference is considered by delegates as the site of the party addressing itself seriously and consequentially, and as a true and total expression of its organisational right and historically informed (and historically sanctified) authority to speak *for* the broad church of leftism in Britain and, by extension, to speak *as* the unarticulated voice of the British people. The delegates at a Labour Party conference, moreover, are normally very aware of this sense of history within the party and the role of the conference within this (certain conferences in particular are remembered as having deep historical significance both for the party and for the history of Britain, the 1960 and 1980 conferences being perhaps the most famous recent examples). The conference is, moreover, the symbolic as well as the actual meeting of the historical family of Labour: the trade unions, the CLPs, the people's representatives – the MPs and MEPs (who all sit together though do not vote), the Cooperative Movement, the socialist societies, the Young Socialists. There is also an international dimension (organisationally expressed in terms of visitors to the conference) which augments further the status of the conference and emphasises the left's internationalism and its formal links with other Socialist and social-democratic parties, and liberation movements. Such internationalism endows the conference with a sense of global historical importance. This international aspect, and the international status it confers, was conspicuously affirmed in 1986 by the warmly received speech of Willy Brandt, ex-Chancellor of the German Federal Republic.

The sense of the party's history, with its attendant sentiments of individual humility and collective greatness, is heightened at the Labour Party conference by the Merit Awards which are conferred upon two 'ordinary' activists within the party; these awards invariably involve people whose commitment, and memory, go back to the early days of British Labourism. They thus legitimate the teleology which underpins leftism, the sense of commitment of those present, the undeniable nature of the relation between the past and the present, and the historical memory of the contemporary party. The Merit Award speeches involve the recounting of particular tales of injustices done to, say, miners or suffragettes, and of the historic struggle of individuals or groups against adversity or oppression. These tellings, along with the touching presence of physically frail elderly people (often inexpert at public speaking on this scale and unused to microphones) who have dedicated (and continue to dedicate) their lives to the cause of the left, bring to the conference both emotion and a link with the past (and therefore, teleologically, with the future). Significantly, it is the leader's speech which follows on directly from the presentation of the Merit Awards, thus linking the leader with the impeccable activist credentials of those who have preceded him on the platform (a link which contributes to the status of leadership persona, as we shall see).

For all of these reasons, both symbolic and practical, the Labour Party conference possesses a fine sense of occasion whose emotionalism can be exploited by leadership discourse on condition that it remain acutely sensitive to the party's historical and ideological parameters. Organisationally, however, the conference also imposes constraints which diminish leadership status and its ability to use organisational and symbolic factors to its advantage, and which add to the doctrinal and traditional constraints upon leaders we discussed above.

The Labour leadership speech is, in organisational terms, nothing more than the NEC's report to the conference. The leadership speech invariably follows the Merit Awards and, therefore, traditionally takes place at a given time (the Tuesday afternoon of the conference). It cannot, therefore, portray itself as the climax of the various discourses and emotions of the totality of the conference itself. As all ritualists know, the most significant speech at any rally is the ultimate one – which is the case with the Liberals, the SDP and the Conservatives, as it is indeed with most party conferences and political rallies abroad. The Labour Party leadership speech is procedurally and traditionally 'held' to a particular and earlier point in the proceedings. This situation makes it extremely difficult for the leadership to orientate the occasion to its advantage. The conference continues, organisationally, symbolically and discursively, for three more days, thus depriving the leader of the opportunity to present himself as a discursive climax, as it were (and, practically, preventing him from effecting any damage-limitation as, say, the Liberal leadership speech had to). At the 1988 conference, for example, Ron Todd the Transport Union leader's widely-reported attacks upon the leadership later on in the week seriously undermined Kinnock's image, and the notion of party unity.

A related factor is that in certain respects the conference cannot represent itself as transcendental at all. It is, as we have mentioned, the site of real power struggles which, by definition, undermine the rally quality of leadership discourse, and the conference's self-representation as a rally. And the presence and the speeches of trade union barons, whether supportive of the leader or not, lend an unconvincing quality to any transcendental flights of rhetoric. We can add that critical floor speakers can themselves use a morally or doctrinally informed style to undermine the representation of the conference as a rally, such as those who draw conference's, and the TV cameras', attention to the emptying conference hall when certain issues (the situation of Blacks or women, for example) are discussed. Nevertheless, at the 1986 conference, partly as a result of meticulous conference organisation, partly as a result of a generalised sensitivity to media scrutiny before a general election, contestatory voices were minimal. And it is interesting to note that in 1986, unlike in 1985 and 1987, there was no heckling during the leader's speech, this strengthening the notion of a party as being a rally around an undisputed leader.

In terms of the speech itself, one of the extra-party, media-cultivated myths which a leftist leadership speech must cope with is the received opinion that the leader's speech, however authoritative, masks the fact that it is the union leaders or, paradoxically, left-dominated CLPs who really control the party and with it the leader himself. The other parties rarely face this problem – a strong leadership speech there is usually sufficient evidence of leadership control of the party. In the Labour Party, the leadership speech must project the idea that the authority revealed therein is not merely an indication of leadership control for the time of the speech itself, but a true discursive reflection of the leader's authority.

There are several other contextual factors which inform the leader's speech at the Labour Party conference. First, the contemporary organised left has few good orators who can provide a cumulative transcendental register for the conference as a whole. At conference the few that there are are usually either ordinary party members or else figures who are themselves critical of leadership, such as Dennis Skinner or Arthur Scargill, or Tony Benn, this last, one of the most brilliant orators the British left has produced. This inability to create a crescendo of conference discourse can cause a certain difficulty for leadership discourse itself because the latter contrasts so strikingly with the pedestrian style of most of the speakers and, especially, with the 'framework' discourse of the conference president, provided, in 1986, by Neville Hough. By the same token, leadership discourse can, of course, stand out above these lesser discourses. It must, nevertheless, take account of this dominant form of conference discourse in order that it avoid the accusation of a demonstrable inappropriateness, inappropriateness in ritual leading very easily to ridicule. To a certain degree, Neil Kinnock is helped in this because his accent is itself appropriate to most rhetorical registers. His (like David Steel's) is a non-English accent, which not only has a real legitimacy within the party (because of the mines and Wales' working-class tradition), but has become far more nationally acceptable since its inscription, along with nearly all middle-class variants of regional accents, into media discourse since the mid-1970s.

Before analysing the text itself, we can make two points here pertaining to this idea of discursive reliance upon Neil Kinnock's 'self'; the first concerns the speaker's style, the second, the way in which the topics in the speech are treated.

In terms of the speaker's style, two factors (of much less relevance in the other speeches studied) take on a particular importance: first, Neil Kinnock's bodily movements, facial expressions, pauses, and, equally significant in terms of the verbalised effort of speech delivery, the impression of deep conviction, and the major deviations from the text in front of him which strengthen the personalised effect of the speech, all increase the personalised quality of the speech. We shall examine in the text the projection of his persona. We can note here, however, that both the tone (which runs the gamut from extreme quietness to shouting) and the projected emotions (which run from humility and sorrow through snarling sarcasm and 'realism' to quasi-religious fervour) reinforce the idea of the speech as springing from the speaker's own personal vision. In the name of the 'conviction politics' forced upon all parties by the style of Margaret Thatcher's discourse, the 'broad church' or 'tolerant' discursive manner of, say, Jim Callaghan is abandoned completely, and this in all aspects of the speech: those which discuss the 'practical' as well as those concerned with doctrinal issues. We shall return to the implications of this for leftist discourse in our conclusion.

The second point is that, in terms of its superficial form and thematic organisation, the speech is straightforward: it is divided approximately (and traditionally) into four near-equal sections which deal, respectively, with government and society, the economy, international issues, and defence (in this it is formally very similar to the other speeches, especially David Steel's). In its deeper structure, however, and in the context of the issues highlighted above – the strong party sense of itself, the elaborate doctrinal tradition, the concerted search for (elusive) power, the strong media presence, and the new exigencies of personalised leadership, the speech is organised around three themes: a dualistic representation of the world, involving essentially a description of the government as the manifestation of one side of that representation, 'the people' and socialism as the other; the presentation of a project or programme which implies a social transformation of mythic proportions; and the representation of Neil Kinnock himself as the legitimate voice of British socialism and (because he is in a privileged relationship to the socialist *movement*, of which the party and conference are the legitimating expressions) the main architect of the project. Bearing this in mind, let us analyse the speech.

THE TEXT

1. The representation of the world

After 1983, the image of the Labour Party (in both the media's representation of Kinnock and the depiction of him by the party's left) was that of a party moving to the right, away from Militant influence on the one hand, and old-style nationalisation on the other, and towards a 'sensible' image, an appeal to the middle classes, and the development of the language and policies of the 'new realism'. The world view offered in the 1986 leadership speech, however, is radicalised dramatically. In essence, the depiction of the world involves a return to a leftist interpretation which predates its entry into government in the 1920s. The main advantage of such an interpretation is that it allows the leader to represent himself as leading a party whose task is, like that of the old ILP and the British left generally in the late nineteenth and early twentieth centuries, to rally the people to power. One of the consequences of this approach, moreover, is that it allows leadership discourse to circumvent the accusations of leadership betrayal (in terms of its image and policies) and bypass the dichotomy set up between party discourse and governmental action as it developed from Ramsay MacDonald's leadership onwards. The policies, as we shall see in the next section of this chapter, can be described (except for those concerning defence) as being, essentially, social democratic and incrementalist. The vision of the world which underpins these policies, however, is itself both revolutionary and populist – the resolution of the apparent paradox being the bizarre idea that the social democratic/incrementalist political tradition and the revolutionary/populist social interpretation are both integral parts of a fundamentally British tradition. It is the deployment in discourse of a patriotic communitarianism which creates the sense of natural liaison between the revolutionary/populist interpretation of society and incrementalist democracy. The notion of patriotism therefore plays a significant role in Neil Kinnock's speech in terms of the justification of *both* social interpretation and political prescription. Patriotism in Neil Kinnock's discourse, much more than, for example, internationalist solidarity, will, moreover, be the fundamental justification of defence policy. This 'rereading' of British leftism will also involve the projection of the speaker as the bearer of a particular half-forgotten historical 'message'.

In the speech, the representation of the world, and of British society in particular, is dualist. We can demonstrate how society is represented by looking at, first, the representation of the right in the speech, and, then, that of the people and the party's relation to the people. We should bear in mind that these two representations intertwine all the time (although the former is dominant earlier, enabling the latter to be directly linked to the exposition of the second main theme of the speech, that of the party's programme which acts rhetorically as a resolution of the dualism depicted). For the purposes of exposition, however, we can analyse them sequentially.

(a) The rulers
The government is presented in the speech, not as a government *per se*, but as a group of *rulers*. Even the personalisation of the main adversary, the Prime Minister, is diminished in this part of the speech in order that this image of a ruling group or caste be elaborated and maintained. The depiction draws upon eighteenth-century European political discourse and eighteenth and early nineteenth century British radicalism, thus, in the first place, underplaying the notion of these 'rulers' having been elected, and, in the second, emphasising that they will be in some way deposed or overthrown. The

first quality attributed to the rule of the rulers is that it divides and weakens, a fundamental myth in populism:

> This eighth year of Thatcherism. Ninety months of Maggie. Ninety months in which our society has become more divided than at any time since the Second World War. Ninety months in which our industry has been devastated as never before (2)

The notion of a period of rule is reinforced, therefore, by the idea of the continuity of the rule, like that of a monarch. But:

> We've had those years of Thatcherism (3)

This is followed by an elaboration of the recovery of the Labour Party (and a scathing reference to the alternative, the Alliance). We shall come back to these in the next section. The link between this elaboration and the return within the speech to the representation of the right as rulers is the reference to the party which asks for:

> The democratic chance to show just what we can do (11)

Given both the depiction of a period of 'rule' and the fact that there is no reference to the democratic nature of the election of the actual rulers, the connotation is (a) that the rule of Thatcherism is illegitimate and (b) that the Labour Party (and its leader as the new ruler) will be just rulers. The status of rulers ascribed to the government is therefore maintained, in part, by the suggestion of the Labour Party as *alternative* rulers. The notion that the unjust ruler will be replaced by the just is one of the myths at the heart of English political culture, connoting the traditional stories of 'good' King Richard and 'bad' King John. The main discussion of these rulers amplifies this traditional idea of bad kingship in that it is based upon their unfitness to rule:

> We have seen, of course, what others do. We have seen their seven savage years. We've seen what they have done to our country (12)

The emphasis throughout the depiction is of a 'they', that is, the ruling caste.

The speaker goes on:

> Given declining unemployment . . . they've increased . . . .

Given record manufacturing investment ... they've cut.... Given a working body ... they've lopped off.... Given a stable world trade position ... they have lost.... Given the fantastic bonus ... they have blown it, wasted it.... That and much more, so much more, makes them a government that is unfit to govern. They are rulers who, in Percy Shelley's words, 'Rulers who neither see, nor feel, nor know, but, leech-like to their fainting country cling' (13)

From the above quotation, it is clear that the judgement upon the unfitness of the rulers to rule or govern is based not only upon the actual effects of their rule but upon their insensitivity and their betrayal of the trust placed in them. The reference to Shelley has four rhetorical effects. First, like David Steel's quoting of Tennyson, it, quite simply, demonstrates the speaker's erudition and sense of the British tradition. Second, it draws upon a poet who is universally regarded as one of England's best, and by the left as a revolutionary poet (unlike the rest of England's best poets who were not, with the possible exception of Blake), in this way offering an English tradition *to* leftism. Third, it enables the speaker to enhance dramatically the notion of the period and quality of rule; that the rulers are quasi-eternal and eternal betrayers. Fourth, it both refers the actual rulers back to the earlier rulers *and* updates the notion of betrayal, thus enabling the speaker to depict the right as the contemporary manifestation of a historically oppressive evil and the eternal treachery of bad rulers.

Unlike David Steel's Tennyson reference, Neil Kinnock's reference to Shelley is developed rhetorically, thus augmenting the referential effects identified above. Picking up on the quotation, the speaker goes on:

Leech-like, they have increased.... Leech-like, they have allowed (14)

'They' and 'rulers' are then brought into the speech again and their characteristics repeated (and their 'eternal' rule brought forward to the Victorian period, thus underlining further the notion of a continuing oppression):

Those rulers who neither see, nor feel, nor know, have cut.... That's what those rulers have been doing in their blindness, their stupidity, their malice, in this last seven years. And all, and all of the time that they've been doing that, we've heard the strident homilies of Victorian values and of morality (14–15)

To the uncaring aspect and malicious evil of these rulers, unfit in terms of both efficacy and morality, is added a further quality essential to their vileness, namely, hypocrisy (and from this we can see that such a representation corresponds with both a populist (rulers are devious) and class (bourgeois ideology is a structural inversion of reality) social analysis):

Strident homilies of Victorian values and of morality. Homilies on the virtues of .... Homilies on the virtues of .... Homilies on the virtues of .... And even then, what is given with one hand ... is taken away with the other by a government that denies resources to the carers of this country (15–18)

This chain of qualities: bad rulers, treacherous rulers, heartless rulers, rulers who usurp the discourse of morality in order to dissimulate their shallowness and their moral bankruptcy, is then focused sharply on Mrs Thatcher and on one of the main images of the speech, that of the family (we shall come back to the representation of the family in the next sub-section):

Mrs Thatcher says that her policies start with the 'freedom and well-being of the family' (19)
The Prime Minister lectures the family, lectures the country on morality (21)

This notion of the 'lecturing' rulers is given as further evidence of the link between the historical and contemporary deviousness of the right, and the Victorian reference is updated to the 1930s, thus reinforcing, once again, the notion of an oppressive historical continuum:

It reminded me of the Tory lady who in the Depression was generous enough to give lectures to the families of the unemployed on what nourishing soup they could make with fishheads (21)

We have seen that the speaker has linked present to past
rulers and built up, through the depiction of a series of
qualities shared by them in the eighteenth, nineteenth and
twentieth centuries, the notion of their common abandonment of their obligations, seen already in their mistreatment
of the country. Their insensitivity to its pain is then developed in the form of examples of the contemporary
manifestation of the consequences of such abandonment:

> We got the lectures on morality when the Silentnight
> Company, when British Coal, when News International
> desert their basic obligations ... the pious sermons, the
> self-righteous homilies ... easier than facing the real
> problems or answering the real questions (21–22)

We have here, therefore, the contemporary manifestation
of the behaviour of the rulers and further evidence that they
are alienated totally from the ruled. This suggested alienation then allows the speaker to claim a contrary relation, that
of true knowledge of the ruled and of the effects of the action
of the rulers upon them. Reference to the rulers' alienation
from the oppressed is therefore reiterated and the speaker's
personal insight, as demonstrated by the interrogative form
(which involves truisms shared by all), are thus presented
simultaneously:

> When it is so obvious that a drugs plague ... why get
> rid ... ? When it is so obvious that dark streets ... why not
> invest ... ? When violence is such a terrible menace ... why
> can't ... ? Why can't ... ? When it is clear ... why ... Why
> ... Why ... ? When it is obvious ... why not ... instead of
> simply saying that it's 'disappointing' or 'one of the great
> mysteries of our time' as Mrs Thatcher does (23–27)

It is in this way that the speaker introduces both a description
of those affected by the indifference of the rulers, namely,
the ruled, and his own and the party's relationship to them.
And we can note here that Labour Party policy will be
subsequently framed in terms as dualist as the depiction of
society itself, that is, as a means of release from the rulers and
from their oppression.

We can see, moreover, from the end of the above quotation how all the qualities of the rulers are displaced on to the character of Margaret Thatcher, especially her inability to 'see', as Shelley noted of earlier rulers, and how the citing of her *words* is demonstrative proof of her possession of these negative qualities (the *speaker's* clear ability to 'see' lending him (and the movement *he* leads) qualities opposite to these). She is, therefore, not simply a bad ruler but the personification of age-old misrule itself. Having thus made an appraisal of what these rulers do, the speaker then proceeds, developing the functional nature of the quality of hypocrisy, to the next consequential act of their treachery, the flaunting of an ideal society which is the negation of reality itself, and which insults particularly groups held dear in any society: the old, the young, and the family:

> These people, these Tories dress up the get-rich-quick society as the 'opportunity society'. They continually represent arrogance and aggression as the only proof of strength. They have dedicated every policy to making the very rich richer and the poor, poorer. They flaunt a commercial paradise before the young people of this country . . . . With their, with their 40p pensions rise and their concessionary fares cuts . . . cuts . . . cuts, they daily, these moralists, breach the commandment that teaches us 'Honour thy father and thy mother'. That's the morality of this government (28–29)

The indignant and highly moral (here, in fact, religious) tone of the speaker is matched by the intervention of the persona of the speaker:

> I, I look at all that and I ask myself just where do they get their idea of morality? (30)

This allows the speaker to link his own persona more strongly to the people, the oppressed, by implying, after mention of:

> The malice and meanness of Toryism . . . dual standards . . . double-talk sermons (31)

his personal identification with the other 'grouping' (the people) which is not 'a narrow, bigoted, self-righteous grouping' (31). We shall come back to the linking of speaker persona to this grouping. Here we can say that the description of the people as not narrow, bigoted or self-righteous is a further indication of the possession of these named shortcomings by the rulers, the rulers who have brought 'hell on earth' (33). This reference to the qualities of the rulers which are not shared by 'the grouping' leads into the speaker's interpretation of (and connection to) the people which we shall analyse in the next section.

The remaining references which serve to depict the rulers are intermittent. They act nevertheless as reminders of the initial dramatic representation of the rulers. It is also worth noting that, from this point in the speech, the characteristics of dissimulation, false homily, blindness, and brutality are displaced unequivocally from 'the rulers' on to Margaret Thatcher as if she were the apogee of this historical movement. Here are the main examples:

> The pious sermons of Maggie's morality (36)
> Mrs Thatcher's rule (42)
> In these years of Thatcherism (54)
> She says she won't . . . because she's not prepared . . . . That is very touching. Or at least it would be touching if it wasn't so cruelly obvious that Mrs Thatcher *is* prepared to leave our children with . . . . Somehow, somehow she doesn't care . . . . You see, it is one thing to say to your children, since she's so concerned about the children . . . . The Thatcher option. That is the imprudent, careless way (61–63)

As we have indicated, this portrayal of the right is mingled with the cataloguing of the perceived qualities of those whom the rulers rule, this juxtaposition throwing into high relief the differences between the two groups, the rulers and the ruled.

(b) *The ruled*

In the speech, the British people, 'the moral majority' as they are called, are divided into three sections: the poor, the average earners and the better off. This three-way division is named just before the party programme is elaborated (paragraphs 38–60), this last being, therefore, as if sanctioned by this 'great grouping' (31). At the beginning of the speech, too, the people are seen as an active, united 'grouping', and as 'our country', 'Britain', 'the people of this country', 'this country of ours', 'the British people', expressions which recur over and over throughout the speech. However, in the evocative initial representation of the three-part ruled entity, it is the first category, the poor, which is given, by far, the largest single rhetorical focus. The second, the average earners, and the third, especially, the better off, are given much less space. The representation of the first grouping alone, moreover, runs in tandem (15–34), as we have said, with the depiction of the rulers, and to dramatic effect, radicalising and polarising as it does the speaker's view of the world and modifying the notion of the Labour Party's preoccupation with the other two depicted groups. The representation of the toiling, wounded masses is prefaced by the last words of the Shelley quotation which vilify the rulers:

'Leech-like to their fainting country cling' (13)

Unlike many contemporary leftist expositions of injustice, the speaker both draws heavily upon eighteenth and nineteenth century depictions of the poor, and focuses upon the poor specifically as individuals and as families (rather than as a category, or as 'the poor' (cf. David Owen's speech), or as a class or underclass). At the beginning of his exposition, the speaker reminds the audience of the lived reality of this suffering:

And these are not just attacks on institutions. These are direct attacks on individuals and their liberties, families and their needs
Millions who would like nothing more than to have the rudimentary means to be self-reliant
Families in poverty . . . constantly humiliated as they try to clothe and feed themselves and their children
Those who care for old and sick and disabled loved ones
Six million people in this country now so impoverished that they can't even afford essential items of clothing. When there are two million children living in families dependent on supplementary benefit. When one in four families in Britain is living in substandard housing. When thousands of homeless families are condemned to the

appalling conditions of bed and breakfast accommodation (15–20)

We can see that all figures or statistics given are always reinforced by the evocation of individuals, families, loved ones, people, children, and homeless families. An illustration of the psychological depth of these wounded millions is given, significantly, in the response to the Tory lady, thus personifying and individualising them further. The voice given to these millions, moreover, modifies slightly the allusions to the more paternalistic eighteenth and nineteenth century depictions (for example Dickens). In reply to the Tory lady, the speaker quotes the woman who said:

'That's very nice, my lady, but could you tell us who has the rest of the fish?' (21)

The register of this essentially eighteenth and nineteenth century (and now 1930s) representation of the British poor is maintained throughout the description of contemporary ills, rhetorically paralleling the ruler analogy:

A drugs plague endangers young people in our country
Dark streets and labyrinth housing estates, and insecure doors and windows
Such terror to people – especially old people
Violence against women
Victims [of] that perpetual fear of the returning brutal husband
Thousands of lives could be saved and terrible anxiety and pain could be relieved.
Death rates, mental and physical sickness rates, suicide and family breakdown rates
They have dedicated every policy to making the very rich richer and the poor poorer
Unemployment and insecurity
A purgatory on those young people (23–28)

We can see that both the historical and the contemporary poor (and the contemporary 'grouping' of people) are portrayed in a Dickensian or evangelist way. They are also endowed by the speaker with an (albeit stereotypical) psychological depth (cf. the 'that's very nice, my lady' retort). We can make three points here. The first is that the endowing of the 'grouping' with psychological depth immediately precedes the reference to the other two groups (the average family and the better-off, the voters whom the Labour Party must gain if it is to govern), thus enabling the speaker to maintain the discourse of an earlier populism in his discussion of the other groups. Second, the psychological depth of the 'grouping' is nevertheless deprived of a *political* awareness until the party's programme is brought into the discourse. And, third, the linking of the three groups and the presentation of a political solution to the historical/eternal dilemma of oppression are linked to the speaker himself:

> I, I look at all that and I ask myself just where do they get their idea of morality? And the British people ask the same question. There's a great grouping in our society that opposes the malice and the meanness of Toryism. There is a huge number which abominates the dual standards and the double-talk sermons. There is in this country, there always has been, there always will be, a moral majority. It is not a narrow, bigoted, self-righteous grouping. It is a broad-minded and compassionate grouping of people (30–31)

This 'great grouping' has the further qualities of being unsentimental and realistic (31). The party itself, and the speaker, are linked to this grouping; because it is realistic, it will rally to the party as if roused by the speech itself:

> We as democratic socialists make our appeal to that moral majority (32)

From our analysis here we can see that the much commented appropriation by the Labour leadership speech of a rightist notion (the moral majority) is a complex one, and involves a series of historical reference points which justify the appropriation. In this passage, 'moral majority', 'moral', 'morality', or 'majority' are repeated nine times in rapid succession (paragraphs 31–36). There is further reference to the toiling people, but two things can be noted in the following quotation: (1) the majority is no longer that of the toiling masses; these are only 'part of' it (although the remainder have not been introduced yet and therefore are not 'part of' the following quotation); (2) the toilers are depicted as possessing self-awareness (but still not political awareness):

> Part of that majority would consider itself well blessed if it had just a roof over its head, if they had a job to go to, if they knew that the colour of their skin inflicted no extra disadvantage on them, they would consider themselves well blessed. If they didn't have to fear electricity or gas bills with all the torturous anxiety of poverty, if they could afford a pair of shoes for the children without being fearful of an economic crisis in the family, they would consider themselves to be well blessed (34)

It is here that the other two groups which make up that majority (and involve virtually everyone, in fact) are introduced. Interestingly, the second grouping (which comprises the vast majority of the British electorate) is given voice (cf. the earlier 'fishheads' direct quotation), the third, that of the better-off, is not. We should note, however, that when the second grouping is given voice, its relationship to the speaker is crucial. We should note that it is this group more than any other that the Labour Party leadership saw as necessary to its electoral success. We should note also its family-centred emphasis:

> They still say to me: 'We're not badly off, but we can't get our Mam into hospital.' 'We're not badly off, but with two younger children at home, we just haven't got the room to accept the daughter and the son-in-law, they can't come and live with us.' 'We're not badly off, I'm working, my husband is working, but our twenty-year-old son has never had a job and our sixteen-year-old is leaving school this year and doesn't even know where to start looking for a job.' (35)

A brief reference is made to the third grouping (the better-off), although this is not given a voice and there are no elaborate images; there is, however, an acknowledgement of its moral sense and the appeal is made in terms of a middle-class moral indignation at the way in which 'others' are treated:

> There are millions too who are not even affected at that range by the problems who consider.... They want a government that doesn't preach the pious sermons of Maggie's morality, but practises the policies of provision.... They want a government that will back up its morality by policies (36)

The speaker then adds:

> We, indeed only we, will provide that government for Britain (36)

This linking of 'they' (the three-part grouping of poor, average, and better-off) and 'we' (the Labour Party) is followed by the elaboration of the party's programme and intentions, the above quotation being the lead into it. We shall come back in a moment to the manner in which this is presented. First, we must go back to the beginning of the speech to see how 'we' (the party) has been legitimated, that is, has been (a) linked to the people as a moral microcosm of it (that is, possessing the qualities of the people elaborated so far), and (b) depicted as an effective political representation of it.

It is worthy of note here that the review of the party comes – unusually – at the beginning of the speech. (More commonly in leftist leadership discourse it appears at the end.) This is an indication of how the establishing of the relation party/people is dependent upon the notion of the party programme which follows on directly, and thereby uncontentiously, from the discussion of party, rulers and ruled. The party review occupies paragraphs 5–11 and comes after an attack upon the other parties and before the exposition of the ruler/ruled discussion. In the review, the party is portrayed as phoenix-like, and is linked to the notion of recovery, a notion stressed again and again in the speech. It is significant that this notion of recovery also appears later in a national and international context, as if the component parts of the whole (the specific, the party, and the general, the world) are organically related. We shall return to this below. Two points to note here are, first, that the distinction between party and people is maintained by recourse to a fundamental myth in English society (the chivalric myth) which allows for the valorisation of the party as the *champion* of an oppressed people who search for guidance, and, second, that the depiction of the party recovery (or rebirth) is mythical rather than simply organisational, that is to say, that the Labour Party is being projected as having been spiritually reborn in 1983 and its aftermath.

The early exposition of the party's recovery begins:

> And, as the Tories fade, and as the Liberals and Social Democrats falter, this party – our party – is entering its fourth year of recovery and of advance. That recovery has been worked for by people right across the movement, in every part of the movement.... And it has been fought for and worked for too by rank and file members right throughout this party who have worked as never before.... We have been making that recovery through a unity of purpose (5–6)

The linking of the party with the people (and the chivalric myth) is then made:

> We have been making that recovery by listening to people and by heeding people, and not straggling behind the lowest and slowest pace of opinion, but never wandering away from the main trail either so far as so lose sight of the main thread of public opinion (7)

And the notion of this organic relation to 'opinion' on the one hand, and a kind of chivalric vision on the other (cf. 'not straggling', 'not wandering', 'the main trail', not losing 'sight of') is strengthened by oblique reference to the action against Militant (there were bad knights just as there were bad kings) – whose presence in the party provided the media and the government with their strongest proof that the Labour Party could not be trusted to govern the British people:

> And we have made that recovery also ... by ensuring that we sustained both our democracy and our socialism.... We have done it because we could not allow our democracy to be distorted (8)

The party is then charged with a mission, again reminiscent of the chivalric task:

But of course there is more to do. There always is more to
do. For us there is no ceiling of satisfaction, no threshold of
support on which we will rest contented (9)

There then follows a refutation of the 'fond presumption
amongst a few pundits' (10) that the Labour Party is trying to
calculate its electoral victory. This is essential to the speech as
a whole because the party must be depicted not only as a
morally-inspired community but as possessing the quality
which can oppose the rulers' hypocrisy, namely, integrity.
The leadership must depict the party both as chivalric (that
is, morally inspired, a characteristic which justifies – and
explains – the party's trials and unpopularity), and as the
preliminary recovery of a rally, that is, as a movement that is
in a privileged and morally-based relation to the people:

We are not in that dangerous game, in fact we're not in a
game at all. We are in the serious and sustained task of
convincing more people, of putting our ideas and our
policies and of persuading people to our view. That is the
way in which we search for power, not by some roll of the
dice . . . . And we'll go on doing that, and we'll go on
gaining and keeping support from everyone who is prepared to hear our message, everyone who is prepared to
give us the democratic chance to show just what we can do
(10–11)

It is at this point that the ruler/ruled representation begins
(paragraphs 12–36, analysed above).

We can see from our analysis that the representations of
the party, of the rulers, and of the people are linked, and this
before the elaboration of the programme and before the
subsequent discussion of wider issues. This linkage not only
enables the speaker to be seen as speaking for the country as
a whole (and subsequently for the country in the wider
context), presenting party policy and intentions as the organised political expression of the people's deep desires, but
also places the elements involved in the relation in a vital, and
essentially mythical, relationship. We have seen how speaker
intervention connects different sections of the argument: the
discussion of the party is linked to the ruler/ruled discussion
by 'We have seen, of course, what others do' (12); the

discussion of the poor to that of the average family by 'And there are many of those – I meet them – who are not' (35). At no point in this part of the speech, however, is speaker *persona* intervention substantially significant, the distinction between the leader (I) and the party (we) being minimal, and reserved for linkages. Rather, it is restricted to the later part of the speech after discussion of the party, the rulers, the people and the programme, that is, after the constituent elements of the myth have been established. As we shall see, the second part of the speech, dealing with international issues and defence, will involve the direct intervention of the persona of the speaker. We shall analyse the rhetorical effect of such intervention in the third part of this analysis. Here we can simply note that 'we' and 'I' portray the rally quality of the party and its leadership in relation to the people, though the strongly moral register underlines directly the moral indignation of the speaker himself.

Let us examine, then, before analysing the strong intervention of the speaker's persona in the second half of the speech, how the party programme is presented, and how it enhances the argument, bearing in mind that the notion of mission, evoked in the 'recovery' theme in relation to the party and the depiction of a people on the eve of liberation from their misery and the oppressive rulers, is central to the exposition of the programme.

2. The programme

Following the depiction of the rulers and the ruled, the exposition of the programme begins with:

> And in doing that [providing government for Britain], we will be guided by four basic facts of our condition (37)

Given the depiction of rulers and ruled and the relation of the speaker/party to the latter, we can see that the 'guiding' principle of such provision is that of inspired reflection on the previously elaborated vision of the world, a guiding borne of both inspiration and party/speaker reflection. We shall, therefore, comment less on the policy substance of the programme itself than on the, here, more significant matter of the way in which it is presented. We should also note, moreover, the certainty of the speaker in the exposition of the programme which, as we intimated earlier, is not just a programme of government but (even though essentially social-democratic in nature) a programme for the liberation of the people from oppression:

> First, there is no prospect . . . unless . . . . Secondly, there is no possibility of . . . without . . . . Thirdly, the length of our relative economic decline . . . presents our country with a new set of . . . . Fourth, none of the . . . is (38–41)

The presentation of four 'basic facts' leads on to the idea of 'an agenda':

> We have to operate on a new agenda and we need new instruments, new policies . . . . We have to combat slump now and simultaneously foster the structural change . . . to reverse the long-term deficiencies
> On that new agenda is our two year programme
> And on that new agenda too there is
> And then at the same time
> For all those reasons it is essential . . . . That is why we shall
> That is why we are establishing
> It is for that reason
> The purpose, the purpose of that practical programme is to produce . . . to sponsor . . . to strengthen . . . to promote . . . to provide (42–51)

At the end of the exposition, which runs for thirteen paragraphs, speaker persona (concerning the need for realism) intervenes:

> Comrades, I have said it before, I'll say it again, and again, and again, and again (52)

This last quoted intervention is a clue to one of the main functions of the exposition of the party programme, namely, the demonstration of the strength of the speaker himself. He admits that, on taking power, there will be 'reservoirs' of injustice built up by the 'years of Thatcherism' (54), and he adds 'I know that. You know that' (54). And over the next six paragraphs he uses this as the main reason for not deviating from the programme (that is, for not attempting to right all

wrongs too quickly), thus further underlining the notion of
the strength of the programme and of the speaker:

> We can empty those reservoirs ... by deliberate and
> persistent policies and by sticking to our strategy. But if we
> tried ... any other way than persistence.... We cannot.
> We will not. And our decisions ... aren't going to be
> governed by obedience to convention.... Those decisions
> are governed by reality ... guided constantly by the
> determination to generate ... to re-build ... to re-
> establish.... That is why ... must be strict and straight
> and it must be sustained. That is, that is how it will be ...
> the direction of those policies, of those decisions will
> unerringly and unreservedly be towards.... That is the
> reason (55–59)

We can see that the elaboration of Labour Party intention
is dominated not just by a sense of realism but by a sense of
personally inspired determination, even though speaker
persona intervention is minimal. The certainty and the
knowledge of the speaker prevail throughout as a kind of
public reminder to the party of the need for resolve. These
qualities, moreover, are not being portrayed as party qualities, given that the 'caution' of governmental realism is
addressed to party as much as to the wider public.

The programme itself, as we have said, is fundamentally a
social democratic one requiring a gradualist approach and
incrementalist policies. However, it is underpinned by an
idea which is both Thatcherite *and* revolutionary; it is a
programme which corresponds to the neo-Conservative idea
of *resolution* in effecting structural change, but the resolute
idea of restructuring the whole fabric of society via the state
has also a revolutionary, even Leninist, ring to it, drawing,
moreover, upon the notion that a revolution is not just an
explosion, a sudden emptying of 'reservoirs', but a long-term
planned project. The earlier populism evoked, therefore, is
functional to the idea of *channelling* an explosion which is
morally justified but practically disastrous if not contained.
In this way, the social democratic and the revolutionary
discursive strains within the party are conflated (to the
exclusion of other revolutionary strains such as syndicalism
or council communism, neither of which has any great

significance in British political culture), and are conflated within the idea of governmental 'resolution'. The notion here, which again has a long pedigree within the organised left, is that one cannot be revolutionary unless one is reformist. This, as we shall see, will have significant implications for the projection of leadership persona in the second part of the speech.

The conclusion of this section is a clear discursive preparation for the next, and involves a refocusing of the discussion on to the rulers and on to Margaret Thatcher in particular. After the discussion of the need for a Labour government to borrow in order to finance the party's governmental programme (60–61), the speaker returns to a reference to Margaret Thatcher, using the metaphor of the family, a version or inversion of a favourite Thatcher image:

> She won't increase borrowing by that 2 per cent of national income . . . because she's not prepared to leave the burden of debt to our children. That is very touching. Or at least it would be touching if it wasn't so cruelly obvious that Mrs Thatcher is prepared to leave our children with a legacy of decay and decline . . . . Somehow she doesn't care . . . . You see, it is one thing to say to your children, since she's so concerned about the children . . . 'I'll leave you with a house and the remainder of the mortgage to pay after my days. . . .' It is another thing altogether to say to your children, 'Because I wouldn't pay the mortgage I will leave you nowhere to live after my days.' That's the Thatcher option (61–63)

This last reference in what has been essentially a discussion of domestic national issues enables the speaker to project on to the consideration of international issues the morality and the dualism used in the first part of the speech. The following declaration is, in this context, highly significant (and follows the family home metaphor of the economy which pointed up the shallowness of Thatcherism):

> We socialists, conscious of the fact that we cannot and do not serve just one generation. Conscious that each generation depends upon another. That one generation inherits in the very course of its preparation for the next genera-

tion. That there is this continual thread of dependence between the generations of human beings. We, as socialists, we always try to leave this place a little better than when we found it. And that attitude is not confined just to our own country. It is a definition of our view of the world. (64)

These remarks allow for the idea of socialism as a concern for *Britain* to embrace the international dimension, while retaining the morality, dualism, and sense of mission which have informed the speech so far. We shall examine the third and fourth main sections of the speech (international issues and defence) in the context of the projection of leadership persona. We can note here, however, that these will be based upon the underlying elements elaborated so far: the healthy recovery of the Labour Party, the dual representation of society, the evil of the oppressors, the mission of the party, the interconnectedness of things, the realism involved, and the idealism which inspires all action. All of these will be appropriated by leadership persona in the later parts of the speech.

Let us therefore make a second reading of the speech (and include now analysis of the second part) to see how the relationship between the idea of a mission and the role of the speaker within it are established.

3. The projection of leadership persona

As we have suggested, one of the essential discursive strategies employed in Neil Kinnock's speech is the creation of a sense of party unity which, avoiding reference to the right or left of the party, reaches back to an earlier leftist tradition. This has several effects. First, it establishes a 'we the party' which is one and indivisible and of a rally nature. Second, it enables the leader to present himself as being at the head of this particular rally in which there are no internal divisions, that is, neither factional quarrels nor contestation of leadership. Third, because leadership is presented as uncontested, the harmonious interdependence of 'I' and 'we' allows the speaker to assert leadership authority without threatening the status of the audience. Such authority can be asserted either by the depiction of the speaker as an ideal type of this 'new' socialism or else by the clear imposition of leadership opinion on to the speech. The speaker is, therefore, a vehicle for a particular socialist sentiment, but in the course of so being displays a series of personal qualities which together make up this character. There is no *direct* lecturing of the party, as we shall see, no declared separation of leadership from party for the purposes of overtly asserting the dominance of the former or of subjugating the latter. One of the effects of this is to underline the confidence and strength of character of the speaker. This means, furthermore, that any disagreement with the leader's speech would involve the conference audience or the activist in refusing their conferred rally status and sense of mission (and, thus, union with the speaker). This offers significant advantages to leadership because it throws into the category of betrayal of the party's rally status and mission virtually any criticism of leadership or leadership portrayal of party policy. Let us look, then, at how the speech itself involves the projection of a particular leadership persona.

The opening lines of the speech display a combination of comradeliness, humility, and ease, which will be exploited throughout:

> Neville, comrades, I always get a little nervous, even though I'm immensely gratified by a reception like that, because I'm always afraid that those who commentate on these things will add together the minute before and the two minutes after and decide I didn't get as much as David Steel. [Laughter] Neville, I, I'll tell you what, following the act that we've just had from Winnie and from Aubrey [the recipients of the Merit Awards] only adds an additional 150 per cent to this task. Winnie the peacemonger, Aubrey the first maker of jams I've met to date that I actually like (1)

The speaker then turns to the serious business with a tone of gravity, thus drawing the audience into the sharing of a contrasting second sentiment:

> We meet now, comrades, in the autumn of this eighth year of Thatcherism (2)

After listing the catalogue of devastation wrought by the Prime Minister and her government, the speaker declares, 'Well she's not going to have another term. [Applause.] We and the British people together will definitely see to that' (2). In terms of the projection of speaker persona, this is an interesting utterance in two respects. First, the initial sentence ('Well, she's not...') reads like a personal conviction, displaying all the single-mindedness of the speaker himself (and it was this which generated the applause); it is only in the second sentence (that is, after the applause) that the partners in this defeat of Thatcherism ('We and the British people') are named. Secondly, such certainty implies a trial of giants rather than an observation on democratic processes, once again revealing the 'character' of the speaker, as well as the symbolic nature of the conflict.

There are several pleasantries at or near the beginning of the speech; that concerning Aubrey (see above), and a little later, comments on Jeffrey Archer's (then deputy chairman of the Conservative Party) 'creative genius', Edwina Currie's 'sweetness and sourness' (there is a later joke about her too (21)), and Mr Tebbit's being a Mr Punch (2), and then a series of ironic remarks about David Owen's personal ambition and shallow opportunism (3–4) which, while undermining Owen, also implicitly carries the suggestion that the Labour leader is free of these unwelcome personality traits. Interestingly, however, because of the powerful nature of Neil Kinnock's speech, humour virtually disappears after the opening paragraphs (there is one macabre joke about a nuclear *entente terminale* near the end of the speech (84)) to be replaced by heavy sarcasm when the speaker is referring to the government or the Alliance, or else by different emotions altogether.

We can see already that the speaker's persona is crucial in the speech but does not necessarily involve self-reference. The overcoming of Thatcherism is linked to an unstoppable movement of which the Labour Party is part and the speaker's conviction, a reflection:

Not all of the ... or the ... can change that course of events. Not even ... not even ... can change that course of history (2)

Speaker certainty is, therefore, enhanced by its being based upon the near-mystical discernment of the teleology of history. This is, of course, strongly reinforced by the dualist view of the world which we examined in the previous section.

The 'course of history' approach returns, after an attack upon David Owen, thus locking the SDP leader into (that is to say, excluding him from) the teleology, as someone who, for reasons of personal vanity, dared to challenge the preordained. The speaker then summarises the teleology:

> And, as the Tories fade, and as the Liberals and Social Democrats falter, this party – our party – is entering its fourth year of recovery and of advance (5)

Once again we have here a combination of a recovered teleology and the party's privileged place within it (a privilege dependent upon its commitment to recovery). The speaker then elaborates upon the recovery (analysed in the previous sub-section). Here we can note the emphasis upon the developing rally as an interdependent gathering of forces:

> That recovery has been worked for by people right across the movement, in every part of the movement. In the local authorities . . . . In the trade union movement . . . . By rank and file members right throughout this party who have worked as never before . . . with an effectiveness that we've never shown before (5)

The last lines of the above quotation are an indication of the surreptitious way in which leadership criticises party. In this example, there is an implication that it was lack of effort which halted the teleology and led to defeat. This is reinforced by a further reference to the idea of unity as an imperative. Again, however, it is offered in the form of a compliment rather than as criticism:

> We have been making that recovery through a unity of purpose without which all else would have been absolutely impossible (6)

We can see from this that it is neither policy nor doctrine, nor even allegiance to leadership, which is being held up to the conference as the key to success, but rather the ideals of

effort, commitment and unity. These last are hallmarks of
rally discourse and of rally leadership discourse because they
heighten the notion of allegiance to a cause while implicitly
downgrading, even criticising, the counter-idea of internal
debate. The 'recovery' of the party (we) is described as being
due to its 'listening to people and . . . heeding people' (7).
There is here also an indirect criticism of past practice (the
suggestion is that 'listening' did not happen in the past), even
though the idea is again put forward positively as is the
suggestion that discussion is now over, and that any *further*
discussion would be an impediment to victory. The speaker
then makes an implied reference to those past practices and
to Militant:

> We sustained both our democracy and our socialism. We
> haven't done it in an authoritarian manner. We have done
> it because we could not allow our democracy to be dis-
> torted, we could not allow our generosity to be abused (8)

Party unity, the prerequisite to the teleology, is therefore
represented as possible, now that the obstacles to 'recovery'
(Militant) have been removed. We can see here that the
Militant issue is functional to the advancement of leadership
status in that it is suggested that the removal of Militant from
the argument means the removal of criticism of leadership
itself.

The notion of recovery as being the aim and *result* of effort
and commitment is then reaffirmed, and in this way the idea
that *further* criticism is acceptable is short-circuited. The
image of the party as committed to a rally unity is, therefore,
reinforced:

> And in all of that we have earned new strength by hard
> work, by effort. But of course there is more to do. There
> always is more to do. For us there is no ceiling of satisfac-
> tion, no threshold of support on which we will rest con-
> tented (9)

It is extremely unclear what this refers to, whether to party
effort and unity or else to national party activity (we have
already seen how such concepts add weight to the idea of a
'quest'). Whichever is referred to specifically, however, the
party is being presented as part of a historic movement. By

this point in the speech, therefore, unity and movement have become fetishised. Policy – though it will not be called policy – will be elaborated, but the commitment of conference and the party to it will have been conditioned by these interrelated necessities, unquestioning unity being depicted as a prerequisite to forward movement. It is now that the speaker goes on to refute the canard put about by 'a few pundits' that the Labour Party tries to calculate its victory:

> Well I can tell them we don't do that. We are not in that dangerous game, in fact we're not in a game at all. We are in the serious and sustained task of convincing more people, of putting our ideas and our policies and of persuading people to our view (10)

This affirmation is above all necessary to demonstrate that the speaker is not an opportunist but the leader of a principled movement. It also, however, reminds the party that a 'sustained task' places a duty on activists to remember that they must persuade rather than wishfully think. It is, therefore, a claim to a kind of inspired realism. In all the statements concerning the party's recovery and intentions, unity and effort are regarded as paramount and, more importantly, in terms of leadership status, are presented pedagogically, even though the ideas presented are held as self-evident truths by the vast majority of party members.

It is at this point that the speaker embarks on the long ruler/ruled passage already analysed. We can see from the present discussion that this is elaborated upon the basis of a discussion of a party which has been represented to itself as possessing a missionary preparedness to right the wrongs of the 'seven savage years' of rule (12). In terms of the leadership question, we can comment further here upon a series of aspects of the ruler/ruled passage.

First, because the rulers are depicted in the way that they are (rather than, say, as a class), the personal nature of the champions of the oppressed (in particular of the champion who is speaking) is thrown into relief. Second, the characteristics of the rulers are, as we have seen, human characteristics: hypocrisy, greed and so on, thus highlighting the human 'virtue' of the champions. Third, the quasi-eternal nature of the treachery of rulers confers upon the Labour Party a chivalric quality (courage, strength, fortitude and moral rectitude) which lends to the party and to its leader the character of a company of knights. Fourthly, the highly individualised illustrations of the rulers' attitudes: the Tory lady who, like the Prime Minister herself, 'lectures' and the working-class woman's reply (introduced as a personal observation of the speaker, cf. 'It reminded me, it reminded me of the Tory lady . . .' (21)) bring out further the personal nature of the conflict. Fifthly, the tone of delivery of this section of the speech is that of an inquisitor at a tribunal; and these 'tribunal' passages ('When it is so obvious', 'When it is clear . . . why . . . ?' (23–27)) are again prefaced with the personalising of the speaker (by the use of 'I') and of the rulers (by the naming of two of them):

> I suppose, I suppose that the pious sermons, the self-righteous homilies from Mrs Thatcher and Mr Tebbit are easier than facing the real problems or answering the real questions. And there are plenty of those, plenty of those real, moral questions (22)

And finally, of course, the issues discussed in this passage are in themselves highly emotional ones, not only in terms of how the discussion is framed (treachery and avarice causing suffering and indignity, privileged self-seeking versus humble integrity, for example), but also in terms of the topics discussed: poverty, injustice, bad housing, children, insecurity, violence, medical care, and government cuts in social provision. Such references go hand in hand with the outrage of affronted morality, and the projection of a deeply personalised Christian sentiment:

> These moralists breach the commandment that teaches us, 'Honour thy father and thy mother' (29)

After the ruler/ruled passage, the link with the discussion of the 'moral majority' is, as we have seen, the speaker himself:

> I, I look at all that and I ask myself just where do they get their idea of morality? And the British people ask the same question (30)

This means that the depiction of the 'great grouping', the

'moral majority', whose qualities, we should note, are described with conviction, is presented as the personal interpretation of the speaker, and is offered as a personal insight, the result of personal reflection. The description of the reasonably well off is also personalised, involves individualised illustration in the form of quotations, and takes the form, moreover, of the recounting of personal addresses to the speaker: 'I meet them .... They still say to me: "We're not badly off ... our Mam ..."' (35). And what they say is, as we have seen, directly quoted, thus emphasising the speaker's relation to the people.

We can see that, in a variety of ways, the speech is highly personalised, even though direct reference to the speaker is limited. The use of the first person pronoun, for example, is infrequent and often without direct reference back to the speaker (the use, for example, of phrases like 'It reminded me', 'I suppose', 'I ask myself', rather than, say, 'I believe strongly', 'I am convinced' and other more emotion-betraying or character-revealing references). The speech is, therefore, for the most part, only indirectly personalised. The overall effect of this is less the imposition of leadership authority upon the party and its presentation to the public (this had already been done in 1985), more the presentation of the party to itself as a transcendent rally community. The significance of this, however, for leadership authority is enormous because such a presentation ties the party to its rally status, its commitment to leadership and its dependence upon leadership guidance. This is why, in the elaboration of party intentions (the programme), there is no attempt at all to focus upon the persona of the leader. The creation of a particular 'we' is crucial to the subsequent imposition of a particular kind of leadership (upon a particular kind of rally). Nevertheless we can note that the use of the first person plural pronoun is ambivalent throughout the speech. The passage on the party programme, for example, begins, 'We will provide that government for Britain. And in doing that, we will be guided by four basic facts of our condition' (36–41). The second 'we' and the many subsequent ones in the elaboration of the policy package (used throughout the description of the programme) refer implicitly to a future government, and, of course, more particularly to the opinions of a future Prime Minister, rather than to the party or to the discursively invented rally. The 'we', in fact, could even refer *directly* to the speaker himself, given both the didactic nature of the exposition and the obvious fact that the speaker would be the Prime Minister of that 'we', with all the power and authority this implies (there is no criticism in the speech of prime ministerial authority *per se*). There is even an implication that the future Labour Prime Minister will be 'guided' even against the siren calls which might have their origins *within* rather than outside the party.

The four 'basic facts', involving economic growth, the development of manufacturing industry, economic strategy, and planning (34–41), are delivered, as we have seen, with all the certainty of personal conviction:

> First, there is no prospect.... Secondly, there is no possibility.... Thirdly, ... a new set of strategic problems ... a new set of strategic answers. Fourth, none of (38–41)

It is the elaboration of the programme, therefore, which allows the speaker to take further the idea of the newness of the recovered party:

> A new agenda ... new instruments, new policies.... On that new agenda .... And on that new agenda (42–44)

The project of the next Labour government is presented as a highly complex procedural change involving: an interconnected two-year programme, a five-year strategy, a ten-year planning horizon, and a whole series of new instruments: Capital Repatriation Scheme, British Investment Bank, British Enterprise holding company, and social ownership. This exposition of ideas which are both new and complex, running over nine paragraphs (42–51), has three effects. The first is that it suggests not only a break with Thatcherism but also a break with traditional Labourism. Second, both the novelty and the complexity of the proposed undertaking substantiate the idea of party dependence upon leadership guidance. The promotion of a long, elaborate, sustained strategy has further implications which we shall return to in a moment. Third, such complexity implies a total undertaking of mutual interdependence which further censors any hint of individual or sectional disagreement.

The next long passage (52–64) is a reminder to the audience of both the practical and the ideological purpose of this multifaceted governmental enactment of the party's mission. And, once again, the reminder links 'I' and 'we'. The passage begins:

> Comrades, I have said it before, I'll say it again, and again, and again, and again, we must literally make our way to recovery, produce our way to recovery, sell our way to recovery in the world. For there is no other way to fully earn the living that we want for ourselves and we want for our children. That's got to be understood. And there's some other factors that's got to be understood too (52)

This passage is significant in several respects. First, it is an echo of the earlier use of the word 'recovery', applied then to the party, in this way making recovery a vast though logical process which moves from party (microcosm) to country (macrocosm) and beyond. Second, it is a kind of forewarning to those in the party (or those imagined by the speaker) who are not wholeheartedly committed either to the notion of Britain as a competitive trading economy or to the 'new realism' of the party. Third, it associates the leader with this 'new realism' (as either its spokesperson or architect). Fourth, the apparent obviousness of the logic of the argument here belies a fundamental revision of the relative values in Labourism between wealth production and wealth redistribution, that is to say, a move towards the kind of language used by the Conservative government. Fifth, there is an implied threat in the last sentence quoted: 'And there's some other factors that's got to be understood too.' From the tone used, one anticipates an attack upon the left or upon dissidence. The speaker goes on, however (and we have seen an example of this anticipated but deferred recrimination in David Steel's speech), to stress an idea close to the heart of the left, namely, the need to impede an explosion of imported foreign goods. The unspoken threat of such a phrase remains, however, as a constant potential within the speech. What this illustrates, and what the whole speech demonstrates, in fact, is speaker strength and power which is always directed outwards from the party but which could, if necessary, and as was demonstrated in 1985, be turned inwards.

The development of the idea of sustained commitment to the chosen strategy continues, and, as we have seen, there is a warning against trying, given the 'reservoirs' of injustice, to do too much too quickly. This is ostensibly a social democratic caution against revolution or maximalism. However, once again, the subject is treated in a way that reverses (and thereby abolishes) the right/left distinction within the party. First, the speaker recognises the existence of the reservoirs ('I know that. You know that.' (54)), then says that they cannot be emptied all at once ('We cannot. We will not.' (55)). The I/we reference is taken further with the ambiguous 'our decisions' ('And our decisions about those things aren't going to be governed by obedience to convention' (56)). These remarks end with: 'If we were to try to do everything at once we would end by doing nothing at all in the end' (56). In a sense these statements imply the classic social democratic or incrementalist response to maximalism, and evoke the classic right/left divide within the left. We should note, however, that, on the one hand, the party has already been endowed with a missionary quality, and that, on the other, the programme to be applied upon the attainment of government has already been elaborated (the two, five and ten year strategy for recovery). The 'plan' has, therefore, already been drawn up. This is, therefore, if anything, a leftist rather than a social democratic argument: the rally-as-government must not be deflected from its long-term mission. The speaker goes on to affirm:

> The direction of those policies, of those decisions, will unerringly and unreservedly be towards economic recovery and structural change all the time (58)

Once again, however, we can conclude that here, as in the discussion of party recovery, it is the sentiment which is crucial rather than the content of the argument; the concept of determined social recovery rather than the specifics of this. The speaker is, in this way, conflating the incrementalist and the missionary strains within leftism. And the whole is presented as being dependent, as we have seen, upon unity of purpose. And the ultimate declared purpose of the mission, though apparently modest, strengthens the idea that this is a mission which must not be deflected:

> We, as socialists, we always try to leave this place a little
> better than when we found it (64)

It is from this deceptively modest idea of a longer-term vision
that the speaker moves on to international issues and defence, 'this place' becoming a metaphor not only for the
nation but for the planet as a whole. It is worth noting here
that it is the concept of a national or nationally-specific
patrimony which acts, not only as the basis for the move on to
a discussion of an international patrimony, as it were, but
also as the discursive condition for the subsequent concerted
appeal to British nationalism or patriotism, which is arguably
the strongest theme in the speech, dominating even that of
traditional Labourism or socialism.

From paragraph 65, the speaker develops the theme of
international issues. We should bear in mind that the continuity (of moralism, dualist interpretation of society and so
on) between this and the earlier part of the speech is
maintained both by sustained emotionalism and by the
creation within the speech of both temporal (the notion of a
patrimony being, by definition, historical) and spatial continuity (from the domestic to the international). In this
speech, as in the David Owen and David Steel speeches, the
international context allows for the amplification of the
moral rhetorical register. We should add that continuity is
also maintained by the continued 'presence', first, of Margaret Thatcher in the discussion of international issues, and,
second, of the dualism which informs the rulers/ruled discussion, and that all of these factors allow the speaker to draw
upon and present himself as an interpreter of a deeply
patriotic British tradition. These thematic cross-references
mean that Neil Kinnock's speech, like the others in this study,
is not one from which the listener can choose to accept or
reject parts, but a holistic undertaking whose different
elements are mutually reinforcing.

The initial picture drawn of the international situation is
bleak, and recapitulates, in an almost identical movement
from oppression to liberation (with the Labour Party as the
instrument of this movement), the earlier discussion of
domestic issues. This has four effects. First, it legitimates,
through repetition, the interpretation of domestic issues.

Second, it is like a second symphonic movement which further builds towards the crescendo which marks the end of the speech. Third, it will allow the speaker to contrast his/the party's integrity with the depicted reality. And fourth, it will enable the speaker to move into the defence discussion as part of the overall need to find a way out of the bleakness depicted in the discussion of international issues, rather than as a traditional discussion of defence within the Labour Party. And we can add that the international debate is treated in the same moral terms, and in the context of the same dualism, as the ruler/ruled discussion. Within two short paragraphs, the following words occur: dangers, famine, pollution, terrorism, warfare, inequality, injustice, exploitation, aggression, oppression, starvation (65–66).

The speaker then begins a concerted and extensive critique of US policy on Nicaragua. This attack drew prolonged applause from the audience. The representation of the conflict is once again that of a ruler bullying, here, 'the innocent of Nicaragua' (67) (the speaker protects himself from the accusation of being predictably one-sided by prefacing this discussion with a one-sentence criticism of the 'invading Empire' in Afghanistan – curiously, the reference to the USSR as 'an Empire' echoes Ronald Reagan – and a one-sentence reference to unjust Soviet action (*vis-à-vis* its sphere of influence in 1946)). The incredulous tone employed when discussing the US attitude to Nicaragua imitates the tone of the domestic discussion (cf. 'when it is so obvious'):

> What it can be that makes the United States of America . . . finance evil . . . . What makes them do that? . . . how can a President . . . ? (67)

When the speaker refers to US action against Nicaragua, he says 'it is wrong' (68), and the same expression is used when he comes on to discuss Apartheid. We can see from these examples that not only are the issues selected (Nicaragua and South Africa) themselves moral as much as political, but they are treated in a highly moral tone.

In the discussion of South Africa, the speaker calls for sanctions which are 'strict and strong' (71), 'strict and stringent' (75). Again this harks back to the reference to 'strict and straight' domestic policy for overcoming Britain's decline (57). Thus we can see that the same images, tone, strong moral perspective and even vocabulary are being used here as in the examination of domestic issues. This also allows the speaker to bring Margaret Thatcher back into the picture, making her 'responsible' for the misery of the oppressed in *both* the domestic and the international context, and to lampoon her claim that sanctions would be 'immoral'. And, once again, as in the domestic discussion, it is 'voices' which intervene and legitimate the speaker's point of view. It is true that these voices are more charged and evocative than those used in the domestic discussion, and the speaker's 'hearing' of them underlined more dramatically. Nevertheless we can see from these examples that the two main parts of the speech, the domestic and the international, are used to legitimate one another thematically and stylistically. In the 'voices' passage, moreover, the speaker positions himself in a privileged manner between the true and the false voices:

> I hear the President. I hear the Prime Minister. I hear the Chancellor [Reagan, Thatcher and Kohl who opposed sanctions]. And I hear different voices too. I hear louder voices. I hear voices of greater authenticity and greater authority upon the business of the future of the people of South Africa. It is the voice that comes straight from that bitter and bleeding land of South Africa. And it doesn't come from the high-falutin politicians or people in hotels or air-conditioned suites. That voice that I hear from South Africa comes from the townships and it comes from the homelands, and it comes from the churches, and it comes from the trade unions, it comes from Nelson Mandela in prison, it comes from Archbishop Tutu in his palace (73–74)

The expression 'we shall overcome', repeated three times, follows the claim that the Labour government will impose sanctions, and is used to end the passage on South Africa, reinforcing the millenarianism running throughout the speech, as well as creating the impression that the election of a Labour government will be a prelude to or expression of a total, global movement of liberation.

After discussion of Nicaragua and South Africa, the third

area treated is the notion of the interdependence between countries. This both makes the domestic and the international mutually dependent, and, later, allows the speaker to move logically into the discussion of defence. Here we can note, however, that the accumulated internationalism of the debate on Nicaragua and South Africa will, paradoxically perhaps, allow the speaker to draw upon a fundamentalist patriotism.

Before addressing the interdependence question, the speaker makes a (completely unscripted) intervention concerning the recently assassinated Olof Palme, Social Democrat Prime Minister of Sweden. Neil Kinnock refers to him as a prophet of interdependence and calls for a continuation of his work. There is, here, quite extensive enhancement of the status of speaker persona, and this just before the speaker's treatment of the interdependence and defence issues. First, of course, the speaker is referring to another leftist party leader (and Prime Minister), this lending to Neil Kinnock something of Palme's status. Second, he refers to him as 'my dear comrade and a friend of the world' (76). Thirdly, he refers to him, the second time, by his first name only, strengthening further the notion of intimacy between the two men. Fourthly, reference to Palme endows the speaker and his task (and the task of the left as a whole) with a religious sense of sacrifice and selflessness. Fifthly, of course, reference to Palme's killing infuses the speech with a further emotional charge (and the speaker at this point seemed, indeed, nearly moved to tears).

The international interdependence theme is illustrated (the speaker returns here to the script) by reference to 'two events, thousands of miles apart' which demonstrated 'the fragility of our world, the interdependence of its countries' (77). The events, both having occurred only weeks before the conference, are the Chernobyl disaster and the bombing of Tripoli by US planes. As with the Palme example, the listener is not immediately sure to whom or to what the speaker is going to refer (cf. 'In this year of 1986, a prophet of this fact, who gave us much more than his prophecies' (76)): 'Within two weeks of April of this year, two events . . . came together to form an equation in the minds of millions of people' (77). This not only elevates these tellings into lessons, almost parables, but creates audience expectation and thus dependence upon the speaker, until a release is effected, as it were, by the telling of what were, in fact, well-known issues: Palme's murder, the Chernobyl nuclear reactor accident, and the American bombing of Tripoli. Reference to Chernobyl and Tripoli allows the speaker to elaborate vivid examples of the dangers to the world (and both of these posed direct threats to the British population, the first because of radioactive fall-out, the second in terms of possible retaliation), but also to emphasise the theme of interdependence, not in terms of its positive desirable potential, but in the context of the interdependence of destruction. This enables the speaker to address the defence issue, not in the context of a discussion of Labour's controversial and, arguably, unpopular defence policy, but as a part of the wider discussion: 'the question of the defence of this country and our system of values' (78).

It is from this point (paragraph 78 onwards) that the persona of the speaker intervenes once again, depicting the speaker as an ideal international socialist, and as the personal interpreter of the questions of national defence and 'our system of values'.

> I hold it to be self-evident that it is a first duty of any government to ensure the security of the country over which it governs (79)

This is followed by another as if a priori truth:

> That duty does not change in any age and we will discharge that duty fully for this is our country and we defend our country as we always have (79)

Not only are declarations such as these reminiscent of the writings of the early American revolutionaries, but the 'we' here, as before in the discussion of domestic issues, denotes the party while connoting the speaker as future Prime Minister (in fact, even the words and style sound more like Margaret Thatcher).

The defence debate is based upon a sustained discussion of defence (more so than of disarmament), thus enhancing the patriotism of the discussion rather than its internationalism; and we should remember that the discussion of defence is

reinforced by the immediately preceding evocation of international threats. As we have seen throughout the speech, the
expressions 'our country', 'this country', 'Britain', 'the British
people' abound. Here the speaker introduces several closely-
packed expressions which are reminiscent of a Churchillian
style: 'defend ourselves ... by land, sea and air' (79), 'the
government is failing to meet the defence needs of Britain'
(82), 'From the Early Warning System at Fylingdales to the
submarine watching station in Pembrokeshire and from
GCHQ to Cyprus, from Hong Kong to Edzell in Scotland
there are essential facilities for ... the collective interests of
the NATO Alliance' (88), 'They [the Americans] are our *allies*
and we honour the alliance' (89), 'We will not bow down' (93),
'We won't succumb' (93), 'We either surrender ... or we
stand and fight' (94), 'We stand and we fight' (94). (Not all of
these expressions refer to defence, and we shall come back to
the significance of this below.)

The criticism of Britain's nuclear weapons is based first
upon the claim that their cost reduces, and will go on
reducing, the strength of Britain's conventional forces (81–
82). As with the other leadership speeches, only two policies
are considered as viable, the third, in this case the SDP-
Liberal Alliance's, treated scornfully (84), 'an illusion of a
policy out of a delusion of grandeur' (84), in this way
focusing the discussion upon the 'true' and the 'false' defence
of Britain. The speaker also has to deal with the problem of
the Americans' attitude to Labour's intentions. At several
points, he refers to Britain's commitment to the NATO
alliance, and claims that the US does not interfere in the
democratic processes of its allies (85), and that the rumours
in 1986 of US disapproval of Labour Party defence policy
were part of an attempt by the Tory government to use the
Americans for their own electoral ends. The implication here
is that the Conservatives themselves betray the nation by
going outside it in order to maintain their power, thus
undermining the nation and revealing, once again, the
extent of their hypocrisy and deviousness.

In the treatment of all of these issues: conventional forces,
the cost of nuclear arms, US security, and Britain's role in the
NATO alliance, it is the loyalty of the Labour Party to the
country's defence interests, and its concern for the country's

security, which underpin the argument. And given, especially, the widely-known discordancy of views on this subject
within the party, particularly over the question of the accep-
tability of US non-nuclear bases and of NATO, the assertions
of the speaker take on the quality of a personal guarantee to
the British electorate, made, if necessary, in the face of
opposition from within his own party.

At this point, that is, only in the closing lines of the speech,
the speaker returns to the traditional Labour Party anti-
nuclear view of the disarmament question, namely, the moral
rather than the strategic reasons underlying it. In this way,
the speaker reintroduces a high emotionalism at this junc-
ture, and this, as we shall see, without abandoning the
strongly patriotic theme that has informed the speech
throughout (and which would eventually enable the party to
abandon unilateralism in 1989). The speaker first elevates
the question, once again, into one concerning the relationship between the actual situation and the course of
history itself:

> We are the first generation in history to have to deal with
> those weapons. The first generation in history.... The
> first generation to have to deal (90)

And in the closing sentence of this utterance affirms:

> That gives us different challenges, requires different re-
> sponses (90)

After the evocation of the idea of the present generation
being in a position unknown to any other in history, the
speaker then makes both his most personalised and most
emotional declaration of the speech:

> I face those questions as the Leader of this party who
> works to become the democratically elected Leader of this
> country. I face those facts too as an adult, as a citizen, and
> as a father.
> And I tell you in no casual spirit, no bravado, like, that like
> most of my fellow citizens, I would, if necessary, fight and
> die, fight and lay down my life for my country and what it
> stands for.
> I would die for my country. But I tell you, I would never
> let my country die for me (92)

This passage, partially drawing upon the high moralism which has informed the speech throughout, reveals the true 'character' of the speaker's persona in discourse as being that of a person whose moralism is boundless, and whose pragmatism is informed, but not deformed, by that same moral quality. There is also an implied contrast here to Margaret Thatcher who, believing in a policy which is the negation of the speaker's, is implicitly likened to those many dictators who have led their countries to ruin through their own egocentrism (this implication is reinforced by the earlier explicit references to her having ruined the economy). Moreover, although the speaker is describing Labour Party policy here and using himself as an illustration of Labour Party sentiment, the image remains that of the man, Neil Kinnock, ready to die for his country.

The defence argument then moves into the closing statements of the speech which are concerned with general reference to 'the weaknesses of our country and ... the menaces to human kind' (94). There is, however, no change at all in the military metaphors used. In fact they increase in intensity, thus maintaining the mental image of the valiant leader, making acceptance of *all* of the views in the speech interdependent (for those who agree with, say, the speaker's views on the economy but not defence, as for those who agree on defence but not on the economy):

We will not bow down (93)
We won't succumb
We either surrender ... or we stand and fight (94)
We stand and we fight

The speaker calls thus upon an idea of combativeness which follows on immediately from the emotional discussion of disarmament but which maintains the aggressive patriotism of the earlier discussion of defence, and underscores the prerequisites to an effective combativeness, namely, unity and obedience to leadership.

5 Margaret Thatcher and the Conservative Tradition

THE CONTEXT

Two very obvious factors influence the Conservative conference, and distinguish it from the other conferences. The first is, quite simply, that the Conservatives were in government. This means that, on the one hand, the symbolism of power in ritual and in discourse is greatly enhanced by the underlying political reality and that, on the other, the conference itself and, in particular, ministerial speeches will be given much more serious attention by the media at the level of policy analysis (we shall comment below on how government uses these conference speeches in a particular way). A related negative effect is that, although a 'government' conference can convey the notion of power, it faces particular problems in the conveying of the idea of a national rally.

The second factor concerns the Prime Minister herself. By the mid-1980s, Margaret Thatcher's persona had taken on, or had had conferred upon it, a status which, depending on individual perceptions and differing media treatment, was of caricatural, historic, or mythical proportions. She was Britain's first woman Prime Minister (regarded as the most significant woman politician in the history of British politics, and one of the most significant politicians in contemporary world politics). Moreover her political persona had gathered around it a cluster of characteristics which were perceived as constituting her personality and explaining her prominence and success: single-mindedness, resolution, an inherent or acquired domineering manner, a visionary quality (hitherto unusual in British politics), a view of the world and a set of personally-held values which were radical in certain respects, highly traditional and conservative in others. To a far greater extent than is the case with the other three leaders – or arguably, with most, if not all previous Prime Ministers – this 'character' preceded Margaret Thatcher's appearance at any public meeting, informing anything she would say. She could, therefore, confirm, add to, or nuance any of these characteristics by saying – or not saying – certain things (conversely, the modification of these perceived character traits would be difficult given that they were widely held to be true and immutable).

Therefore, unlike the other three leaders, even though these too, to a much lesser extent, possessed a public 'character' which went before them, Margaret Thatcher did not have to 'invent' herself in her discourse. In fact, the amalgam of characteristics ascribed to her are rarely, and rarely need to be, mobilised fully in her discourse because of the strength of the assumed public understanding of that character. So powerful was the ascription that this perceived character was sometimes, and 1986 was a case in point, regarded as a possible electoral liability by her colleagues and by Conservatives in the country, thus fuelling the idea of the leader who, through 'resolution', has become single-minded to the point of isolation and, therefore, vulnerability. This myth is a strong one in Western culture: Julius Caesar, Louis XVI, Robespierre, Tsar Nicolas, and, more recently, Peron, Kruschev, the Shah of Iran, Anwar Sadat, Nikoli Ceaucescu are all leaders whose arrogance, blindness, or isolation were seen as having cut them off from their own support and occasioned their downfall. The related notion of 'regicide', moreover, has a strong tradition within the British Conservative Party, the most recent victim of this being Edward Heath. The drawing of knives against the leader within the Conservative Party is, however, usually associated with a leader who has been considered as, or as having become, 'weak', as well as a political liability. The former quality clearly did not apply to Margaret Thatcher's leadership.

Nevertheless opinion polls towards the end of the Conservatives' second term in office suggested increasingly a popular disaffection with Margaret Thatcher, her uncaring and insensitive attitude repeatedly stressed by those whose views were canvassed. And, given the focus upon personal leadership since 1979, her possible vulnerability to a strike against her by her colleagues in an embattled government and party was obviously increased. It is true that her position was strengthened by the fact that she had few, if any, real rivals, and certainly no dauphin (or dauphine) to contend with. Nevertheless she would clearly be open to attack if, for example, any political or economic disaster occurred and was ascribed to her leadership, or, obviously, if the Conservatives lost the following election, or assumed themselves to be in danger of losing it.

In terms of the media-vehicled assessments of popular support, it was clear from the polls that the second Thatcher term (from 1983) had not been regarded as being as 'successful' as the first in terms of the projection of an image of either government efficiency or government innovation. It was, by and large, the first term (1979–1983) which was retrospectively seen as occasioning the 'Thatcher revolution' (although the reality of this is debatable). The first term had also been provided with enormous popular appeal, with the resultant landslide election victory which led to the second term, by Margaret Thatcher's perceived steadfastness (and the success achieved by the military) during the Falklands War of 1982. The second term, on the other hand, had witnessed few major policy successes, and had seen an acceleration of the departure of senior members of the government; by the second term these included high-ranking ministers (James Prior, Francis Pym and Michael Heseltine, in particular). A series of negative popular and media impressions had also been established: the miners' strike of 1984 had not, in spite of the 'resolution' demonstrated by the Prime Minister in particular, enhanced the government's standing; the pound was under severe pressure throughout 1985 and 1986; unemployment was still very high; monetarism was no longer a popular idea; there had been major riots in Britain's inner cities in 1985; the Trident programme, with its projected massive increase in Britain's nuclear firepower, was not universally popular; the Queen herself was reported as being opposed to the Prime Minister on the question of the government's attitude to the Commonwealth; even Margaret Thatcher's own Cabinet were believed to be at odds with her over her opposition to sanctions against South Africa; the government had been forced to retreat on the question of allowing parts of British Leyland to be sold to the Americans; and the permission granted to American bombers to use Britain as a base from which to attack Libya in April 1986 had been, according to the polls, an extremely unpopular measure. The Labour Party, moreover, was doing relatively well in public opinion polls, sometimes overtaking the Conservatives, and with Neil Kinnock's status as a potential Prime Minister increasing.[1]

There had also been the Westland affair, potentially highly damaging for the Prime Minister's 'character' status, with its echoes of a Watergate-style cover-up and the doubts which arose concerning the integrity of the Prime Minister. The affair had blown up in early January 1986, and in June the Defence Select Committee's report had seriously criticised both the Prime Minister's Press Secretary and the Cabinet Secretary. The Westland affair undermined the 'character' of Margaret Thatcher in part because of its implication that she had misled, perhaps even lied to, the House of Commons. It is true to say that the affair had had little actual resonance in the wider public but it had, nevertheless, a potentially harmful effect upon government, a government, moreover, whose success was seen as resting with one person, the Prime Minister. It also, however, had a further effect upon leadership by creating the opportunities for Michael Heseltine, the then Defence Secretary, to resign very publicly from the government, and therefore set up, or begin to set up, both a real and a symbolic rival pole of attraction within the party and the country. This idea was compounded by the fact that Heseltine, the traditional darling of the Conservative conference, was absent, because of his resignation, from a central place at the 1986 conference (before this he had invariably used his conference speeches as a means of generating a rally form of support within the party). In the month before the conference, moreover, James Prior, formerly Employment and then Northern Ireland Secretary under Margaret Thatcher, had published his memoirs in which the 'character' of Margaret Thatcher had been taken to task.

We should add, however, that the climate which the Thatcher years had helped bring about had, in certain respects, enhanced both the government's and Margaret Thatcher's position. Much of an ideology which hitherto had apparently been exclusive to Thatcherism had been accepted and adopted more generally. The early privatisations, for example, had met with virtually no resistance at all (BT's troubles (and, of course, the 1987 Wall Street crash) did not occur until after the 1987 election). And the left had made very little headway with the patriotic notion that privatisation was a selling off of the nation's heritage. Council house sales had also proved very popular (and were quickly adopted as ideologically acceptable by the Labour Party). The 'business culture' as an idea was no longer something that had to be appealed to, but was largely accepted as a given of British life. It was as if the political culture had moved towards Margaret Thatcher, rather than her towards it, with all the attribution of visionary qualities to the Prime Minister that such a revolution implies.

At the conference itself, the notion of moving on to a further phase (the conference slogan was 'The Next Move Forward') allowed for justifications of the government's seven year record to be minimised, and references to it to be represented as consolidations, as preparations even, while allowing the focus of the conference to project the idea of forward movement. This, the presentation of the conference as a rally rather than a debate, actually informed the 1986 conference significantly, enabling it to show itself as transcending the belief (weak in Conservatism anyway) that the conference was a party-related, rather than leader-related, expression of organisation, and thus enhancing the idea of the conference as the prelude to an unmediated rally of the faithful around the leader on the eve of the reconquest of power. In this way, the 1986 Conservative conference offers a good illustration of how a government party copes with the traditional problem of disenchantment by the *further* radicalising of its discourse and by its self-presentation as a political movement making an appeal to the idea of a crusade.

One of the main motifs of the conference itself was that of privatisation, which through the public sale of British Telecom shares had been popular in the country, and which had been used to interlink two very powerful notions in the political culture: the liberation of the people (and energy) *from* the state; and the liberation of the people *by means of* state intervention. Phrases used by conference speakers when referring to privatisation were those which spoke of an idea 'whose time had come' and one which had 'caught the imagination of the British people' (and we can note here that by 1986 the positive term 'privatisation' had itself completely replaced the more negative one of 'denationalisation' in political discourse). This helped to strengthen the idea that Thatcherism was now part of a vast long-term project allied to the liberation of the British people and of their energies from previous constraints. The image of a crusade at the conference was, therefore, based largely upon this concept of privatisation, which was able to appeal to traditional Conservatism but also to Liberal and SDP and leftist notions of people deciding their own fate, being responsible for themselves, circumventing the faceless bureaucracy, bettering themselves, and so on. And, as we shall see, it is privatisation as a *theme*, rather than as a policy, which is the essential constituent of Margaret Thatcher's speech.

In the context of the above discussion, let us, therefore, examine the conference itself as the immediate context of the leader's speech.

The majority of the speakers, while supporting the existing government, stressed repeatedly the idea of Conservatism as being *anti*-government and *pro*-people (even though the Conservatives had been the government for seven years). This constantly-referred-to theme created the idea of a movement which needed to attain *real* power in order to liberate the people from government itself by handing conquered power back to the people. Most of the speakers also praised the Prime Minister herself, either by making reference to her as an integral part of their argument or by departing from their main argument to accord her due credit, and often making specific reference to her vision. Interestingly, Margaret Thatcher attended the greater part of the conference herself, listening attentively throughout as a leader who had come back from the lonely heights of power to listen and to heed her people (even though the quasi-totality of what she listened to was uncritical praise), before embarking once again on her mission, strong in the confidence of her supporters. It is worth stressing here that the leader's near-continuous attendance at the conference is unusual in Conservative Party history. Many previous leaders had often appeared only intermittently or at the end of conference. Margaret Thatcher, therefore, is not only viewed as a leader who has returned to gain fresh insights;

she, as a party leader in government, enhances even further the idea that she is making time for 'her people'. And obviously the Prime Minister's presence when a delegate or minister speaks increases the perceived importance of those concerned and of the occasion itself.

The conference itself, like all Conservative conferences, was clearly stage-managed in terms of the minimising of a critical discourse. One of the effects of this was to reaffirm the image of a well-run party (and therefore, by implication, of a well-run country). Moreover the notion of stage-managing, always associated with the Conservatives, had itself become normative, given that even the Labour Party had now moved away from its traditional untidy democracy to a similarly smooth self-presentation. Before the conference, many motions highly critical of government had been received by Conservative Central Office, most of them expressing the locally-felt worry that the government was becoming increasingly unpopular; that its public relations were bad (that is, that its media and public image, and therefore its policies and leadership, were at fault). The Conservative Agenda Sub-Committee, however, on which Norman Tebbit sat, did not find it hard to deflect these and select for discussion more anodyne motions or those less critical, more supportive of government. Moreover certain speakers at the conference were able to claim that any shortcomings were the fault of the party rather than of the government (claims which invariably met with applause. Delegates at all conferences respond positively to self-criticism on condition that it is delivered by speakers from the floor). And, for Conservative delegates (or representatives, as they prefer to call themselves), and indeed for most Conservatives, the notion of direct public criticism of government and especially of the leader, whether from the right or from the left within the party, is normally considered anathema.

At the conference, the most significant speeches in policy terms during the week were, of course, those made by government ministers. And it was clear from the ministerial speeches that what was being elaborated was not a defence of past performance but, essentially, an election manifesto. Nigel Lawson (Chancellor), Douglas Hurd (Home Secretary), and Norman Fowler (Social Services minister) all made major and forceful speeches which involved what amounted to a programme for future government. Moreover, the high-spending ministries (Transport, Social Services, Housing, Education, Health, Defence, Environment) were all given a very high profile, thus consolidating the notion of the conference as a pre-election rally, and, moreover, promoting the government as 'caring' while, nevertheless, at the same time offering radical change (we shall come back to this point in our analysis of the speech).

Throughout the week, direct attacks upon Neil Kinnock (whose rating in the opinion polls was rising steadily at this time) had been continual (at fringe meetings too), along with disparaging reference to the Labour Party's claims to morality, this the strongest theme of the Labour leadership's speech, as we have seen. Margaret Thatcher's speech is, therefore, 'conditioned' in a way that none of the others is: the speeches both of ministers and of grassroots speakers set the scene for her own in a way that none of the conference speeches at the other party conferences does for their leaders. The detailed policy initiatives presented by other ministers (all given much higher media profile than shadow ministers or spokespersons) solve for Margaret Thatcher the problem of having to elaborate policy herself (and thereby force her discourse 'down' into the realm of the practical, the rhetorically mundane). Several media commentators, commenting Margaret Thatcher's 37-minute speech, observed that it was a 'thin' speech in this regard, thus, perhaps, missing the rhetorical point that she did not need to address herself to such issues – these had been dealt with for her throughout the week (similarly, she did not need to refer by name to Neil Kinnock (thus effectively downgrading his status) – others had been only too willing to do this as well for her). She was thus able to develop in a relatively short speech two or three themes which acted as illustrations of her personal view of the world, of her prescription for the future, and of her personality.

The Conservative conference was the last of the 1986 season, thus allowing the major speakers to reply, as it were, to the discourse of and claims made at the other conferences. This gave the Conservative conference a major rhetorical advantage. By the same token, the Prime Minister's address was itself 'the last word', dismissing and commenting upon the preceding conferences and leadership speeches. Margaret Thatcher's address was in fact the final speech of the thousands of conference and fringe meeting speeches, press conference statements and interview responses of the whole season, and could thus, and did, portray itself as the summation of them all.

This idea of the Prime Minister's speech as the most important of the whole conference season is reinforced by several factors. First, it was the most well-attended; queues began forming more than two hours before she spoke. On her arrival, the Prime Minister was announced and walked in from the side of the conference hall (unlike David Owen and Neil Kinnock, who were already seated on the platform before standing to deliver their speeches), accompanied by music ('A red rose for a blue lady'). Significantly also, she walked in at ground level and *up* on to the platform (rather than from the wings of the platform itself as did David Steel). Moreover, possibly incongruously, even this notion of walking in (and walking among the floor delegates afterwards – again, the only leader to do so) was valorised further by the fact that the Prime Minister had sprained her ankle earlier in the week and was reported as being in pain. When introduced (not by a new Conservative of the type epitomised by Norman Fowler but by the rather old-fashioned Sir Charles Johnston, President of the National Union), fulsome praise was heaped upon her with statements such as 'you have impressed yourself on government like nobody since the war years of Churchill' (cf. Neville Hough's asking Neil Kinnock to present the NEC's report, and the deflating return to 'party business' after his speech was delivered). Let us look than at this so-called thin speech, the last leadership conference speech before the third successive Conservative victory at the British general election of 1987.

THE TEXT

From the above discussion we can see that the two factors informing Margaret Thatcher's discourse (that she was in government, and that her political persona was already, if not legendary, then a nationally recognised phenomenon), free her from the main imperative operative in the other three speeches, namely, the construction of a political persona within the speech itself. Paradoxically, her already elevated status is thrown into even higher relief by the particularly 'quiet' and intimate way in which she begins her speech, observing, with determined *politesse*, the protocol of a major public speech, and revealing her knowledge of the more ordinary things of conference:

> Mr President, I would like to thank you for your welcome and also like to thank our Chairman, Patrick Lawrence, for his splendid work during the week. He's brought a light touch to the proceedings. We also want to thank Norman Tebbit, our party could not wish for a better Chairman. And we've all been delighted that he's been joined by Margaret (1)[2]

And the use of 'Mr President' to begin many subsequent paragraphs is a constant reminder of the nature of the occasion. Margaret Thatcher does not need to reassure the conference, as do the other leaders, as regards its perception of its own significance. Attention to detail, the display of awareness of the conference's tone, a touching reference to Margaret Tebbit, are confirmation enough for a Conservative conference of its ritual function. Observance of the formalities is a major indication of the speaker's being a 'true' (properly behaved) Conservative. Moreover, irrespective of disquiet in the constituency associations in the country over Margaret Thatcher's leadership, the Conservative Party conference is traditionally a site where leadership is symbolically portrayed as unfettered. It is not the role of Conservative leadership to handle a Conservative audience, nor the role of the conference to intimate any party dissatisfaction *vis-à-vis* that leadership. And the speaker refers (patronisingly?, dutifully? The distinction has no meaning in this kind of Conservative ritual) to the (ideal) role of a Conservative conference in a complimentary reference to the actual conference: 'A most responsible conference ... from the body of the hall has come speech after speech of advice, encouragement and commitment' (2). This quiet friendliness brings us to a related point concerning her national persona.

Margaret Thatcher's national reputation was in part built upon the idea that she was 'not like everyone else', was not even an ideal-type representative of the ordinary activist mythified into greatness (cf. Neil Kinnock), but was in some sense apart from the people, apart from her party too; that she possessed a 'vision' which predated its acceptance by others, even by the party itself. This will allow her to speak in the bulk of her speech as if offering or recapitulating 'her' ideology in a one-way self-assured manner. This, in a sense, is expected of her. And she has little need to respect traditional party ideology as this had become, through the particular treatment and perception of her both within and outside the party, whatever she happened to be saying at any particular time – at least for the 1980s. We can see, however, from her opening remarks, that this also involves her, paradoxically, in behaving in accordance with Conservative Party tradition and stressing the conference's importance. And this she does by observing the niceties of public speaking in a manner reminiscent of the Townswomen's Guild rather than of visionary leadership. In the course of the speech, she will also exhibit the quality ascribed to her of harshness on certain issues (defence in particular), but not on others (hospitals in particular). The harshness is in fact mitigated in that her persona is, in part, that of the ordinary person: the tradesman's daughter, the person who talks of 'little' issues, housekeeping for example, expresses 'little' emotions, perpetually giving voice, as we shall see, to the desires and anxieties of 'ordinary people', often to the point where she conveys the notion that she, like them, is not interested in politics, but is simply the woman we see bustling about with her handbag on her arm (this latter mannerism having been developed considerably *since* she became Prime Minister). And this ambivalent character (ordinary yet considerably powerful) is underscored by her taking time to observe the clichés of politeness as required by an address to the Conservative faithful.

The sum total of this is that, given the respect accorded to the conference delegates, and the traditional view that the delegates are not there to constrain the leader but to support her, Margaret Thatcher has very little *need* to mediate or be seen to mediate her speech *through* the party, and, equally, little need to take discursive account of the dual ideology in Conservatism. By ignoring what can be described as the country squire/estate agent divide in Conservatism, she neither threatens the former nor represents the latter as a deviation from traditional Conservatism. And, as we have said, given her supremacy, her speech is, in a sense, the ideology itself. Ironically, therefore, Margaret Thatcher's speech is in certain respects the least doctrinally sensitive, her discourse the most difficult to put an 'ism' next to. Even more ironically, even though it is the speech which is the least concessionary to the idea that leadership discourse reflects party ideas and which is the most manipulative of the plural personal pronoun as indicative of the singular, it is the most impersonal of the four speeches.

The speech, less restricted than the others we are studying – and much shorter – concentrates upon one notion, that of government, in terms of both its political function and its vocational base. Despite little personal reference, it will, however, be directed towards the enhancement of the status of the speaker herself. At its most banal level, this will allow Margaret Thatcher to tell her audience about government and of some of its secrets. All issues in the speech are treated in relation to this apparent interpretation of government not as a political institution but as an inspired activity and personal vocation. An unscripted indication of this relationship of the speaker to her particular interpretation of 'government' is given at the beginning of the conference:

> Mr President, before I begin there's just one thing I would like to make clear. The rose I am wearing is the rose of England (1)

Apart from the focusing upon herself (all eyes and cameras inevitably focus upon the rose on Margaret Thatcher's suit jacket), and the dismissal of the Labour Party's adoption of the red rose, we observe here the provocative defiance of the speaker when, in the context of a 'polite' conference framework, she considers such bluntness necessary. Over and above this, however, is the notion of the *reclamation* from other false claimants of the nation's identity. This notion of reclaiming and protecting the heritage will become, along with protection of the people and the particular treatment of privatisation, the dominant theme of the speech.

Underlying the speech (the topics covered are: the Labour Party; the Alliance; the government's record and intentions; the Health Service; education; and defence) are four referents, all of which are related to government and are presented as organising the world view which Margaret Thatcher's government reflects. These are (1) the relationship of government to people, (2) the moral basis of government, (3) government as a task, (4) that which government must protect and protect against. Let us examine the speech in relation to these four organising principles, and then comment upon the significance of all this in the depiction of Margaret Thatcher herself.

1. Government and people

After the introductory paragraphs concerning the conference itself, the speaker attacks the Labour Party on the grounds of its pretension to a special relationship to the people. Referring to the Labour Party's conference slogan, she says acidly:

'Putting people first'. Putting *people* first? (3)

We shall come back to this treatment when we describe the way the Labour Party is depicted. Here we can say that the initial attack is upon the Labour Party's claim to represent people (and, throughout, it is 'people' rather than 'the people' as a category that the speaker refers to). This not only gives the speaker the opportunity to highlight the sinister hypocrisy of the left but will later allow her to claim to be truly representing people's interests. The ridiculing of the Labour Party's slogan is achieved by repeating it three times in question form (as above), and repudiating the claim over three issues: Labour's wish to deny trade unionists a secret ballot (3), its wish to take away people's shares (4), its wish to take away the council houses people now own (5). All of these were traditionally highly 'ideological' issues for both parties, but we can see that the speaker is treating them in a deliberately non-ideological, 'everyday' manner. It is also worth noting here that all of these issues had often been questioned by the public, and highly criticised by the left, but had all, by 1986, become generally accepted, and even partially adopted by the left. In this way the 'right before her time' visionary quality of the speaker is further underlined without any *actual* reference to her. Moreover, the speaker does not refer to trade unions but to the individuals in them (trade union members), not to privatisation as a concept or shareholders as a category but to the 'millions of people who have been able to own shares for the first time in their lives', not to local authorities and housing but to saving people from the Labour Party's wish to 'kill the hopes and dreams of so many families'. In this way, Margaret Thatcher allows the entry into the discourse not only of the idea of the effects of her policies on real people but also of the idea that all along, when her government was being seen as doctrinaire and uncaring, the rationale of its action was, in fact, the protection of the people with whom it was in a secret, unspoken relationship. This idea of appearance (unpopular resolution) being a mask for or *apparent* inversion or misperception of reality (a caring attitude towards the people) will recur several times in the speech to the point where reference to all topics will imply that the opposite of what appears to be the reality is in fact the case.

The speaker returns to this relationship of government to people after a brief reference to the deviousness of the Labour Party and the irrelevance of the Alliance; and gives voice to the notion of government action as a kind of secret pact with the people or rather as a pact whose reality is scandalously undermined by others:

> The charge is sometimes made that our policies are only concerned with money and efficiency (9)

Not only is the efficiency of government implied here as given, but also at this point four issues, again all traditionally doctrinal ones, are framed in the same manner, that is, in terms of revealing a truth through the non-ideological refutation of a misperception. The notion of revelation of a truth (to those who did not realise) and confirmation of a truth (to those who did) is put in a question and answer form:

> Why are we Conservatives so opposed to inflation? Only because it puts up prices? *No* (10)
> Why have we limited the power of trade unions? Only to improve productivity? *No* (11)
> Why have we allowed people to buy shares in nationalised industries? Only to improve efficiency? *No* (12)
> And why are we setting up new kinds of schools in our towns and cities? To create privilege? *No* (13)

Once again, the reasons given as negatives complement the idea of a well-run administration in the two middle examples, and the four 'No's' define the speaker's need to explain patiently, though slightly exasperatedly, to the uninformed. Moreover, in all of the replies to these false or incomplete explanations (cf. the four 'only' sentences quoted above), individualism is again stressed, thus echoing positively the earlier negative accusation levelled at the Labour Party's lack of concern for individuals. Here are the answers to the four questions:

> *No*, because it destroys the value of people's savings. Because it destroys jobs and with it people's hopes (10)
> *No*, because trade union members want to be protected from intimidation and to go about their daily lives in peace – like everyone else in the land (11)
> *No*. To spread the nation's wealth among as many people as possible (12)
> *No*. To give families in some of our inner cities greater choice in the education of their children (13)

We can see here, moreover, that, once again, the relationship of government to people is presented as an unmediated one (later, the role of government will be widened to include the idea of protection), and government presented as a kind of facilitative social instrument, or personally-controlled entity, which acts on behalf of people, even in the absence of their being aware of this. The expression 'go about their daily lives' underlines this: the people *should* go about their daily lives, government must ensure that they are able to do this even to the point of the people's unawareness of the quiet, powerful solicitude of those who represent their true in-

terests. The depicted series of appearance/reality dichoto-
mies, moreover, is a prelude to the major theme of the
speech, namely, that (Margaret Thatcher's) 'strong' government is, in reality, simply (the custodian of) popular self-
government.

The notion of government and people is developed further (17 and 18). Here the discussion involves the deployment
of the idea of what the Labour Party would do if it were
allowed to gain power. We shall come back to this in our
consideration of how the Labour Party is represented in the
speech. Here we can say that the government/people relationship is always depicted in terms of what the Labour Party
would do *if* it gained national power. In this way, the crucial
nature of the government's relationship to the people is
emphasised in that the government is portrayed as trying to
protect the people, and that relationship, from an outside
force. Furthermore resistance to Labour's intentions and
beliefs is itself presented as non-ideological: 'What supreme
folly! It defies all common sense' (16), further underlining
the non-political nature of the relationship of the speaker to
the people. We can see from the examples we have given,
however, that a privileged relationship is being established
between government and people, and, more significant in
terms of our study of the relationship of leaders to the
public, that this relationship is being revealed by the speaker
as a hitherto not understood or misunderstood secret. The
government/people relationship continues in the speech, and
is clearly central to it. This exclusive relationship, however,
implies a further quality of government, namely, the morality which informs it in order that it does not deviate from this
relationship into a position of wanting power for its own
sake, the idea that power is a corrupting force being a
particularly strong one in British political culture. Let us
then continue our analysis, as does the speaker, from this
perspective.

2. Government and morality

The concept of 'people' is itself a moral one, the normative
value of the people and the mythical notion of its possessing

a fundamental virtue (often abused by leaders, and not always perceived by people themselves) being central to democratic theory. The notion itself is taken, in this speech as in the others, as unquestionable. And such an implicit view is enhanced by a high moralism which informs the speaker's depiction of the government/people relationship. Interestingly, however, as we shall see, it is the moral rectitude of the government (the speaker) in this relationship rather than of the people that is stressed. In fact, as we shall see, it is the assumed morality of the people which allows the speaker to make a claim for the explicit morality of the government.

The explicit introduction of government as a moral entity or undertaking prefaces the question/answer paragraphs mentioned above. Government policy is stressed as morally-inspired (arguably, personally morally-inspired) rather than as efficiency-inspired action:

> But just now I want to speak about Conservative policies, policies which spring from deeply-held beliefs (8)

The 'deeply-held beliefs' are, in part, Conservatism's (cf. 'our Conservative tradition' (13)). Given, however, what we have said concerning Conservative ideology and Margaret Thatcher's perceived persona, and given also the context of the claim (the speech itself), the deeply-held beliefs are as much, perhaps more, *her* beliefs as they are organised Conservatism's. There then follow the four question and answer issues, all of which concern, potentially, efficiency-related, morally neutral issues: monetary policy, industrial productivity, privatisation of industry, rationalisation in education. All, however, as we have seen, are transformed into moral contexts involving ordinary people's lives and government's acute awareness of them. After these passages, the speaker refers to a whole series of issues which we shall return to in our analysis of government as a task (14–29). We can say here that all of the issues are addressed in moral tones and all are, moreover, depicted as issues which the speaker must explicate as being other than they might seem, that is, as issues which might appear as administrative or efficiency-related, but which are in fact morally inspired and related to people.

This continuation of the moral theme also involves a long

passage which ridicules once again the Labour Party's claim to morality by reference to the left's moral insensitivity (striking miners depriving the old of heating, striking teachers depriving children of education, Labour councillors undermining the police). The speaker concludes:

> Mr President, we're not going to take any lessons in caring from people with that sort of record. We care profoundly about the right of people to be protected against crime, hooliganism and the evil of drugs (29)

The apparent logical relationship of miners, teachers and Labour councils to crime, hooliganism and drugs, given the temporal proximity of the two series (each containing three evocations), and the mutual ascription of wrong-doing, is clear. And, from this point, the words 'care' and 'caring' recur many times, and their moral relation to political action (as well as the idea that the opposite to caring embraces miners, teachers, the Labour Party, criminals, hooligans and drug pushers) is stressed. Here is an example:

> And it's *because* we care deeply about the Health Service, that we've launched the biggest hospital building programme in this country's history (30)

In this way, the discussion of the Conservatives' (Margaret Thatcher's) political Achilles' heel is prefaced by a discussion of the evil of that which she opposes. This is, moreover, given a very personal touch concerning Margaret Thatcher's own experience of hospitals. Such focusing upon the self enhances the 'I know, I was there' quality of the argument. We shall come back to this example of personal experience in the next section. We can say here, however, that addressing the morally-charged issue of medical provision in a 'personal', that is, non-political way, allows the speaker to discourse upon *others'* lived experience, thus undermining the notion of Margaret Thatcher's attitude to the Health Service being either an ideological or a personally insensitive one:

> This government's record on the Health Service is a fine one. We're proud of it and we must see to it that people know how much we've done. Of course there are still problems to be solved. The fact that there's no waiting list in one area doesn't help you if you have to wait for an

> operation in your area. It doesn't help if there's a new
> hospital going up somewhere else, but not where you'd
> really like it. We're tackling these problems (32)

This is only a small extract from the passage on the Health
Service. In fact, in terms of the speech as a whole, the topic of
the Health Service is one dealt with at some length. We can
see, therefore, that such an approach allows for the personal
'descent' of the speaker into ordinary lived experience
(which we shall detail in the next section), while permitting
her to obviate the accusation of a moral vision that is *so*
inspired that it fails to see the morally significant issues of
daily lived experience. The claim to the 'fine' government
record is also strengthened by the now well-established
rhetorical form of the speech (that appearance – here, a
government uncaring about the Health Service – belies the
true reality). It is also worth noting that the extensive
discussion of the Health Service enhances the status of the
speaker's courage, in that Margaret Thatcher is here devoting a major part of her speech to an examination of the issue
for which she and her government were most unpopular. It
is interesting also that the conference itself is brought in here
as a *caution* to government, and given its full symbolic role as
counsellor to the speaker ('us'):

> The debate we had on Wednesday, with its telling con-
> tributions from nurses and doctors in the Health Service,
> was enormously helpful to us (32)

This aside enhances the notion of the speaker's relationship
to conference, and implies that the Conservative government
can 'listen' to the Health Service, not via the Health Service
unions, nor even the BMA, but through the government-
legitimating conference speakers who belong to the medical
profession. The 'us' of the quotation, moreover, suggests the
counsel offered to a thoughtful monarch. The reference to
conference, moreover, triggers the recollection of one of the
most theatrical moments of the conference, Norman Fowler's (the then Social Services minister) throwing forward
over the rostrum a long computer print-out (to an ostensibly
incredulous press corps) of a list of new hospitals which had
been built or which were under construction as part of the
government's hospital programme. The discussion of this

topic ends, as it began, by the creation of a liaison between feeling and practical action:

This is Conservatives putting care into action (33)

Because this long (in terms of the speech) discussion comes from the head of the government, this idea of linking feeling and action has an added implication (over and above the speaker's awareness of a topic of which she was popularly supposed to have little knowledge), which is that the morally indignant criticism by those politicians who are *not* in government can be discounted as empty idealism. This further enhances the exclusive status of the speaker, first, because it personalises government by underlining its moral (that is, human rather than institutional) quality and, second, because 'government' by 1986 meant, in the public's perception, one person: the speaker.

The 'care' theme prefaces three more dimensions of the argument:

And we care deeply that retired people (34)
And we care passionately about the education of our children (35)
Mr President, we care most of all about our country's security (39)

We can see, therefore, that these several issues are not simply portrayed as important, but are further illustrations, on the one hand, of government as caring, and, on the other, of the speaker's *need* to demonstrate the real relationship between misleading appearance and true reality.

We shall come back to the second and third of these issues (education and security), but we can see here from the way in which the issues follow one another, and are similarly prefaced, how caring/morality allows for the shift to the defence issue as a fundamentally moral issue which is inextricably linked (as in the other leadership speeches) to a moralism concerning domestic issues. In this way, Thatcherism's 'toughness' (the defence issue being both one of the most popular Thatcher 'tough positions' and the opposition parties' most vulnerable) is legitimated in that it is presented not only as a prerequisite to effective moral action on other issues but as synonymous with a discursively established morality itself, and as the (tough) moral complement to a (caring) moral concern.

A barely perceptible change, however, has taken place by the time the defence issue is addressed: the notion of government has been implicitly extended from the earlier one of the government/people relationship to that of government of the people. This change is rhetorically possible partly because the previous discussion of the government/people relationship was, as we have seen, dependent upon the idea that while government was there to free people and allow them to govern themselves, it was also there to protect them, given, in particular, the hypocrisy and deviousness of other claimants to government (there is also, of course, as we have seen, given the speaker's insistence on the theme, the implied notion of the people as being unaware of the necessary responsibilities of government itself). This allows for what is essentially a social democratic notion (paradoxical in that it justifies an aggressive nationalism) concerning government's role as being that of guardian of the people. Thus the notion of Thatcherism as a kind of free-for-all Darwinism is mitigated, and the ground prepared for the discussion of defence by the implication that on the domestic front, the government is a shield which protects the people from those who threaten them.

The link between these two contradictory notions, government as giving itself over to people/government as caring for people in a social way, is resolved in the speech, and, we might add, in Thatcherism generally, by the representation of government as not really being government at all. We have already seen how government is depicted as a shield for the people from the left, as if the left *were* the government. The link is, therefore, that government in Conservative form is in fact anti-government. This will inform significantly the notion of government as a programme (see next sub-section), lending to a government which had been in office for seven and a half years the ability to depict itself and its intentions as breaking down the institution of government. The notion of a crusade is thus discursively deployed. Let us now see how government can be non-government.

We have already noted the great stress placed on the notion of handing government back to the people. This is interwoven in the text with – and there is an irony here because the whole speech is about government, *is* government in discursive action – the representation of government itself as a force of oppression:

> Labour may say they put people first, but their conference voted to put *government* first and that means putting people last (5)

It is the Labour Party itself which is presented in the text as 'government' in this form. The speaker then extemporises upon the programme of such a government, representing it as a kind of ideological mindlessness:

> What the Labour Party of today wants is: housing *municipalised*, industry *nationalised*, the police service *politicised*, the judiciary *radicalised*, union membership *tyrannised*, and above all – and most serious of all – our defences *neutralised*. Never! (6)

This contrasts sharply with the depiction of 'Conservative policies' (8) (not 'government' policies) which, as we have seen, have been concertedly represented in an 'ordinary' way. This distinction is reinforced by the idea of Conservative government as having as its central – until this point in the speech its only – focus its relation to the people, the protection of the people, and the liberation of the people (in the sense of allowing them 'to go about their daily lives'). We shall come back to the way in which the nature of government as represented in the speech changes significantly from the point at which defence is discussed, and what the implications of this are for the representation of the persona of the leader. Here let us examine how government policy (elaborated throughout the week by *other* speakers) is presented as a task in its deeper, chivalric sense.

3. Government as a task

The idea of future intention follows on uncontentiously in the speech from the idea of what has been achieved. What is interesting, however, is that it is not a question of mere policy proposals, but, as we have seen, of a moral undertaking which relates government to people (and which, as we shall see, protects both ancient and newly-acquired freedoms). In this way, government policy can be represented as a crusade (and will be named as such) and as a moral task, as yet unfulfilled. This, moreover, has special implications for the status of the speaker, as the next section of this chapter will demonstrate.

Thus we may observe that the problem – named by nearly all media commentators as the government's major stumbling block, that is, the defence of the record – is sidestepped by the speaker's depiction of a cycle which goes beyond (because it operates in mythic time, like all crusades) the cycles of parliaments (which operate in real time). It is interesting to note in this context that the prefacing of the justification of past policy (cf. the initial references to monetary policy and industrial productivity (paragraphs 10–13)) involves the mixing of tenses ('Why are we . . . ?' (10), 'Why have we . . . ?' (11), 'Why have we . . . ? (12), 'Why are we . . . ?' (13)), as if the parliamentary cycle is secondary to a longer mythic one of a crusade to fulfil a task. We can see from this notion of mythic continuum that, for the speaker, it is not just a question of defending a government against an opposition but of defending from illegitimate attack a morally-inspired project which transcends the cycles of parliament. Government intention as a crusade is introduced (paradoxically, because it momentarily returns us to real time) by the speaker's picking up on the conference theme:

> Mr President, as you've said, the theme of our conference this week is the next move forward. We have achieved a lot in seven short years. But there is still a great deal to be done for our country (14)

Over the next twenty-five paragraphs (14–38) government policies are not, however, put forward as such (and we can see here how the context of the conference, the major speeches by government ministers throughout the week, is functional to leadership discourse – the policies have already been given), but are presented as illustrations of a progressive movement, to which the previous 'seven short years' are but a prelude.

The depiction of what is involved in the next move

forward is prefaced by two cautionary references, the first to the world context of government action (15) – that Britain is in a period of major technological change – and the second to the need for Britain to remain a trading nation (16) (which is accompanied by several references, which we shall analyse below, to the fact that the Labour Party would put back this movement (17)). These domestications obviate the danger of 'the crusade' being implied as 'ideological' or unrealistic, the crusade of a megalomaniac leader divorced from reality (such accusations are further deflected, as we have seen, and the status of the speaker enhanced, by the already strong implication – never explicit assertion – that the speaker 'sees' (desired) reality before anyone else, the evidence being the subsequent acceptance by others of the rectitude of earlier decisions). References to the mission of Conservatism are, therefore, constantly linked here to the idea of government action as having real effects. It is, therefore, a crusade which incorporates 'reality' into it:

> The government has created the climate that's produced a million extra jobs over the past three years. Here in Britain, it is encouraging that more of the population are in work than in Italy, or France, or even Germany. Nevertheless, as you heard yesterday, more has to be done, and is being done . . . . For only modern, efficient industry and commerce will produce the jobs our people need (18)

This notion of tough realism (prefaced by a 'No other country in Europe can rival' (17), and underlined by reference to the technological revolution and the trading context) reaffirms the idea of 'a task' undertaken.

The speaker then continues on the theme of the rightness of the government's action, in this way underscoring its unquestionable legitimacy in terms of its having triggered an international reaction:

> This government has rolled back the frontiers of the state, and will roll them back still further. And so popular is our policy that it's being taken up all over the world. From France to the Philippines, from Jamaica to Japan, from Malaysia to Mexico, from Sri Lanka to Singapore, privatisation is on the move, there's even a special oriental

version in China. The policies we have pioneered are catching on in country after country. We Conservatives believe in popular capitalism – believe in a property-owning democracy. And it works! (20–21)

The speaker then returns immediately to the domestic context, in turn justifying it by the reference to the international context. And, of course, what is also suggested by the above quotation is the delicate interdependence of the domestic and the international (cf. 'and what's more'). This is also a precursor of the extension of the crusade (from the national to the international). The speaker declares at this point, in relation to the domestic context, as if carried forward by a series of logically-related concepts:

And what's more, millions have already become sharehol-ders. And soon there will be opportunities for millions more, in British Gas, British Airways, British Airports and Rolls Royce. Who says we've run out of steam? We're in our prime! (23)

What we see here is not simply a justification of a past record, nor even a programme for the future, but the explanation of a task which is being undertaken and must be fulfilled because, as an exemplary model, it has become part of a complex global process led and stimulated by Conservative government (and, in the global context, the speaker's status is heightened in that all coverage of foreign reports in the British media on British governmental decisions involves a determining 'Iron Lady' factor in all decisions). The speaker then takes the next logical step, namely, the inscribing of Thatcherism itself (as a political undertaking and as a vision) into an unfolding, historically-legitimating, process. And the inscribing is strengthened by the triumphalist tone (cf. the exclamatory tone of the delivery in the previous two quota-tions) which precedes the insight:

The great political reform of the last century was to enable more and more people to have a vote. Now the great Tory reform of this century is to enable more and more people to own property. Popular capitalism is nothing less than a crusade to enfranchise the many in the economic life of the nation. We Conservatives are returning power to the people. That is the way to one nation, one people (24)

The speaker then dismisses the opposition, but not as she had earlier, that is, as a direct threat, but here as that which attempts to trivialise the greatness of the crusade. Thus the opposition is marginalised still further as not only a political, but, given the previous passage, a historical irrelevance:

> Mr President, you may have noticed there are many people who just can't bear good news. It's a sort of infection of the spirit and there's a lot of it about. In the eyes of these hand-wringing merchants of gloom and despondency, everything that Britain does is wrong. Any setback, however small, any little difficulty, however local, is seen as incontrovertible proof that the situation is hopeless. Their favourite word is 'crisis'. It's a crisis when the price of oil goes up and a crisis when the price of oil comes down. It's a crisis if you don't build new roads. It's a crisis when you do. It's a crisis if Nissan does not come here. And it's a crisis when it does. It's being so cheerful as keeps 'em going. What a rotten time these people must have, running round running everything down. Especially when there's so much to be proud of (25–26)

The speaker then lists at length the reasons to be proud: low inflation, few strikes, research, job creation, the arts, music and sport. The passage ends:

> The triumphs of our sportsmen and women, they all do Britain proud. And we are mighty proud of them (27)

It is interesting here to note a rhetorical point concerning the build-up to this quotation, the crescendo which ends on the very human and colloquially (personalised) expressed sentiment of pride: 'Lowest ... lowest ... lowest ... advances ... achievement ... outstanding ... triumphs ... proud ... mighty proud' (27). We can see here, also, how the clear conflation of government preoccupations (eradicating inflation, reducing strikes, promoting research and job creation) and concern with wider issues (the arts, music, sport) allows for the concomitant conflation of government and Britain, as if Conservative government were part of a near-mystical process involving the energies of the whole nation. The claims made for 'our sportsmen and women', therefore, are not a crude attempt to appropriate to government extra-governmental achievements, but, on the contrary, a discursive attempt to inscribe the Conservative government into a wider cultural process of regeneration and renewal.

It is after this long passage that the speaker refers to the moral inadequacy of the left (striking miners depriving the old of heating), and to its own record of 'caring'. We can see from our analysis so far how government policy is being framed in terms of a moral crusade, a crusade against an opposition which would diminish (because it is morally impoverished) not only everything which has been built up, but also a morally envisioned future.

4. Government as protector

We have seen how the 'caring' theme leads on to the defence discussion (schematically, you *are* caring, you care *about* something, you therefore *defend* it). We have seen also how policy and morality are perpetually intertwined to the point where past and future policy are depicted as moments in a moral crusade, and how the notions of people and caring are linked by the idea of government as non-government. It is in this way that the idea of a crusade *for* people is transformed into that of a strong government *defending* people. This involves not just, however, the proposing of strong defence policies (and all the implied strength which this ascribes to the speaker) but also the notion of government as a form of protection for the people against all their brutal, alien, and sly opponents. This portrayal of a besieged protection in fact legitimates government defence strategy itself. We have noted already (and shall return to in the next section) examples, in terms of domestic policy, of this notion of protection of the people against the Labour Party, whose policies would 'put out', 'blight', 'could not afford', 'could not give', 'close down', 'lose', 'would destroy' (all of these terms are from one paragraph (17)). Such references are a further demonstration of protection of the truth against would-be falsehoods, of clear thinking against muddled thinking, of advance towards a new society against retreat from it. Therefore, in spite of the concerted idea of government as non-government, we can see that the 'strong' idea of government as protective is also prevalent throughout the speech;

in the second part of the speech this is portrayed explicitly, in the first part implicitly through the constant references to the notion of threat to government. When the notion of protection is transposed on to the wider issue of defence, government, in all its strength (and solitary responsibility), returns. Moreover the speech has portrayed the Conservative government as being not interested in government as the site where self-interested pressure groups meet, only in government as the expression of higher moral issues. From this point, and because of moral commitment, it is as if government must be *reluctantly* assumed. This will link up with the idea of the great leader who must remain in office (continue the crusade) in order to fulfil a task:

> Mr President, we care most of all about our country's security. The defence of the realm transcends all other issues. It is the foremost responsibility of any government and any Prime Minister (39)

The speaker then draws heavily upon the theme of the Labour Party's betrayal of trust (of its own past and of the country), a rhetorical effect which has been foreshadowed by the speaker's reference to the desire of the Labour Party to run down Britain (25):

> For forty years, every government of this country of every political persuasion has understood the need for strong defences.... Last week, Mr President, the Labour Party abandoned that ground (40–41)

The 'forty years'/'last week' juxtaposition is, moreover, a dramatic suggestion that the country is at a historical turning point. In this way, the speaker dramatises the historical significance of her own discourse. She then enlarges on this idea of the 'gravity' of the decision (this word, referring to Labour's unilateralism, is used twice as if the left was not only irresponsible but not even aware of the importance of its decisions), and on what she sees as the 'nuclear blackmail' and 'surrender' which would be occasioned by such decisions if they were ever implemented. In this way, the folly of a party not fit to govern is reinforced, as well as the present government's distinctive qualification to govern. The speaker then states, as if offering the conclusive maxim which flows from such observations:

You can't be a loyal member of NATO while disavowing its fundamental strategy. A Labour Britain would be a neutralist Britain. It would be the greatest gain for the Soviet Union in forty years. And they would have got it without firing a shot (43)

This concept of allowing an enemy to gain advantage as the result of irresponsible decisions is a strong one in British political culture because of Neville Chamberlain's ill-fated policy of appeasement in 1938–39.[3] The speaker then continues her attack on the Labour Party in terms of its having abandoned the country. We shall look at this in more detail in the next section. Here we can note the dramatic refocusing upon the speaker as the only protector of Britain as she closes the discussion:

As Prime Minister, I could not remove that protection from the lives of present and future generations (48)

This echoes the sentence which begins the defence discussion ('Mr President, we care most of all about our country's security' (39)). There is also an echo here of Neil Kinnock's idea of not letting his country die for him. We can see from this example not only how the speaker takes advantage of the previous conferences but also how the personalisation of issues has become a central rhetorical device, and how the image of the lonely exercise of power is exploited to the full, because, on the one hand, it involves responsibility for protecting against the destruction of humanity, and, on the other, it strongly implies the centrality of the speaker because of the finger-on-the-button nature of decision-making on the question of nuclear attack. It is clear that the depiction of the Labour Party is fundamental here to the idea of the government as protector and, by extension, to that of the Prime Minister as supreme protector. Let us, therefore, look at how the Labour Party has been depicted as the enemy of 'the task' before considering how the persona of the speaker reinforces the defence argument and is reinforced by it.

We have seen many examples of how the presentation of the Labour Party throughout the speech has been that of an entity which the people have to be warned against and protected from (in terms of both the Labour Party's deviousness and the people's absence of understanding of such deviousness). The Labour Party is referred to constantly throughout the speech (the Alliance is barely mentioned). This goes beyond the simple desire to undermine an opposition. The depictions of the Labour Party as false, inadequate, devious and irresponsible are necessary to the speaker's presentation of (Conservative) government as morally inspired. Let us list here the ways in which the Labour Party is represented in the speech and see how all references point to these notions of falsehood, deviousness, pettiness and danger which government must guard against:

> The Labour Party made the bogus claim (3)
> Labour voted . . . regardless of the millions of people (4)
> Labour may say they put people first, but their conference voted to put *government* first and that means putting people last (5)
> What the Labour Party of today wants is: housing *municipalised* . . . . Never! (6)
> They want to put back the clock and set back the country. Back to state direction and control. Back to . . . . Back to . . . . Back to . . . . What supreme folly! (16)
> Labour policies which, far from putting people *first*, would put them *out* of jobs. The prospects of young people . . . . A quarter of a million jobs could be at risk. Many thousands of jobs would go . . . . And then Labour want . . . . Tens of thousands of people could lose their jobs . . . . And out would go jobs at . . . . On top of this . . . . Labour say . . . . But those policies would destroy . . . . (17)
> And our opponents would have us believe (19)
> Mr President, you may have noticed there are many people who just can't bear good news (25)
> And then our opponents, having lost the political argument, try another tack. They try to convey the impression . . . . So let's take a close look . . . They're the ones . . . . They're the ones . . . . They're the ones . . . (28)
> Education . . . infiltrated by a permissive philosophy of self-expression (36)

And then the Labour Party's abandonment of the country's interests:

> Last week, Mr President, the Labour Party abandoned that ground. In a decision of the utmost gravity, Labour voted

to give up Britain's independent nuclear deterrent unilaterally (41)
Labour's defence policy ... is an absolute break with the
defence policy of every British government since the
Second World War (43)
The Labour Party of Attlee, of Gaitskell, and of Wilson is
dead (45)

Taken together, these statements concerning the Labour
Party's attitude to both the people and the defence of the
country amount to a dismissal of the relevance of the Labour
Party at a moral level (abandoning the centre ground is
synonymous with abandoning the nation *militarily*) and a *mise
en garde* against the Labour Party at the level of its *potential*
nefarious power (they also give play to the notion that it was
only the earlier strong leaders of the Labour Party who
prevented it from assuming its true, bad, character). The
cumulative effect of this is to suggest that on the domestic
level, through scheming, and on the international level,
through incompetence, Labour Party intentions amount to a
betrayal of the country – and this is underlined by the notion
of its betrayal of its own past, as we have seen, and of its
people (44) (this latter claim will allow the speaker to make a
subsequent appeal to 'traditional' Labour Party voters). The
government's position is portrayed as not simply holding
different views from the opposition, but of holding the line
against an insidious and irresponsible aggressor. We shall
come back to this point below.

From the above discussion we can see that the essential
notion is not simply one of defending a particular government, but of government as a concept; 'government' rather
than 'the government' (in this it resembles certain aspects of
David Steel's speech). We can also see that it is being depicted
as a personal calling. The level at which the discussion of
issues is pitched: its moralism and individualistic, people-
orientated and protective emphases, and all these in the
context of the conclusions we have drawn before concerning
the pre-speech national status of the speaker, facilitates the
impression, not only through the personal delivery of the
speech and the fact that it is the Prime Minister speaking, but
also through the ideas deployed which correspond to hu-

man, emotional reactions, that 'government' in fact means the personal, and institutionally-derived views of Margaret Thatcher herself.

We have in Margaret Thatcher's speech a major illustration of the personalisation of discourse which does not involve the concerted intervention of the persona of the speaker herself (there is personal intervention but this is essentially, as we shall see, of a very 'localised' nature). When the theme of nationalism is developed beyond the defence debate, there is not the same need to personalise, as in the other speeches, the speaker having become – from the initial remark concerning the red rose onwards – synonymous with the protection of the nation and its heritage. There is, however, as one might expect, a major rhetorical deployment of nationalism, but this, because of the Falklands War and the Brighton bombing, does not need personalised discursive justification (although, as we shall see, there is a 'quiet' reminder of Brighton). Let us, therefore, turn to the discussion of the ways in which the portrayed character and character traits of Margaret Thatcher inform the speech, and then look at how these inform the major demonstration of nationalism towards the end of the speech.

5. The character of the speaker

In our analysis of the other speeches we have seen how maxims are, by definition, impersonal yet serve to improve speaker status. In the case of Margaret Thatcher, and the notion of Conservative and government ideology as 'hers', maxims will elevate her even more, especially given the fact that these will necessarily be seen as 'truths' subscribed to by the country's national leader. When such maxims link up with fundamental beliefs of the British people or the conference audience, they will, in this context, further enhance the speaker herself in that they will be the leadership expressions of these widely-held beliefs. There are several maxims in the speech:

> We are a party which honours the past that we may build for the future (2)

> Without choice, talk of morality is an idle and an empty
> thing (13)
> Without the rule of law, there can be no liberty (29)
> The defence of the realm transcends all other issues (39)
> You cannot deter with conventional weapons an enemy
> which has, and could threaten to use, nuclear weapons (41)
> We do our best for our country when we are true to our
> convictions (53)

These six maxims, moreover, relate to issues of national
importance, rather than to individual conduct, thus underlining, in the context of a highly individual-orientated
speech, the exclusive national status and global vision of one
particular individual: the speaker.

Apart from and in contrast to the maxims, there are also
several interventions of the speaker's persona. What is striking about these is that there are as many homely interventions, concerning 'little' issues, as there are strident national
and international ones:

> Mr President, before I begin there's just one thing I would
> like to make clear. The rose I am wearing is the rose of
> England (1)
> Mr President, I would like to thank you for your welcome
> (1)
> I'll have rather more to say about defence later. But just
> now I want to speak about Conservative policies (7–8)
> I am the first to acknowledge that morality is not and never
> has been the monopoly of any one party (9)
> And I would just like to say, Mr President (18)
> In Scotland recently, I was present at the sale of the
> millionth council house: to a lovely family with two chil-
> dren (22)

And the most extensive personal intervention:

> Over the past year or so, I've visited five hospitals. In the
> North West, at Barrow-in-Furness, I visited the first new
> hospital in that district since the creation of the Health
> Service forty years ago. In the North East, I've seen another
> splendid new hospital, at North Tyneside, with the most
> wonderful maternity unit and children's wards. Just north
> of London I went round St Albans hospital where new

wards have been opened and new buildings are under way. I visited the famous Elizabeth Garrett Anderson hospital for women, which this government saved. And the service it provides is very special and greatly appreciated. And then last week I went back to the Royal Sussex County hospital in Brighton, to open the new renal unit. Many of us have cause to be very thankful for that Brighton hospital (31)

And later at a less personal level:

I believe that this total reversal of Labour's policy for the defence of our country will have come as a shock to many of Labour's traditional supporters (44)
As Prime Minister, I could not remove that protection from the lives of present and future generations (48)
I believe it totally misjudges the character of the British people (50)
I believe that we have an historic duty (57)
I believe that our party is (58)
I believe the interests of Britain (59)

Many of these interventions, moreover, in spite of their personalised quality, imply that Margaret Thatcher is not really in government, but is simply the spokesperson for ordinary people. Furthermore, we can say that the 'inappropriateness' of the homeliness of some of the interventions (given that she is the national leader) is rhetorically very effective. It creates an image of a leader who, although she has, historically and in relation to rival leaders, been considered as, at worst, a fascist, at best, bossy, is in reality the most homely of them all, the most publicly given to the observations and pleasures of the ordinary person. Given also that personal intervention (the use of the first person singular) is restricted to either homely or wide rhetorical claims, these two categories of claim are mutually reinforcing and suggest the wide range of characteristics contained in the speaker's persona.

In terms of the speaker's persona, there are, moreover, several expressions of humour in the speech. These, along with the lightnesses of touch, the homeliness, the observance of thanks, the treatment of the conference as a nice little meeting, increase the humanity and individualism of the speaker. They also, along with one or two political jokes (for example, 'They [the Alliance] appear to be engaged in a confused squabble about whether or not Polaris should be abandoned or replaced or renewed or re-examined. And if so, when, and how, and possibly why?' (7); 'And we shall complete the manifesto for the next election [pause] within the next eighteen months' (52)), demonstrate the ease with which she carries her national responsibility. In the closing discussion of the defence issue, all of these characteristics are omitted and yet the overall impression is that of a composite character who is able to be concerned, simultaneously, with the minor issues of everyday life and with the major issues of planetary significance.

We have seen how the introduction of the defence issue surreptitiously reverses the depiction of government-as-non-government while simultaneously conveying the notion of the lonely exercise of *personal* power:

> Mr President, we care most of all about our country's security. The defence of the realm transcends all other issues. It is the foremost responsibility of any government and any Prime Minister (39)

We have also noted how this responsibility is portrayed as having to be shouldered by the speaker, given the Labour Party's betrayal of a forty-year tradition. This is an interesting illustration of how the speaker posits herself and her party as being in a consensual centrist tradition and the Labour Party as deviationists from this (this reinforces the subsequent conjecture that the Labour Party's having 'abandoned that ground' (41) means its having abandoned a notional centre (and sacred) ground). The scorn clearly felt here by the speaker is underlined by her never referring to Neil Kinnock by name, in spite of the fact that attacks upon the Labour Party itself take up a substantial part of the speech. She mentions Attlee, Bevan, Gaitskell and Wilson by name (in the case of Bevan and Gaitskell, their forenames are given also), all of these thereby being accorded a place in the traditional national consensus of which the speaker herself is part. In this way, the speaker presents the Labour Party as having betrayed both its past *and* its traditional supporters (cf. 'a shock to many of Labour's traditional supporters' (44)). Moreover, given the topic under discussion, namely, defence, the association with betrayal of the country, 'the realm', is clear.

The speaker then gives some lessons concerning the nuclear issue (which amount to the revelation of the secrets of good government which themselves, of course, can come only with experience and insight, thus underlining the governmental inexperience of the Labour leader): first, that weapon development and production is a long and complex process which, if arrested, 'would fatally weaken' the country's defence potential (46); second, that the nuclear balance has saved Europe from war for forty years (47); and third, that the Reagan/Gorbachev summit (of 1986) would never have taken place if the West had not been strong (50). This is reinforced by a reprise of the speaker/people relation in a reference to the Labour Party's misjudging (as revealed in its policies), as well as the speaker's own understanding, of the people/government relation:

> I believe it [Labour policy] totally misjudges the character of the British people (50)

And the role of the speaker herself as a protective shield, as it were, is then stressed, linking up with the personalised sentence opening the passage on defence (39):

> As Prime Minister, I could not remove that protection from the lives of present and future generations (48)

The defence of the country (as in the other speeches, references to 'our country' are legion) and the internal, domestic issues are, therefore, treated in the same way at one level (both involve protection) and differently at another (one involves strong government, the other what we have described as strong non-government). We should also mention here the enormous constraint placed upon listener disagreement with the speaker, given that the issue being discussed here is one involving the potential destruction of the globe, an issue the details of which few Britons could claim detailed knowledge of. It is also an issue which the speaker has already underlined as being exclusive to government, involving the lonely exercise of power, and which she will soon refer to as the 'awesome responsibility' (56) of government, given the abandonment of it by those who are opposed to the government's defence policies and in whom she gives the impression of being very disappointed.

The speaker then fuses all the three government themes: government as being for the people and the country, government as moral, government as a programme. The latter, moreover, is given, even more clearly, its status as a crusade, and involves a vision of the future. In addition, all the human qualities involved (cf. 'deeply held beliefs', 'our convictions', 'we look forward', 'we have a vision', 'we wish to see', 'we all serve') highlight the essential element of this crusade: the speaker herself:

> That manifesto will be a programme for further bold and radical steps in keeping with our most deeply-held beliefs [cf. reference to the same, paragraph 8]. For we do our best for our country when we are true to our convictions. As we look forward to the next century, we have a vision of the society we wish to see. The vision we all serve (53–54)

And the vision, unspecific as all visions are, is elaborated into a statement of an ideal nation (the 'Britain' the speaker envisions is mentioned eight times here), and, given the suggestion throughout of the speaker as being in possession of and, occasionally, sharing a 'secret' – the secret which both governments as entities and visionary leaders as individuals possess – the image of an ideal Britain is implied as personally offered as well as personally envisioned (irrespective of the 'we' involved in the envisioning):

> We want to see a Britain where there is an ever-widening spread of ownership, with the independence and dignity it brings, a Britain which takes care of the weak in their time of need. We want to see a Britain where the spirit of enterprise is strong enough to conquer unemployment North and South, a Britain in which the attitude of 'them and us' has disappeared from our lives. We want to see a Britain whose schools are a source of pride and where education brings out the best in every child. A Britain where excellence and effort are valued and honoured. We want to see a Britain where our streets are free from fear, day and night. And above all, we want to see a Britain

which is respected and trusted in the world, which values the great benefits of living in a free society, and is determined to defend them (55)

This is the Britain which, according to the speech, already exists in partial reality (because of previous governmental action) and in the mind and thoughts (given the speech and the implied vision) of the speaker/Prime Minister herself.

Through the speech (and rhetorically reinforced through the discussion of defence which further focuses upon the Prime Minister as potential button-pusher), the speaker has constructed the view that the present government must go on because there is no one else to fulfil the task of protecting, directing, and leading the nation. This is stressed again very near the end of the speech:

The failure of the other parties to measure up to what is needed places an awesome responsibility upon us (56)

This 'what is needed' implies, and therefore rhetorically relates, all the issues discussed in the speech, but focuses specifically upon the idea of the defence of Britain from attack – and particularly connotes the defence of a Margaret Thatcher-protected Britain from attack by the massive forces of Communist Russia (that is to say, of the country possessing all the values antithetical to those of the speaker). This claim to the failure of others to 'measure up' to their responsibilities is followed by 'I believe' – as if it were the product of personal reflection – and the 'I believe' prefacing the above claim that 'we have an historic duty' (57) is repeated three times. Such personalism is mitigated by the further claim that 'our party' is equipped for the task (58), and that 'the interests of Britain can now only be served by a third Conservative victory' (59). This last statement hands the conference back to the party and to the audience and offers *them* a task, that of working to recreate in reality all that the speaker has created in discourse.

6 Conclusion

From the foregoing analysis of contemporary leadership discourse in a particular ritual setting, we can make three brief general conclusions. We can also make a series of concluding remarks concerning each of the parties and the role of the party conference in political life and its relationship to leadership. We can also itemise the shared characteristics of contemporary leadership discourse in the conference setting. Finally, and from these conclusions we can make brief mention of the political role of language, ritual, and leadership in contemporary politics.

The first conclusion relates to all the parties' adaptation or attempts to adapt to the Conservative Party's continuing political success, a success seen as resulting in great part from its leadership style. After 1979, all four of the parties analysed, including the Conservatives, were forced to respond to what we might call the 'Thatcher factor', that is, the assumed role of Margaret Thatcher's persona in the Conservatives' gaining and retaining governmental control. The various responses involved some notable alterations in the parties' discourses, and, concomitantly, alterations in the relationships between leadership, organisation, policy formulation and policy presentation. Second, the modifications within these relationships have involved in each of the parties not only the enhancement of the ritual significance of the party conference but also the presentation of party life generally as a rally of forces which will lead to a morally-inspired national revival or awakening which is leader-led. Third, all the conferences involve the ritually-framed and discursive exploitation of the notion of making real the apparently impossible: in the case of the Labour Party, of overturning a huge Conservative majority (and bringing the people to power); in the case of the two Alliance parties, of becoming a truly national phenomenon (and of redrawing the map of British politics); in the case of the Conservative Party, of winning yet another decisive and consecutive electoral victory (and moving into the next phase of a politico-cultural crusade).

To turn our attention to the particular, it is arguable that, in the SDP, the focus upon David Owen *as* the SDP helped fashion a perceptible SDP ideology. Given the fragility of the young party and the strong media interest, it is also arguable that the transmission of this ideology through him was necessary and inevitable. In terms of national organisation and local implantation, and, by 1986, of policies, the SDP, as a party, had done a great deal. It was still true, however, that the presentation of this achievement involved an extraordinary conferring of significance upon David Owen. As far as leadership is concerned in this context, we can speculate on whether, irrespective of ideological and policy differences between the two parties, the creation of the Alliance was, in terms of both ideology and leadership persona, a historical mistake. Briefly, the personalisation of David Steel's leadership was out of place in the Liberals but was made necessary to counter David Owen's strongly personalised leadership and to lead the Liberals forward into the Alliance. The personalisation of David Owen's leadership was necessary to give a focus and semblance of ideology to the young SDP. In the context of a national political leadership, Margaret Thatcher's, which was highly individualistic and morally-inspired, there could only be *one* symbolic challenger, leadership rivalry between Steel and Owen therefore becoming inevitable, and ultimately, after the 1987 election, critical. It is also arguable that the Alliance was itself necessary because of local political conditions, the dominant two-party system, and the first past the post electoral system. If both of these views are valid, we can say that *practically* the Alliance was necessary, but that the equally necessary personalisation of leadership worked against its success. Moreover the focus upon David Owen created the potential for him to 'walk off with' Social Democracy and claim an even more *personal* relationship to it in the post-1987 period, even though only a minority of the SDP walked off with him. The idea, one to which even Owen's personal supporters would subscribe, that Social Democracy was not 'him', is not the point here. Of course social democracy is not David Owen (indeed, the creation of the SDP was a reaction *against* the social democracy of the Labour Party); social democracy is a worldwide phenomenon, arguably the quintessential leftism of parliamentary democracies. Nevertheless the keystone role accredited to Owen in the mid-1980s facilitated his 'appropriation' of British Social Democracy, particularly in the context of a political culture which was ascribing special significance to the notion of leadership 'vision'.

In the case of the Liberals, the political conditions of the early and mid-1980s led the party into a relationship with another national party, the SDP, and into potentially governmental association with the policies of that party, thus compelling it to modify its style and its image (not least as these related to leadership), as much as its policies, in order to offer itself as a governmental party. The defence issue in particular, therefore, harmed the Liberal Party considerably. Before the creation of the Alliance, defence had never been a divisive issue on this scale, the pros and antis co-existing in relative tranquillity, irrespective of the long, strongly Quaker, pacifist strain in British Liberalism. The Alliance forced into the forefront of Liberal Party discourse, however, not only the question of the style and range of leadership authority but also leadership as an emanation of both the Liberal 'tradition' and a personally inspired 'vision'. In the context of the Alliance, moreover, where the other partner manifested such a strong emphasis upon leadership, the Liberals could not become governmental if they placed only limited emphasis upon personalised leadership, which they might possibly have done in the absence of the Alliance (in retrospect it is impossible now to calculate the ultimate political and electoral effect of all the opposition parties refusing overtly personalised leadership and cultivating collective leadership as a challenge to Thatcher's style). The leadership factor forced David Steel to behave in a particular way, and the national context forced the party to define itself in a particular way. It is arguable, although this is difficult to measure, that the defence vote at its conference profoundly shocked the Liberal Party, undermining not only its image but also its self-confidence, and this in part because the party had not been fully aware of the road it had travelled in terms of the new exigencies of leadership. The defence vote was implicitly a vote of no-confidence in David Steel both as party leader (in terms of his subscription to certain policies) and as a leader of 'vision' who should not have allowed David Owen to make him seem secondary, impressionable, or unaware of his (Owen's) assumption of greater status.

This is why there was such a deliberate upgrading of personal leadership in Steel's speech in order to resolve the defence issue. Such upgrading was, however, to have a series of unforeseen effects when the next phase, namely, the merger of the two parties, developed. In order to reassert his authority over his party in 1986, the Liberal leader drew upon all the discursive resources at the disposal of leadership. One of the effects of this was not only the disproportionate upgrading of leadership status but, as we have seen, the redefining of the mythical and discursive resources to which leadership within Liberalism can lay claim. Illustrative of this was Des Wilson introducing David Steel and his reference to the qualities of a great leader in the 'last twenty years of the twentieth century', and his claim that it was 'our unique distinction in British politics to be able to offer the country such a leader, our leader, the leader of the Liberal Party, David Steel'. Enhancing the leader in this way was not only an attack upon David Owen and the SDP but also a mythification of the notion of leadership within Liberalism itself, a concession which subsequently allowed the leadership to attempt to completely redefine Liberalism on the eve of the merger conference of January 1988. This attempt was refused by the party, and the refusal had a further damaging effect upon the governmental status of the party, upon the merged party, and upon David Steel's own status as leader which by this time had become untenable.

In the case of the Labour Party, this new trend in leadership style and the heightened significance of public political ritual was to have similarly imperceptible but far-reaching effects, not least because of the generally-held and therefore unguarded assumption on the left that emphasis upon leadership was acceptable because it was merely cosmetic and that the party could use it as a tactic which would not change the fundamentals of a Labour strategy or, most certainly, those of Labour doctrine. Such an emphasis did, however, have very real effects. Labour Party discourse since 1983 has annihilated Labourism in its predominant twentieth-century form, and replaced it with a paradoxical combination of 'new realism' and millenarianism, drawing upon old and new ideas which accord with the notion of the leader as visionary, a change which, in its turn, had significant influence upon, basically, who decides what within the party. The new 'designer' leftism (which, in fact, as we have mentioned, was a conflation of 'new realism' and very old millenarianism) was operated largely through the persona of Neil Kinnock, and had real effects, one of which was that (as with Thatcherism) the notion of right and left within the party no longer existed in its traditional form. One of the consequences of this was the further radicalisation (and marginalisation) of the party's traditional left.

The personalisation of Labour leadership has meant, therefore, more than is generally assumed, that it is Margaret Thatcher who has defined the Labour Party's agenda. Two perceived major problems haunting the Labour Party in the 1980s were the image of a minor but virulent extremism in the shape of Militant on the one hand and the widely mistrusted trade union connection on the other. Organisationally, the party leadership could not free itself from one without using and strengthening the other, that is, it could only crush a perceived ultra-left with the help of the trade unions, who would take the opportunity to strengthen their own position. Symbolically, however, the leader still had to represent the party as something other than a trade unionist party, in terms of both its presentation of itself *to* a national electorate and its self-image as representative *of* a national electorate. The resulting personalisation of leadership extended and modified the discursive parameters of the British Labour Party and allowed the leadership (in the light of the 1987 election defeat) to initiate a policy review, which was in fact rather a doctrinal review of British Labourism. Opposition to this doctrinal revision was the essence of the subsequent challenge to Neil Kinnock's leadership, in 1988, by Tony Benn. By the 1990s, the various groupings of the left within the party (one of which Neil Kinnock had once been a member of) had been either crushed or rendered impotent. The next task was to redefine, that is reduce, the trade unions' influence within the party in order to ensure that the Labour Party became electorate-friendly by the time of the next general election.

For the Conservative Party, its governmental status (coupled with the fact that its was the last of the four conferences, and Margaret Thatcher's speech the last of the whole conference season) meant that it could combine the presentation of its proposed policy with unbridled mockery of the other parties' conference performances. Paradoxically, it also presented itself as attempting to conquer power in order to give itself a crusading spirit reminiscent of parties out of power. One of the effects of this was the displacing of *governmental* discourse to the right, and the acceptance by the near-totality of British Conservatism that it was inextricably associated with, if not defined by, Margaret Thatcher's persona and discourse. The use of conference to project government (both actual and proposed) involved Conservative discourse in the creation of a renewed, more extreme radicalism embracing the discursive enhancement of the idea of a (personalised) mission. We can see, therefore, that the new radicalism of mid-1980s Conservatism was also an effect of what Thatcherism had itself done to British politics. Thatcherism as a personally-inspired crusade or task had created the idea in British political culture that the political pendulum does not have to swing. The effect of this at the level of representation is that policies are transformed into projects, crusades, missions, and mythical tasks which transcend the cycles of parliamentary government. The traditional image of the Conservative Party as the articulated voice of a particular conception of Britain thus takes on a new, more revolutionary form (and, of course, from our analysis, we have seen that such a view has also been incorporated into the other parties).

It is interesting that, in all the speeches we have examined, the opening (usually unscripted) sentences are used to enhance leadership status in relation to the conference itself. In the case of David Owen, humility and a joke about the weather lessen the tension involved in the party's relationship to leadership, yet increase leadership status through the contrast with the ensuing address of the leader out past conference to the nation. In the case of the Liberals, David Steel exploits the context of the conference, by referring to the ritual of the standing ovation, thus using irony to create an albeit arched collusion with the audience. When he then destroys that collusion, his singular status is highlighted. Neil

Kinnock reminds the audience of the media treatment of conference by joking in a similar manner to David Steel about ovations, and, like David Owen, he is humble in his opening remarks (exploiting rhetorically the occasion of the Merit Awards) thus portraying a deceptive humility before his long and highly emotional speech. Margaret Thatcher, prefacing her speech with a reference to the rose she is wearing, undermines the Labour Party, but also draws attention to herself physically before her conference speech proper ('before I begin . . .'). And she, as Prime Minister and undisputed leader, by observing the traditional thanks, treats the conference as nothing more nor less than what it is, a gathering of Conservative Party delegates, thereby maintaining throughout her speech her relationship to it, and her extraordinary relationship to wider issues.

In the context of our analysis, all of the conference leadership speeches prefigure the immediate future of the four parties' fortunes: in the case of the Alliance parties, the split by which the Alliance would be riven after the general election of June 1987 because of the clash of its two leaders; in that of the Labour Party, the further heightening of leadership status, which would find reflection, not only in the projected image of the leader during the 1987 election campaign, but also, negatively, in the contestation of leadership in 1988; in the case of the Conservative Party, the consecration of the leader's undisputed authority and the presentation of a (further radicalised) election manifesto, as well as the beginnings of a series of long leadership struggles anticipating a post-Thatcher era, exemplified by the long-term strategy of Michael Heseltine which would use both the constituency parties and the media in the deployment of a new 'visionary' leadership persona.

Let us then, finally, identify the fourteen shared characteristics of this contemporary political discourse which we have identified in the leaders' speeches to conference:

1. All the leadership speeches screen out as far as possible the third alternative (we have seen that even the Alliance leaders do this, even though the non-leadership discourse of both the SDP and Liberals places itself consciously between the two 'extremes'). This screening out of the third alternative is a prerequisite not only to the establishment of the idea

that there are only two choices, one bad and one good, but, more importantly, to the depiction of personalised leadership in the context of a dualist 'vision of the world'.

2. All the leadership discourses, therefore, have a (dual) vision of the world.

3. All the leadership speeches involve discussion of the economy and of society, that is to say, of practical issues, but all invert the practical and the utopian, thus enabling not only the depiction of the ordinary as somehow special (say, a slight tax reduction as the trigger of radical change), but, more importantly, the depiction of a 'brave new world' in deceptively pedestrian terms.

4. All the leadership discourses sacralise the people, suggesting that simple people are the wisest, that those who are slightly more informed are dangerous (that is, the luminaries of other parties) and that 'wisdom' itself can be encapsulated in the persona of a political leader.

5. All the leadership discourses attempt to create an essential relationship between leader and people which goes well beyond the party's more contractual relationship to the people.

6. All the leadership discourses treat leadership itself in a particular way, lending to it an elevated status. The precise kind of status, the role models it implies, and the way it is depicted, will depend upon the respective doctrinal traditions of each party. All, however, enhance leadership while never evoking a leadership principle which explicitly recalls the Europe of the 1930s.

7. All the leadership speeches involve a high moral tone in the evocation of the leader/people relation.

8. All the leadership discourses use moral indignation as well as quieter or more self-evident moral justification of action and sentiment, thus giving credence to the idea that fundamental moral principles are shared by the party, the leader, and the people.

9. In the leadership speeches, the combined emphases upon moralism, people, and leader increase the reference to nationalism which brings to the fore the discussion and significance of the defence issue.

10. All the leadership speeches deploy the notion of personal certainty, thus reconciling, in the persona of the

speaker, the contradictory ideas of voluntarism and of a teleological interpretation of history.

11. All the leadership discourses pretend to unmask false realities imposed upon the people by rival movements and leaders, and depict enemies as ravening wolves (in sheep's clothing).

12. All leadership speeches are in some sense anti-organisation, anti-state, even anti-party, and thus enhance the notion of an unmediated relationship between leader and people, and suggest the New Testament themes of the clearing of the Temple, of redemption and of deliverance.

13. All the leadership speeches involve one dominant subject or theme which is presented as a kind of societal release mechanism: the SDP, tax reform; the Liberals, good government; the Labour Party, national recovery; the Conservatives, privatisation.

14. All the speakers (Owen, Steel, and Kinnock) enhance Margaret Thatcher *nolens volens* in some way while trying to enhance themselves. They do this by referring inordinately either to her or to the style she personifies (she, on the other hand, never mentions the other leaders).

In conclusion, we can make three comments concerning the three essential issues analysed in this study: language, ritual, and leadership, and their place in the political process. In the first case, it is clear from our study that language is integral to the political process and to political change within organisation, over and above its assumed effect upon Britain as a media-dominated society. Certain issues are addressed obliquely (for example, exalted leadership), others directly (for example, national defence). The overall effect of this interplay of the implicit and the explicit in political language influences perceptions of, and therefore alters, the political topography.

In the case of ritual, it is clear that in the political context, ritual not only reinforces values in the generally accepted social anthropological sense, but is also causative of change: Social Democracy used ritual to enhance leadership status which in turn allowed leadership to offer an ideology to the movement; Liberalism used it to create a leadership principle which it had not possessed since the time of Lloyd George; the Labour Party used it to attempt a transition from the

crushing of the ultra-left of the party (1985), via a channelling through personalised leadership (1986), to a review of
British socialism (1987–); Conservatism used it to enhance
leadership status even further and present it as the prerequisite to a new politico-ethical crusade.

Finally, on the question of the discursive and ritual depiction of exalted leadership, we should note that neither a
Fascist undertaking nor a presidential system are necessary
to it; the notions of a leadership principle within political
organisation and national allegiance to it seem to be compatible with representative democracy and a parliamentary regime. Indeed, in the British case since 1979 the exaltation of
political leadership in one form or another has been positively encouraged, not only by the manner in which the media
reports political life, and by the way in which public opinion
has responded to the various manifestations of personalised
leadership, but also by the representative political parties
which operate within it.

Appendices

Appendices

Appendix 1: Speech by the Rt. Hon. Dr David Owen MP, Leader of the Social Democratic Party, to the SDP Council for Social Democracy and Consultative Assembly, Harrogate, Wednesday 17 September 1986

1. Shirley, to whom we, and I, owe so much, friends, this has been the largest and best ever conference. We had the sun out for us in Torquay. I don't think any of us thought we could get as much sun as we have here in Harrogate. Someone up there seems to love us. [Laughter. Applause. Pause.]
2. I want to talk beyond this hall to the people of this country. I want to talk about achieving prosperity and ending poverty.
3. Let us hope for all of our sakes that the Election is not postponed until 1988. For the further away the Election, the more the decisions that are essential for our national well-being will be delayed.
4. We are already in the midst of a cynical pre-election consumer boom. In 1955 and in 1959, the Conservatives bought votes then only to take harsh economic measures once the Election was over. The message will be the same this time. 'Vote now and pay later'.
5. Will voters fall for it again? I doubt it. For this is going to be a very different Election from any that we have known since 1929. There are now three major contenders jockeying for position instead of two.
6. Repeated polls and, more importantly, by-elections, local and national, over the last few years all show a persistent three-way split in the minds of the electorate.
7. There is not now, and I suspect there will not be, even during the Election, a clear favourite or an obvious winner. Though, like all the other contenders, I would be, of course, preferring to be able to claim now outright victory for our Alliance, you know and even the other

parties know in their heart of hearts that the forecast of a balanced Parliament, with no one party holding absolute power, is the likeliest outcome.

8. Yet what a spectacle the Labour and Conservative Parties present, trying to pretend that nothing has changed in British politics. They act half the time in cahoots, desperate to hold on to their swing of the pendulum of power. They are like old entertainers trying to keep alive music hall routines in seaside halls.

9. Our new politics is about partnership, about sharing power, about co-operation not conflict in industry, and above all about national unity.

10. Now what about the Labour Party's new image? It first goes grey. It then pretends to haul down the red flag. And now it intends to bring back the socialist symbol of the 1960s, the red rose. Not the white rose, not the thistle or the daffodil. And what we have to remember is that behind that red rose is the clenched fist. As a party Labour are balanced only in the sense of having a chip on both shoulders. Today their defence policies are far more dangerous even than in 1983 under Michael Foot, and that's saying something. Labour now threatens the very existence of the Atlantic Alliance and they combine it with hostility to everything European. After the Election Labour's Parliamentary Party will be dominated by the hard Left, the bitter, neutralist Left. It's like a submerged iceberg. Labour, like the Titanic, is doomed to hit it.

11. Now what of the Conservatives? By the time of the Election, they will have had eight years in office. They can neither sing nor dance to a new tune, even if one was capable of being written for them. They have no option but to swallow and to digest their own record. The unspeakable in pursuit of the uneatable. They have no option either but to defend their own record. The unbelievable proclaiming the indefensible. Now let's leave them alone.

12. All over the country the thing that people ask me most is 'What is the real truth, David, about the state of the British economy?' I tell you, the situation is neither as bad as Labour pretends nor as good as the Conservatives claim. Let's be objective.

13. New jobs are being created, but nearly half are part-time and the underlying trend of unemployment is still up.

14. Over-manning in British industry has been reduced, but unit labour costs are rising at twice the rate of our competitors.

15. Trade union power has been curbed, but there is little sense of partnership yet between unions and management.

16. The service industries have expanded, but manufacturing capacity is still shrinking.

17. Investment is up and so is productivity, but it is still woefully insufficient to make us internationally competitive.

18. So the true picture is that all is not gloom. There are rays of sunlight beaming in. Some brilliant scientific and technical breakthroughs, some excellent labour relations. But our underlying economic weakness is alarming. We are still in economic decline. Now take North Sea

oil out of the accounts and our balance of payments would be more than £10 billion in the red, compared with a surplus of a billion in the Conservatives' first year of office. Our share of world exports remains stagnant at its 1979 level.

19. Productivity is rising at an annual rate of about 2 per cent in 1986, while average earnings have been increasing at 7 per cent. We won't continue to compete at home or abroad on that basis for very long. The truth is that no honest Conservative can claim that Mrs Thatcher has stopped Britain's underlying economic decline. We have now sunk to being the nineteenth industrial nation in the world when 35 years ago we were the third industrial nation. Last year Italy overtook us. If present growth trends continue Spain will have overtaken us in the early 1990s. Why is this happening to us?

20. We are not an idle nation. There is great inventiveness and imagination amongst our people that can still beat the rest of the world. How is it that we cannot harness the talent we *know* lies within our nation? A clue comes if one listens to the farmyard noises of the House of Commons. I am convinced that Social Democrats and Liberals are right to argue that a major part of our problem is the old-fashioned, rigid, unrepresentative parliamentary system in which we conduct our national affairs. You know, outside the Communist countries, we are the most suffocatingly centralised nation in the world. Far from encouraging energy, enterprise and innovation, the dead hand of Whitehall and Westminster kills it – very often stone dead.

21. Why do we go on allowing Conservative and Labour controlled local councils and the national governments to impose their political dogmas on us when they can only command minority support amongst the voters? Are we afraid of change? I am convinced now, that the push for change will have to come from you, the voters. The tiny minority of people who form the hard core, left and right, who live, breathe and dream nothing but politics risk making our country one of the most ideological of all democracies. To the political zealot – and zealots they certainly are – it is an offence to admit that any other party can ever be right. That sort of political play-acting is puerile waste of the nation's time. I refuse to say that everything that either Neil Kinnock says or Margaret Thatcher does is always wrong. Even David Steel is right [Pause. Laughter. Applause. Pause.] sometimes. [Laughter.]

22. Now we've got to stop this self-destructive dogmatism. We have damaged ourselves as a nation by our failure to sustain economic and social policies for long enough for them to show results. The chopping and changing of our economic and industrial policies prevents us meeting the challenge to our trade and our jobs from the newly industrialised nations, let alone the competition from Japan, the United States and Western Europe. We have got to stop being afraid of competition, whether in business or in our schools. There is no escape from the discipline of competition. Of course we can and should temper market effects from time to time. But we are, as a great trading nation, in business to generate more wealth. That should be

the dynamic behind all our economic policies.

23. It is our persistent lack of competitiveness that undermines our capacity to finance the caring services which shield the weak and strengthen the social cohesion of our community.

24. Violent crime, drug addiction, and vandalism are plaguing this country, the rich as well as the poor. The latest menace is the drug 'crack' poised to sweep into this country. Too many of our politicians and our pundits scoff at other countries' systems of government. Can we not learn? Can we not adjust and adapt to modern experience? Let us remind ourselves that most of our partners in the European Community have achieved far more for the standards of living of their people than successive British Governments in our post-war period.

25. Let us remind ourselves that, that whereas from 1940 to 1980 we had a bi-partisan defence policy, there is now a more bitter division between the political parties over national security than at any time since the Boer War.

26. Yet to us it is obvious that the only way to greater national unity and better government is Proportional Representation, decentralisation and freedom of information, but we have to persuade others. Persuade them that is the best way to regain our self-confidence at home and abroad, to reverse our economic decline, to end racial prejudice and class divisions within our own country, to persuade.

27. The elusive goal of national unity will certainly be frustrated if we allow the Conservative and Labour Parties to combine together to prevent at least a third of the electorate from having their say. If there is a balanced Parliament and at least a third of the people have voted for the Alliance, are Social Democrat and Liberal MPs really expected to let either Labour or Conservative parties take absolute power on a minority vote? Labour constantly say they will never negotiate with the Alliance or for that matter anyone else. I will believe that if and when I see it. But if they petulantly refuse negotiations, they will be betraying their own supporters.

28. We, for our part, are ready to negotiate, within a balanced Parliament, to achieve as much as [sic] our programme as we can with either Labour or Conservative. We will take into account – in deciding who to talk to first – the views of the electorate as democratically expressed in the number of votes they have cast for the different parties. For the first time ever, we will have made it clear in advance of the Election – in marked contrast to the situation in 1924, in 1929 and in 1974 – that we will vote on your behalf, the behalf of the voters, against any Queen's speech at the start of the new Parliament that is not negotiated with us.

29. Now in a balanced Parliament the Alliance might easily have the largest number of votes, even though, through the lunacy of our electoral system, we might not have the largest number of seats. Equally important, it is very possible that Labour or the Conservatives might well find themselves in third place in terms of votes and even in the number of seats won. I wonder what they'll say then?

30. If Labour or the Conservatives want to do a shabby deal and let the others govern as a minority – let them do it and risk the consequences

at the following election. They'll pay a heavy price.

31. We have a duty not to allow the voters' wishes to be ignored. We can risk a second election. The voters are not stupid. They will know that any such election will only have been brought about by those politicians who refuse to listen to their views, the views of the voters. We will trust the voters and they will trust us.

32. The extreme left within the Parliamentary Labour Party after the Election may well dictate, dictate that there be no dictations [sic], no negotiations. But what will those who have voted Labour think then?

33. Will they want Labour to let the Conservatives continue to ignore the three and a half million unemployed and not negotiate a sensible programme for creating jobs with the Alliance? Will they want to ignore the neglect of the National Health Service and the Education services and not negotiate improvements with the Alliance. Will they want to ignore the nuclear arms race and not negotiate cancelling Trident but keeping Polaris?

34. Does the same contempt for the voters' wishes prevail in the new Conservative Party? Amongst Conservative MPs? You know it's time people throughout the country ought to start, start asking them, and doing it now.

35. When a Cabinet Minister, Kenneth Clarke, said recently on 'Any Questions' to me that he feared the prospect of coalition-making with the Alliance above all others, then, you know, one must ask what are Conservative values? But more importantly, what will those who have voted Conservative think about letting Labour in? Do they prefer Labour in Government risking a financial crisis to negotiating with the Alliance? Do they prefer Labour in Government trying to kick out the United States from nuclear bases and abandoning nuclear deterrence to negotiating a sound and sensible defence policy with the Alliance? Do they prefer Labour in Government attempting to repeal trade union legislation? To pose the question in this way is simply to expose the absolute absurdity of Labour and Conservative politicians' positions. They want to ignore the voters.

36. The Alliance, the Alliance, by contrast, is determined to listen to the voters. Determined to convince the voters that the eradication of poverty and the enhancement of prosperity are two sides of the same coin. Our determination to do this stems both from realism about the present and hope for the future. There is no joy in simply documenting Britain's national decline. Our task is to offer a way forward. Forward to a more self-confident and united Britain. Our country is capable of developing the inner strength and unity to fight back and revitalise our fortunes. It will take time, but we know it can and it must be done.

37. We all know too that to find the money for the health service, for the expansion of higher education, we must sell more of our goods in world markets. Our task is to motivate the nation to win against world competition and to do so without building a harsh, uncaring society which ignores the needs of those who cannot compete. Now we cannot do this, one cannot do this, without reforming our tax system.

38. Mrs Thatcher is trying, by a conjuror's trick, to focus your attention only on income tax and has the brass neck to lecture us about taxes. [Applause.] She wants you to forget that she has put up taxes. By a supreme irony the Conservatives now have become the party of high taxes in Britain. The average earner is now paying a higher direct tax bill than in 1979. Also, by doubling VAT, incidentally, in spite of telling the electorate that she had no intention of doing so, she made sure you are paying higher levels of indirect tax. Every penny they have taken off the basic rate, they have put back on through the back door tax of national insurance.

39. But not satisfied with that, in order to fulfil Mrs Thatcher's electoral pledge, somewhat out of date now, to do something about rates, they now propose a poll tax. A tax so notoriously unfair that no government has tried it for centuries. Tory tax policies seem to be shifting from the Victorian to the Medieval. But they also force others to raise taxes for them at every turn. They force the gas and electricity boards to charge more than the commercial rate to people who can ill afford it. They cut the rate support grant, forcing even sensible and responsible councils to put up rates, including the 23 councils we in the Alliance run and the more than 80 that we in the Alliance influence. The truth is: 'The lady giveth and the lady taketh away.'

40. Now, before this Government took office in 1979, our taxation system penalised high earners. They were right to remove that disincentive. At the same time to increase the disincentive for lower earners was totally wrong. The poverty trap is perhaps the most cruel of all the anomalies in our taxation system. But it is also very economically damaging to this country.

41. Conservatives have been as blind to the damaging effect of relatively high taxes on the low paid as Labour was blind to the damaging effects on the high paid. This country's tax and benefit structure is unfair, inefficient and incomprehensible. Those who depend on it – even more, I might say, those who have to administer it – don't understand it, let alone think it fair. It destroys dignity. It damages family life. It defies all logic.

42. Now reform of the tax and benefit structure is part of economic revival. Reform would help to release the energy and the vitality of those in work, and to restore the self-respect and freedom of choice of not only those who are out of work but of the handicapped, the pensioner and the one-parent family, as well as the low paid.

43. Twenty years ago, the total tax burden – direct and indirect taxes combined – was less than a fifth of average earnings, so people started to pay tax well above any defined 'poverty line'. In 1986, tax swallows up more than a third of average earnings, so people start to pay tax at levels well below the poverty line. In all conscience – and this is still a country of good conscience – we must act to end that injustice. [Applause.] The right to grow rich must be balanced by the duty to end poverty. Our tax system has multiplied and mutated like a virus – you'll be glad to know that I checked with doctors that viruses still do mutate [Laughter] – an allowance here and an allowance there and

with it, a social security system becomes one of mind-boggling complexity. The result is a depth of poverty in Britain which should be seen as a national disgrace. The Government's own figures show that between 1979 and 1984, the numbers living on or just below [should be 'above'] the poverty line increased from 11.5 to 16.6 million. It is a staggering rise. Nearly one-third of the population, many of them young children now live in families struggling to feed, clothe and decently house themselves. We cannot go on ignoring that. We must not pass by on the other side [Applause].

44. Yet, yet, yet, not only do we have a social security system which provides too little for those who are genuinely in need, it is also so complicated and confused that millions of low-income families are failing to claim over £1 billion of benefits that they are actually entitled to. The same complexity which denies so many their rights enables the less scrupulous, the free-riders, to draw benefits to which they are not entitled. The inefficiencies and injustices of our taxation and social security systems can only be solved by a radical structural reform. That either costs new money which we cannot afford, or means using existing money as we have done in our scheme to restructure the whole system. Nothing is for nothing in life.

45. The Conservatives dare not ask even for a modest contribution from those who are reasonably well-off and who they see as their voters. Not for the first or the last time, the Tory Party underestimates the conscience of the British people.

46. The Labour Party dares not talk straight to skilled workers, preferring to pretend that all the money can come from the rich. Labour rejects selectivity, yet because of the crippling costs of giving universal benefits for all – many of the poor actually grew poorer under Labour Governments. It is time for a change. High time for a change! [Applause]

47. I predict, I predict tax will be a major issue at the next Election and I relish the prospect. Whereas Mrs Thatcher hopes to bribe voters for a few months, I might add, we intend to tell the voters the truth. She points backwards; we point forwards. She believes the British people can be blindfolded and bought. We believe they are ready for the plain unvarnished truth and will respond generously.

48. The Conservatives are now praising the United States' radical tax reforms while criticising the SDP reforms. They forget that reform in America has only been possible because of agreement between the parties. The Democratic Party as well as the Republican Party. Support freely given because more than 6 million of America's poor will come out of the tax net altogether. Because a massive reform of allowances will sweep away tax distortions and loopholes as well as providing a fairer system for low-income earners and the poor.

49. We want all party agreement on our reforms here too. But the difference between us and the United States is that they have a profitable business sector that can foot the bill. Whereas we cannot weaken our industry and commerce to anywhere near the extent necessary to pay for our reforms.

50. We, therefore, decided not to raise taxes. [Pause.] I repeat, not to raise taxes. [Pause.] Do you journalists want that in code? [Laughter. Applause.] I can offer you morse code or semaphore.

51. The restructuring we propose is costed by adding up the present direct tax and present total benefit cost. We have not put up any rates. We have not taken money from any other source. If business thrives we may be able to rely on extra money from that source to improve the position of some groups we would like to help more. But where the Conservatives are in for a big shock is that our reforms are designed so that they would apply whether the standard rate we inherit was 27 pence in the pound or even 25 pence in the pound after the next election.

52. That means if the Conservatives take a few pence off the standard rate of tax before the Election, we would simply fit our structure on to that basic rate. A lower basic rate, let me remind you, provided we judge the economy can finance it, would actually help soften some of the harder edges that are inevitable in any radical reform, and particularly the one we have set out at present base rates. Our integrated tax and benefit scheme is well designed. Its architects in our party have our full support. [Applause.] It is fairer and simpler. And it will not be easily evaded by the accountants for the rich or abused by the few who draw benefits to which they are not entitled.

53. Our basic benefit will be targeted on those who need help. Such substantial help could never be provided unless the benefits came selectively, both for low paid families and the unemployed. Our proposals will make it far harder for people to make false claims. Our reforms grapple directly with the genuine problem of low pay, and we do so without Labour's inflationary folly of a statutory minimum wage. By merging National Insurance Contributions and income tax, we are not raising tax rates but making taxes simpler and more sensible. National Insurance 'Contributions' are nothing of the kind – they are a tax – and a tax that bears hard on the lowest paid. For the first time, for the first time, everyone will be honestly told their true tax burden.

54. By restructuring personal allowances, and introducing separate taxation for women, we both end sex discrimination and strengthen equality.

55. Now to pay for this, to pay for this we phase out the married man's tax allowance. We restructure personal allowances and introduce higher capital taxation. We keep mortgage tax relief at the basic rate of tax, and only those on the higher rates will pay more for their mortgage. The result of such restructuring is dramatic. The poverty trap is abolished and the direct tax burden on families earning less than £180 per week substantially reduced. The Government boasts that under its new Family Credit Scheme an extra 200 000 families in poverty will benefit. By comparison, our Basic Benefit scheme would help 6 million families and do far, far more to tackle poverty. The, the single person would get £12 per week more from Basic Benefit than under the Conservative's Family Credit.

56. No one will any longer pay employees' national insurance contribu-

tions and for the great majority the burden of direct taxation will not be increased. As a result, at least two out of three standard rate taxpayers will be better off. All non-taxpayers will gain. Practically all pensioners, except the richest, will be better off. The basic pension will go up by £2.30 per week for the single pensioner. The phasing out of the married man's tax allowance will not affect pensioners. The disabled and handicapped will receive at last proper help from the Carers Benefit with £16 a week more than the invalid care allowance. These are truly radical, reforming actions not just to make Britain fairer but also to make Britain more efficient and more prosperous. It alleviates poverty and it enhances prosperity.

57. Beyond these measures, in Government, the direction of our tax strategy is to shift the burden of personal taxation from an income to an expenditure base. This is, however, to be done gradually, so as not to increase inflation.

58. Reducing unemployment too, remember, both attacks poverty and increases prosperity. We desperately need selective public sector investment and private sector incentives to encourage job creation particularly for the long-term unemployed.

59. We need increased spending in higher education to invest in the skills and brainpower that are the engine of our future prosperity.

60. An incomes strategy and an exchange rate strategy through full participation in the EMS are also essential. Without such measures we risk sucking in imports, increasing inflation and triggering a balance of payments crisis. It is in these areas that the Alliance parties are almost alone in advocating sensible, sound money policies.

61. We are right to introduce incentives to encourage management to keep pay, particularly in the private sector, in line with productivity.

62. We are right to hold an inflation tax in reserve as a novel way of helping to keep pay in line with productivity. We hope we can avoid using an inflation tax. But without such a reserve power we could be forced back into living with intolerable levels of unemployment. And we are not prepared to do that.

63. We are right to keep reminding the trade union movement of the need for more arbitration to avoid strike action and to champion the role of the postal ballot instead of relying on the workplace ballot.

64. We are right to promote profit-sharing and partnership. We believe in the 'right to own', just as much as the 'right to buy'.

65. We are right to put industrial revival as our first priority, our first call on scarce funds and to emphasise with it the absolute need to invest in skills training.

66. We are right to stress in all our social policy – whether for the NHS, Education, or Housing – our commitment to caring about people and caring about costs.

67. We are right to be unashamedly internationalist. This government has made this country like the moral leper of the world over Apartheid. This country [sic] – this government has made this country the most laggardly nation within the European Community, look, in NATO, apart from the United States, as the country least interested in

defence, but more particularly, disarmament; and within the Commonwealth its most disinterested and half-hearted member.

68. We are right to insist that Trident is both too expensive and too large in terms of megatonnage and warheads and that instead we should seek a European minimum deterrent.

69. Our attitudes are far closer to the true heartbeat of the British people. The nation can trust our Alliance, trust us to tell the truth, trust us to negotiate in good faith, trust us to defend our freedoms. Above all, we are determined to forge again a new sense of unity within this nation.

70. Far too many of our neighbours have their pride crushed by unemployment. Too many of our neighbours have their dignity violated by racist attacks. Too many live in constant fear of crime and violence. Too many families see their children's future diminished by lack of money, lack of support, and crumbling schools and medical services. It's time for all our people – North as well as South – Scots, Welsh and Irish – women as well as men, whatever their class, creed or colour – to enjoy their fair share in the fruits of Britain's success.

71. Yet, there will be anxious times. Our problems are deep-seated but our strengths are soundly based. Given unity, there is nothing that our nation cannot together achieve. We will best help the aspirations of the British people: a happy home life, rising living standards for their families, a pleasant environment and a thriving economy around them, if we are seen to stand for individual success and harmonious communities.

72. These are not opposites in a decent and ordered society. They complement each other. Let Labour stir up envy. Let the Conservatives glorify meanness. The job of Social Democrats, working in close partnership with Liberals, is to give voice to the ambitions and hopes of the British people.

73. After the Election, our job as an Alliance, participating in government, will be to enable those hopes, those ambitions, to be fulfilled.

74. Trust us and we will not fail you.

Appendix 2: Speech by the Rt. Hon. David Steel MP, Leader of the Liberal Party, to the Joint Liberal Assembly, Eastbourne, Friday 26 September 1986

1. Well, Mr President and fellow Liberals, one of the traditional sports of party conferences is guessing the length of the Leader's ovation. And I don't advise anyone to take a bet on that this afternoon.

2. I had planned to address my speech to a wider public on the serious social and industrial problems which confront Britain today. I shall do that anyway, but that part will now have to be shorter, because I want to address some very particular words to the Liberal Party and our allies in the SDP. People outside understand that applause is no substitute for getting our programme right.

3. There has been a special urgency to our deliberations this week, because an election cannot be far away. The destructive years of Thatcherism are drawing to a close, and a very large slice of the electorate have not yet decided how they are going to vote. Now we will be ready for that election just as soon as the Prime Minister nerves herself to call it, because for us campaigning is a way of life.

4. Our opponents are both aware and frightened of our strengths on the ground. Whatever the ups and downs of the national polls, we have been the election-winners in this Parliament. We've polled more votes in parliamentary by-elections than the Tory or Labour parties. And this year we have achieved the great triumph of Ryedale, and we gave the Tory and Labour parties the fright of their lives in West Derbyshire and Newcastle-under-Lyme. Yet again we have shown that there is no such thing as a safe Tory or Labour seat against the challenge of the Alliance. And we are ready to join battle in Knowlesley North, just as soon as the slogan 'Kilroy *was* here' becomes a reality [Applause].

5. In local government elections our performance has been even more impressive. And I say 'even more' because the absolute consistency of progress and success in local government in every part of the country cannot be written off as a flash in the pan. In over 250 by-elections since the general election, Liberals and Social Democrats have swept

the board. These are the polls that matter, these are the real polls. In every part of Britain we are advancing and the other parties are retreating. And in many authorities, for the first time, for many years, local people are getting a sample of Liberal government, and they are coming back for more. And notice something about our 3000 elected councillors. We have a higher proportion of women than the other parties, and a very much higher proportion of councillors under the age of 45. And now that this Assembly has changed our selection procedures, I expect to see more women among the MPs who will join us at the general election. Now let us be clear about what the general election will be about. It will of course be about who will form the next government. But it will also be about the sort of government that the country needs. As well as the choice between Tory, Alliance and Labour, Britain will also be choosing between good government and bad government. I hardly need to explain to you what bad government is. We've had bad government for decades from Labour and Tory governments alike, but, rather confusingly, they call it 'strong government'. Now what does this strength consist of? It consists of a highly ideological minority party of one variety or another using a corrupt electoral system to grab the whole power of the state. That isn't strength, it's fraud.

6. When I look at the vast Tory majority in the House of Commons, when I see those serried rows of smug faces, I like to remind myself how they got there. Not by their merits but thanks to the distortion of the electoral system, and I remember Tennyson's line, 'Their honour rooted in dishonour stood'.

7. Real strength in a parliamentary democracy doesn't consist of imposing a minority view on the majority, it consists of finding the policies and giving the leadership which can unite the nation. Democratic government is about consent, not about domination. And the essential prerequisite for good government is the introduction of a fair voting system. Proportional representation is the way to get the strength of the majority behind the government, and of ensuring that minorities are protected at the same time. And that's why we are committed to electoral reform. Not for any short-term party advantage but for long-term fair representation and good government.

8. Now our opponents must be under no illusion. Our commitment to a reformed electoral system is unqualified and absolute. We shall use all our weight and power at the earliest opportunity to introduce PR because it is the key to the door to good government [Applause].

9. Let me define what I mean by 'good government'. First, it should be constructive. Governments should build on the achievements of their predecessors, however few and far between they may be. For instance, we should build on the trade union reforms of this government, which are one of their few positive achievements. It would be a tragedy if Labour are allowed to revert to a cosy carve-up with the union bosses, against the democratic interests of their members. And it would be a tragedy if good government is not far-sighted. It is a disgrace that the British economy at the present time is being manipulated to help the

prospects of the Tories winning the next election. Assets are being sold, investment is depressed, money is being printed, consumption is being boosted and taxes are to be cut, not to help the long-term future of our economy, but to buy votes. And Nigel Lawson, the Chancellor of the Exchequer, is the ringmaster of this election circus. There is no government strategy in any of the policy areas that matter most: energy, industry, education, housing or welfare. The long term and the future of the next generation are being mortgaged by this moral myopia.

10. Good government should be de-centralised. We've been told by the Institute of Directors that ministers are overloaded, staggering under the burdens of office. So they may be, but the obvious reason doesn't yet seem to have occurred to them. Central government is trying to do too much, and a very great deal of what is being forced through the Whitehall machine should be done at local level, at regional level, and in Scotland and Wales by their own elected governments.

11. Good government should be open, not secretive. The point of a Freedom of Information Act and repeal of Section 2 of the Official Secrets Act is not to punish Civil Servants who make mistakes. We want better government and we have to learn from experience, see what works and what doesn't work, and avoid making the same errors again and again. We would never have got so far down the path with the Trident missile, for instance, if full information had been available and if the Cabinet and Parliament had been able to review the double escalation, of both warheads and expense, which it represented.

12. Good government should be in the general public interest, not in the vested interest of one section or class in our country. And as long as the Tory and Labour parties are bound hand and foot to the two sides of industry, Britain will be badly governed. And as long as both the old parties continue to stir up class envy and suspicion because it suits their electoral interest, they cannot claim to speak for the public interest. As long as Mrs Thatcher and Mr Kinnock continue to refer patronisingly to 'our' people, they show what they think about everyone else.

13. And lastly good government should help people to help themselves. Our idea of government as enabling or empowering people to run their own lives successfully is miles away from what the other parties believe in. There used to be Tories who believed in helping people, in a rather superior paternalistic sort of way. But Mrs Thatcher has made them an extinct species. She believes in sink or swim. And Labour on the other hand like to keep people dependent rather than giving them the tools to become as independent as possible. That's the difference between Labour and Liberals in local government. They like to keep power to themselves so that local residents have to come to them for everything. And we are never happier than when they don't need us any more, when a local housing association, or tenants' association, has got off the ground with a bit of help from us, and we can move on to help others towards self-reliance.

14. So just ask yourself whether the sort of government I have described,

far-sighted and constructive, open and decentralised, enabling people
rather than controlling them and governing in the public interest, is
possible in Britain today?

15. Well I tell you this much. It is not possible as long as the power of the
British state is bounced between the Tory and Labour parties. They
like things just the way they are because it suits their party interests.
And the result for the country has been decade after decade of decline
and degeneration. If you want good government only our Alliance
can provide it. But we aren't going to get an Alliance government
unless the Alliance is credible. And that brings me to Tuesday's
debate. And before I turn to the subject of defence and disarmament
itself, I must tell you bluntly that two characteristics of our debate on
Tuesday disturbed me. One was the sight of the Liberal Party
reverting to a habit which I thought we had kicked ten years ago, of
being seen sitting in a corner polishing and burnishing our policy to
get it nice and pure and shining in the context of the ideal world we
would all desperately like to see, rather than dealing with the real
harsh world in which we live. [Applause.] It is one thing to declare our
goal of ridding our country, our continent, our world of nuclear
weapons. That we must assert with all the passionate intensity at our
command.

16. But if we are ever going to be in a position to influence our destiny in
that direction, we must also convince the electorate that we have
carefully thought through the painful steps we must take to reach that
non-nuclear goal. Declaring the objective [Applause], declaring the
objective isn't enough because the objective is not a policy. The
Chernobyl cloud drifting over Europe and over parts of Britain
carrying its dread fall-out in the wind should have taught us, if we
didn't know it before, that you cannot create nuclear free zones by
putting up signs on the lampposts of Lambeth. [Applause.] And our
Assembly resolution as amended is the equivalent of one of these signs
and it will convince no one [opposing voices, counter-applause], it will
convince no one [Applause], it will convince no one that we are
capable of advancing from where we are now to a genuinely nuclear-
free world. [Applause.] So there is no point in trying to blame what
happened on the press. As Jo Grimond wrote on Wednesday: 'For
Britain alone to abandon nuclear weapons would be to retreat from
those doctrines of international collaboration and collective security
which have been a main aim in Liberalism.' And I too want intellectual
consistency and integrity in our policy.

17. One of our delegates said yesterday that the trouble with this
Assembly was that it had too much heart and not enough head. Well
by God after seven years of this benighted government the country
needs a party with a lot of heart, and I am proud to lead it. [Long
applause.] But it needs its head as well. [Applause.]

18. And the second point which troubled me was the no doubt well-
intentioned but completely misguided belief that in some way this
Assembly's task was to accentuate the few remaining points of difference with the SDP in order [protesting voices], in order to, in order to,

in order, in order to 'strengthen my hand' in manifesto negotiations with David Owen.

19. That is a breathtaking misjudgement. We are either in alliance or we're not. We must live and breathe the Alliance. It's unthinkable that we enter the election with two defence and disarmament policies. But neither David Owen nor I are prepared to arrive at any election policy as a result of some botched-up bargaining, haggling process. We wouldn't convince the country. We wouldn't convince you. We wouldn't even convince ourselves. We will arrive at our election policy by applying our common judgement to the problems which will face the next government on taking office. We have repeatedly stated our goals very firmly and we will have them firmly in view as we do that.

20. I am reported as being angry with this Assembly. My emotion is not one of anger but of profound frustration that what you hope for and what I hope for, namely electoral victory for Liberalism and the Alliance, may have been temporarily and unnecessarily put at risk.

21. But I say 'temporarily' because yesterday two events took place which sent a clear signal to the public that we are on our way again. The first was your overwhelming endorsement of our joint Alliance document, 'Partnership for Progress', and your massive vote of confidence in the democratic procedures by which we will determine our manifesto for the election – involving the policy committee, the parliamentary party and the candidates. Both David Owen and I are well able to move forward now on all policy issues including defence on the basis of that document, and that is a clear message I give to you, the SDP and the electorate.

22. The other event of yesteday concerns David Owen. We had what the *Sun* would call secret talks in London – watched by about 7 million people. [Laughter.] It was a good meeting, confirming my belief that the bonds of our Alliance will hold. Neither of us subscribes to the doctrine of infallibility of party leaders – at least I don't [Laughter], but nor does he. And in fact no one should be worried by differences in style, or even occasionally of opinion between David Owen and me. The reality is that this relationship will work and the two leaders and the two parties are growing steadily closer together.

23. But turning now to defence and disarmament policy itself, let me reiterate the fundamentals on which we are agreed.

24. We are firm in our support for the NATO Alliance – full support, not the lip-service the Labour Party pays to it while undermining it with the actual policies of chucking the Americans out. That's our agreed policy.

25. We want a moratorium on any further deployment of cruise missiles in Britain, and indeed we expect to see a negotiated reduction of those already here before we even get to a general election. That's agreed.

26. We've accepted that we want to put Britain's Polaris system into the next round of the strategic missile reduction talks. That's agreed.

27. We will strain every sinew to make these talks succeed, but it will take some time, and we would be in a hopeless negotiating position as an Alliance government if we went into them with the Russians believing

that all they had to do was to drag out the negotiations over the years – as they could – until the Polaris submarines rusted away. If we are to get reductions in the missiles pointed at this country as well as those based in it, the Russians must know that we are able to maintain and, if need be, update our nuclear capability, until such time as these negotiations succeed. That's the negotiating position.

28. And if we are not so prepared, we might as well follow the Labour party's logic and abandon the nuclear deterrent system unilaterally, hoping that out of the goodness of their hearts the rulers in the Kremlin will kindly destroy theirs. In the 1970s there was a party leader in Denmark who achieved some limited success for a while by arguing that he would save costs and reduce taxes by withdrawing his country from NATO and installing a taped message in Russian at all his country's airports saying 'We surrender.' Denis Healey's tape is a good deal longer but its message is basically the same. Liberals place a higher value on the defence of liberty than that.

29. And [Applause] we are agreed that we will oppose the replacement of Polaris by the Trident system because it represents an enormous escalation of nuclear firepower from 64 to 512 warheads. That escalation is quite unacceptable to both our parties. We are seeking to contribute to disarmament. And I want the Tories to have to defend their commitment to Trident on every doorstep at the next election, because the public are on our side on this issue. But they won't support us unless they know that we are prepared to retain a minimum deterrent capacity no higher than the present Polaris force. [Applause.] And I, and I believe we can achieve this through collaboration with our European neighbours. Now nothing in that, nothing in that is designed to create a new European super-power, or a Eurobomb, or a committee of fingers on the button, as some people have sought to suggest. Securing greater European co-operation to get better value for money in defence, to promote world disarmament, to switch global resources to development, is wholly in tune with the European ideals of this party, that we have proclaimed consistently since the 1950s.

30. Now my two parliamentary colleagues who spoke against the policy resolution, both said that a non-nuclear Europe was a final aim and that their amendment was not intended to frustrate the efforts we are making to find an effective European policy. Very well, we shall go on doing so. But how I wish that the texts approved by our assemblies would more often match the speeches made in their support.

31. The international context in which we have to make defence policy doesn't stand still. There are some hopeful signs of lessening tension. And I welcome the agreement in Stockholm last weekend. And I hope we will see further progress towards the control of armaments at a US–Soviet summit in the next few months. But there are also less hopeful signs. Mr Gorbachev, for all the freshness of a new face in the Kremlin, has not yet abandoned the old militarism or the old police state. And we have to accept that the Americans, who have been Western Europe's protector and ally for the past 40 years, may not

remain as committed to European interests or European defence. And the American troops are not likely to be around in their present numbers in five or ten years' time. And that means that we Europeans must take much more responsibility for our own security. [Applause.] And we all know that defence will be an important issue in the next general election. And with Labour having nothing credible to offer, the choice will therefore fall between Conservative defence policy and the Alliance alternative. And let me spell out that choice.

32. The Conservatives will make an eightfold increase in Britain's nuclear firepower. The Alliance will maintain a minimum deterrent and only until the success of arms control negotiations renders it unnecessary.

33. The Conservatives will starve conventional forces of the equipment that they need in order to find the money for Trident. The Alliance will safeguard the real interests of our army, navy and air force by sharing costs and equipment with our European partners.

34. The Conservatives will lock Britain into United States technology for another generation, through the purchase of Trident and through British participation in the star wars project. The Alliance will contribute to a stronger European effort in high technology, from which Britain as well as our partners will benefit.

35. The Conservatives will leave Britain over-dependent on the judgement of whoever occupies the White House. We haven't forgotten the bombing of Libya. And the Alliance will place defence within the wider European context, through which we will also pursue concerted economic and industrial recovery.

36. The Conservatives will continue to frustrate every initiative for disarmament as they have for the last seven years, particularly if British nuclear weapons are involved. The Alliance will use the whole weight of British government power and influence to bring about comprehensive arms reductions. These are the differences between the two sets of policies.

37. Some people seem to see the issues of defence and disarmament as purely a discussion of hardware – of missile technology. But a fixation with hardware also betrays a wholly distasteful, macho obsession with nuclear firepower. And such is Mrs Thatcher's inexhaustible enthusiasm for it. This obsession often serves to disguise the contraction of what should be the real power of Britain – the power of a nation at peace with itself, the power of a nation fully employed, the power of a country with civilised standards, caring for its old, investing in the education of its young, providing for proper housing and medical care.

38. I don't doubt that when the Spaniards of the sixteenth century planned their Armada there were many who discussed in the minutest detail the galleons and the guns that were to reduce England to servitude. And these preoccupations hid from them the truth of Spain's national weakness – the sterility of its social order, the bankruptcy of its economy.

39. We in Britain need a defence which is appropriate, which guarantees our safety. But our burning concern is to tackle – in power and in

government – the real causes of our national vulnerability, and it is to these that I now turn.

40. You'll have seen that education is given pride of place in our draft programme. A far-sighted government that wants to enhance opportunity for its citizens by giving them the skills for success could do nothing less. Economic recovery and our future prosperity depend on education. And we can't go on wasting the human talent of Britain the way we do at present.

41. One in fourteen British youngsters goes to university. In Holland it's one in seven, in West Germany it is one in five, in Japan and in France it is one in three. The chances for a young person to go to university in Britain are spectacularly lower than in any other major industrial country. It isn't just the individual who loses out, it's our whole society that's impoverished. In education, too, the Thatcher years have been the destructive years. At every level, British education has been starved of resources, from pre-school and nursery right through to the training, retraining and continuing education that were essential. But the main debate concentrates inevitably on the schools. And what an indictment of past governments, Labour and Tory, that at the very time schools should be taking advantage of lower pupil numbers to improve the quality of education we find that we are being plunged into a crisis: a crisis of low teacher morale, low standards of achievement and low investment of resources.

42. An Alliance government will initiate a new partnership in education. We need first of all a new partnership between the government and local education authorities, to ensure that teachers are properly paid, that their professional status is enhanced, that their views are respected. And just like the repair of and renovation of school buildings, and the provision of adequate books and equipment, that of course will take more resources. It may take some time, and it may create pressure on other spending priorities, but we won't begrudge the extra resources because this is long-term investment in Britain's future. And we can't [Applause], we cannot afford to continue to lose over 100 qualified teachers every day of the school year, particularly when so many of the losses are in maths and science. Mrs Thatcher has been ready to break cash limits for the police and the armed services, arguing that the quality of the men and women was vital. The quality of the people who teach our children is vital too. [Applause.] Only our Alliance is ready to introduce an incomes strategy. And only an incomes strategy can protect large and important groups of public employees like teachers from losing out. That's the way to keep morale high in the profession. There is no future in a pay free-for-all, where the only way to protect teachers' incomes is by harming pupils' prospects.

43. The Tories, in a panic at the mess they have made of public education, are talking now of centralising the whole service and putting the man in Whitehall in charge of local schools. That would be a disaster. Certainly minimum national standards of excellence should be required, but local accountability of education should be made stronger.

That is why the second element of the new educational partnership must be greater parental involvement in schools. As those schools who have taken the plunge can testify, far from being a problem for the teachers, partnership with parents is not only merely for the benefit of their own children, but of all children in the school because it can create entirely new resources of enthusiasm and commitment on all sides. We have got to invest in the future of education. And we've also got to invest in housing.

44. I can think of nothing more demoralising than bleak substandard housing, nothing that makes people feel more degraded than to have to eke out their daily lives in conditions which, frankly, deny any possibility of a good life.

45. The facts are deeply disturbing. In the seven years before the Thatcher government came to power, over 2 million houses a year were started. In exactly the same comparable period of seven years since Mrs Thatcher became Prime Minister, only 1.3 million houses have been started, a fall of nearly 40 per cent over these seven years. It is our policy to match the sale of council houses with replenishment and renovation of the stock of houses available for people to rent. [Applause.] Over one in four homes in Britain are substandard and the Government's own report last year showed that 18 billion pounds are needed to bring local authority housing up to an acceptable level. What do these figures mean in human terms? Over a million families and individuals on council waiting lists. A doubling in the number of homeless in the Thatcher years. Artificially inflated house prices which stop young people from purchasing their own homes. And half a million homes without a bath or an inside toilet.

46. I don't know what effect statistics like this have on you, but, twenty years after *Cathy Come Home* and twenty years after I became more personally involved with the problem as Chairman of Shelter in Scotland, they fill me with fury. Fury [Applause], fury at successive governments whose neglect has created this mess. And fury above all at this government whose policies have made the mess and misery so much worse.

47. But what we've got to do is to turn our fury into positive action. And I promise you that an Alliance Government will deal with this growing problem as a matter of urgency. A nation that doesn't house its citizens properly is not entitled to call itself a civilised nation. And all too often the people degraded by poor living conditions are also without jobs. And this combination creates levels of human wretchedness which Mrs Thatcher in her tours of the Tory luncheon clubs of Britain never even bothers to see. And that's why she simply doesn't understand how this lethal cocktail of unemployment and squalid housing has led to the explosion of vandalism, crime and drugs in our society.

48. There are four immediate steps that we will take to create both jobs and houses. First, councils will be allowed to spend the 6 billion pounds locked in their bank accounts. Most of that money came from the sale of council houses and should be spent mainly on housing. Second, more money must be available for home improvement grants,

which are an enormously effective way of attracting private investment into housing, encouraging people to tackle the problems of deterioration for themselves. This government has actually cut home improvement grants since 1984 at a time when it should be increasing them. Third, we will introduce a Tenants' Charter which would give tenants the right to run their own estates and manage their own affairs. And this, as I have seen, can transform the quality of life for millions of people. Fourth, we will carry out a long-term plan to galvanise building activity, using partnership schemes like housing co-operatives, housing associations and neighbourhood trusts to encourage private investment in new homes. When our economy is languishing, when 400 000 workers in the building industry have been rendered idle, when resources are under-utilised, it is not only unacceptable in human terms, it is economic madness not to build and renovate houses.

49. And don't let people tell you that we can't afford it. The most significant Commons vote in this parliamentary session was, in my view, on the 24th of March when the Alliance MPs divided the House against the Chancellor's giving away one billion pounds from his budget by taking a penny off the income tax. Of course all of us paying income tax like such reductions. But we voted against it because we believed that any available money this year should have gone where it's really needed, to projects that would have provided work. Now the Labour Party, note this, no don't applaud, note this, the Labour Party makes speeches about doing exactly that, but when it came to the crunch they sat on their benches and abstained during the division rather than face the possible unpopular stance of denying the taxpayers their penny. Our words and actions match each other squarely and honestly. And theirs don't. That's the difference.

50. The Alliance is about to launch a great housing campaign. Let's all support it. We must act to end this national disgrace.

51. Now I've been talking about the internal condition of Britain. Abroad this government has chosen isolation and impotence.

52. Isolation, first, in the European Community, where brawl and bluster have been the substitute for getting on with the real task of building European political and economic union.

53. Isolation in the Commonwealth, where the Prime Minister, with apparent equanimity, had ceded its leadership which was Britain's traditional role to Canada, Australia and India, but only after causing grave offence to the wider Commonwealth.

54. Isolation in NATO, by choosing to place devotion to President Reagan above our own European defence interests. The Thatcher foreign policy has rightly been dubbed as poodle-ism. And I agree with Gary Hart in criticising the 'Credit Russia first' mentality, which is seeing the hand of a Soviet puppeteer behind every local conflict in the world, a view which has led them to support fascist dictatorship in Chile and reactionary terrorism in Nicaragua. [Applause.]

55. Isolation also in the United Nations, in the General Assembly on the Falklands; in the Security Council, repeatedly and shamefully, on

South Africa; and in joining in a crude and senseless vendetta against international agencies like UNESCO, a body which Britain itself helped to establish.

56. So, isolationism and narrow nationalism, in preference to rekindling the spirit of internationalism which Britain so actively fostered in the early post-war years, that's the hallmark of this government.

57. But isolation, above all, from the instincts of the people, who were moved – and moved governments – on the great global challenges of poverty and famine. In this 40th anniversary year of UNICEF Britain ought to be leading the way in support for world development. But what chance is there of that?

58. Timothy Raison in an open letter to his successor as overseas aid minister wrote the day after his sacking, this: 'The Prime Minister has many qualities but I can't say that over-enthusiasm for the aid programme is one of them. I couldn't help thinking as we had our amiable farewell chat last Wednesday that it was about the first time I had ever had a conversation with her about what I'd been up to as Overseas Development Minister'. What a commentary on the real values of our Prime Minister. [Applause.] And her values are seen at their worst in dealing with South Africa. Even through a shackled and muzzled press, the horrifying and violent realities of Apartheid have come home to the British public. They understand the special duty to the majority – a duty to act – which arises out of our historic and commercial links with South Africa. But Mrs Thatcher, on the other hand, prefers to enjoy the remaining short term profits of that link. In response to the call for action, she talked gloatingly of accepting no more than 'teeny weeny sanctions'. And when the Commonwealth Group of Eminent Persons reported no prospect of the South African Government being prepared voluntarily to dismantle Apartheid, she prevaricated.

59. Sanctions – the only peaceful form of pressure on Pretoria – she described as 'immoral'; but that's not a phrase we ever hear from her about the Apartheid system itself: about the infant mortality and the malnutrition of the 'homelands', or of the 60 per cent of black Africans currently unemployed; or of a system which, by virtue of their colour, condemns the overwhelming majority of the people to scratch a living on 13 per cent of the land area. The Dallas-style affluence of Cape Town or Johannesburg lies alongside that other sub-world of the black townships. And William Gladstone's famous phrase, 'the negation of God erected into a system of government', applies to South Africa – but the overwhelming impression left by our Prime Minister throughout the world is sympathy, not for the oppressed, but for the oppressor. [Applause.]

60. But of course the Prime Minister's attitude to South Africa is the mirror image of her profound racism at home. And I am glad that our Assembly condemned the proposed visa system for visitors from Third World countries with the closest family connections here. You know, successive governments, but especially this one, have imposed the most repressive and inhuman restrictions on all visitors from the

New Commonwealth, treating them as potential law-breakers, and not as genuine visitors. And then inevitably long queues have been the result and, when they arrive, it's imposed strain on immigration officers, but inflicted enormous hardship on thousands of innocent people. So, instead of humanising the laws, making them even slightly more in harmony with those principles of family life which the Tories claim to uphold, they merely compound their inhumanities by removing the victims of it out of public view.

61. That's part of the growing racism of officialdom in Britain. The occasional racist taxi driver is a minor social irritant; but any racist policeman is a major social menace. [Applause.] And there has been an appalling, ever-increasing number of cases of police harassment of innocent coloured people. And even journalists of the right like John Junor, Bernard Levin and Peregrine Worsthorne have been scathing in their condemnation. We know there are thousands of dedicated policemen working to promote racial harmony and to protect minorities from racial attack. And their task is made more difficult by the failure to discipline and eradicate racists within their ranks. This country needs and values the quality of its police force. But that quality has got to be maintained, unblemished. But Mrs Thatcher remains impervious to criticism and reality, cosseted in a cabinet from which she has removed all independent minds.

62. She is candidate for No. 10 again. Or is she? Because on November 14th last year she gave a much under-noticed review to the *Financial Times* in which she said that she needed another five years to complete her task. 'After that', she said, 'someone else will carry the torch'. So even if the Tories won the next election she's going by 1990. And if she leaves the election until the autumn of 87 that would give her only three years. If she delays till 88 it would be only two years. At least when they vote for us the electors know they're getting Steel and Owen for the full four or five years. But who will they be getting if they vote Conservative? Thatcher and Howe? Thatcher and Tebbit? Thatcher and Gummer? [Laughter.] Thatcher and Cecil? [Laughter.] Or that truly well-matched duo, Thatcher and Currie? [Laughter. Applause.] I'm not sure that that's quite what John Biffen had in mind when he called for a balanced ticket. At the next election the Tories will have the handicap of promoting not only Mrs Thatcher but a successor best kept unidentified, a joint leadership of a truly mysterious kind.

63. Now, fellow Liberals, the country *hungers* for a change of government. The Liberal Party has advanced from the fringes of politics to the very centre of the stage, to the heartlands of Britain, to the edge of power, thanks to you, the people in this hall, and to tens of thousands of people who are not here today. In town, city and county halls, Liberals are grappling with the realities and problems of power, bridging the gap between the ideal and the real, especially in the harsh reality of the government's restrictions on local government finance.

64. Many Liberal ideas are no longer just in pamphlets. They are visible on the ground. Here in Eastbourne I opened a partnership housing

scheme last year which was at the innovation of the Liberal Council. Last week in Rochdale I visited a tenants' co-operative in a scheme of 300 houses started by the Liberal-led council three years ago. They've reduced vandalism, by the way, by 80 per cent in that time. I've visited several industrial partnerships inspired by the Liberals. There is living proof of Liberalism working all over Britain. But Britain as a whole is not a Liberal country, and we cannot convert it to one until we achieve power.

65. Now I am not interested in power without principles. But equally, I am only faintly attracted to principles without power. [Applause.] Without power, all our resolutions, all our idealism, all our passion will remain mere intention, mere hope, mere dream. We have so much to do, so much to change, great tasks to achieve. But we will do nothing, change nothing, achieve nothing unless we can first gain power and then use it wisely.

66. Ten years ago I became Leader of this party, the first leader of any party to be directly elected by its members throughout the country. And when I became Leader there were a number of promises I did not make. I didn't promise to be a new John Stuart Mill and re-write the party's philosophy. I didn't promise to be a new Lloyd George and raise the wealth and resources of our organisation. [Laughter.] I didn't promise to be a new Gladstone running four administrations to the age of 85. But what I did promise was to lead the party to the achievement of power for Liberalism in our generation.

67. I made that commitment to you. And I will keep it. But you made a commitment to me. And I require *you* to keep it. [Applause.]

68. Beyond this hall people are waiting and *willing* us to win. [Applause.] Willing us, you and I – together. The parliamentary party and the party in the country – together. Liberals and Social Democrats – together. The British people – together. My commitment is to turn hope into fact, intention into achievement, and dream into reality. I will honour that commitment. Together we have made a commitment to the people of our country and they require us to keep it.

Appendix 3: Speech by the Rt. Hon. Neil Kinnock MP, Leader of the Labour Party, to the 85th Annual Conference of the Labour Party, Blackpool, Friday 30 September 1986

1. Neville, comrades, I always get a little nervous, even though I'm immensely gratified by a reception like that, because I'm always afraid that those who commentate on these things will add together the minute before and the two minutes after and decide I didn't get as much as David Steel. [Laughter.] Neville, I, I'll tell you what, following the act that we've just had from Winnie and from Aubrey only adds an additional 150 per cent to this task. Winnie the peacemonger, Aubrey the first maker of jams I've met to date that I actually like.

2. We meet now, comrades, in the autumn of this eighth year of Thatcherism. Ninety months of Maggie. Ninety months in which our society has become more divided than at any time since the Second World War. Ninety months in which our industry has been devastated as never before, in which our economy has been weakened as never before. And still after all that the Prime Minister says that she seeks another term. Well, she's not going to have another term. [Applause.] We and the British people together will definitely see to that. And not all of the creative genius of Mr Jeffrey Archer or the sweetness and sourness of Mrs Edwina Currie can change that course of events. Not even the Chairman of the Conservative Party, Norman Tebbit, Mr Punch, set to control all the puppets, not even he can change that course of history, for all his scare tactics which are such proof of a scared party that he chairs.

3. We've had those years of Thatcherism, and we are also, of course, in the sixth year of the coagulation of the Liberals and the Social Democratic Party. At last, David Steel and David Owen are finding out that it takes more than fishing trips and Edinburgh Festival visits and French leave to make either a policy or a party. If they didn't know before, they certainly know now after a Liberal gathering last

week which will long be remembered as the Assembly that put the lie in Alliance. It shouldn't really have come as such a surprise that they voted as they did on defence and civil nuclear power and many other things. They did, after all, have the inspirational experience of being addressed by Dr Owen at their very first session of the Assembly.

4. To be fair to Dr Owen, he is unique. He wanted to dominate the Labour Party – and he failed in that. He's trying to dominate the Liberal Party – and he's going to fail in that too. Now they do tell me that there are some Conservatives who fancy an association with Dr Owen. I think he ought to carry a political health warning to political parties. In any case, the Conservatives should be cautious. After Mrs Thatcher – once bitten, twice shy.

5. And, as the Tories fade, and as the Liberals and Social Democrats falter, this party – our party – is entering its fourth year of recovery and of advance. That recovery has been worked for by people right across the movement, in every part of the movement. In the local authorities where people have had to endure the most crushing pressures and have still fought their way through. In the trade union movement which has been subject to incessant attacks from every quarter. From unemployment, from the courts. From the prejudice made statute that is so much part of the Tory codes against free trade unionism in this country. And it's been fought for and worked for too by rank and file members right throughout this party who have worked as never before to get our message of jobs and justice to the British people with an effectiveness that we've never shown before.

6. We have been making that recovery through a unity of purpose without which all else would have been absolutely impossible.

7. We have been making that recovery by listening to people and by heeding people, and not straggling behind the lowest and slowest pace of opinion, but never wandering away from the main trail either so far as to lose sight of the main thread of public opinion.

8. And we have made the recovery, also, in this democratic socialist party by ensuring that we sustained both our democracy and our socialism. We haven't done it in an authoritarian manner. We have done it because we could not allow our democracy to be distorted, we could not allow our generosity to be abused in this democratic socialist party. [Applause.] We have, we've done it by natural justice to them. And, yes. And we have done justice to ourselves.

9. And in all of that we have earned new strength by hard work, by effort. But of course there is more to do. There always is more to do. For us there is no ceiling of satisfaction, no threshold of support on which we will rest contented.

10. There is a fond presumption amongst a few pundits that we hide ourselves away and do fancy arithmetic to find out what neat arrangement of Tory, and Liberal, and Social Democratic support will give us the highest number of seats with the lowest number of votes. Well I can tell them we don't do that. We are not in that dangerous game, in fact we're not in a game at all. We are in the serious and sustained task of convincing more people, of putting our

ideas and our policies and of persuading people to our view.

11. That is the way in which we search for power, not by some roll of the dice, but on the basis of the effort that we are prepared to make to gain the mandate in this democracy. And we'll go on doing that, and we'll go on gaining and keeping support from everyone who is prepared to hear our message, everyone who is prepared to give us the democratic chance to show just what we can do.

12. We have seen, of course, what others do. We have seen their seven savage years. We've seen what they have done to our country.

13. Given declining unemployment in 1979, they've increased it by over 2 million. Given record manufacturing investment in 1979, they've cut investment and destroyed capacity, so that manufacturing investment is still 20 per cent below the level that it was when they took over. Given a working body of manufacturing industry in 1979, they've lopped off whole limbs of manufacturing industry. Given a stable world trade position in 1979, they have lost 22 per cent of our share of world trade. Given the fantastic bonus of 50 000 million pounds worth of oil revenues, they have blown it, wasted it on the massive bills caused by the unemployment which their policies have generated. That and much more, so much more, makes them a government unfit to govern. They are rulers who, in Percy Shelley's words, 'Rulers who neither see, nor feel, nor know, but, leech-like to their fainting country cling'.

14. Leech-like, they have increased interest rates and the tax burdens. Leech-like, they have allowed the drain-off of investment capital from this investment-hungry country. Those rulers who neither see, nor feel, nor know, have cut housebuilding, training, research and development, the health service, education.

15. And these are not just attacks on institutions. These are direct attacks on individuals and their liberties, families and their needs. That's what those rulers have been doing in their blindness, their stupidity, their malice, in this last seven years. And all, and all of the time that they've been doing that, we've heard the strident homilies of Victorian values and of morality.

16. Homilies on the virtues of self-reliance, when millions would like nothing more than to have the rudimentary means to be self-reliant.

17. Homilies on the virtues of thrift, when families in poverty are constantly humiliated as they try to clothe and feed themselves and their children.

18. Homilies on the virtues of responsibility, when the rights of those who care for old and sick and disabled loved ones are secured only by the interventions of the European court, and even then, what is given with one hand by the judgement of the court is taken away with the other by a government that denies resources to the carers of this country. [Applause.]

19. Mrs Thatcher says that her policies start with the 'freedom and well-being of the family'.

20. When there are six million people in this country now so impoverished that they can't even afford essential items of clothing. When

there are two million children living in families dependent on supplementary benefit. When one in four families in Britain is living in substandard housing. When thousands of homeless families are condemned to the appalling conditions of bed and breakfast accommodation.

21. The Prime Minister lectures the family, lectures the country on morality. And she has a sort of clone now as Under-Secretary of State for the Health Service who has recommended but last week that a high fibre diet should replace the National Health Service. [Laughter.] It reminded me, it reminded me of the Tory lady who in the Depression was generous enough to give lectures to the families of the unemployed on what nourishing soup they could make with fishheads. Until one woman in the front said 'That's very nice, my lady, but could you tell us who has the rest of the fish?' [Applause.] But we got the lectures on morality when the Silentnight Company, when British Coal, when News International desert their basic obligations to those people who have given them faithful years of service. It is the people outside who are lectured on morality and never those who sit in the offices inside.

22. I suppose, I suppose that the pious sermons, the self-righteous homilies from Mrs Thatcher and Mr Tebbit are easier than facing the real problems or answering the real questions. And there are plenty of those, plenty of those real, moral questions.

23. When it is so obvious that a drugs plague endangers young people in our country, why get rid of one in nine customs officers? Why sack nine hundred customs officers whose job it is to restrain the importation?

24. Another question, another question. When it is so obvious that dark streets and labyrinth housing estates, and insecure doors and windows give such freedom to criminals and such terror to people – especially old people, why not invest in repairs and strengthening and lightening those streets so that people can enjoy real security, and the criminals can be defeated?

25. When violence is such a terrible menace, especially violence against women, why can't the laws against beating and abuse that already exist be fully and rigorously enacted and enforced in this country? Why can't that be the case so that it can free victims from that perpetual fear of the returning brutal husband so that the guilty can be punished, or treated for whatever sickness it is makes a man hit a woman? We will see that those laws are enforced. We'll make the investments in security. We'll see that the customs officers are there as part of the partnership against the drug menace. And there are other areas too where there are moral questions.

26. When it is clear that thousands of lives could be saved and terrible anxiety and pain could be relieved by an effective system of cervical cancer screening, by an increase in the treatment of kidney ailments by the maintenance of medical research, why close down the cervical and breast cancer screening facilities? Why make cuts that prevent dialysis and treatment? Why impose reductions that terminate re-

search programmes and send some of our best young scientists abroad to work in other countries away from our land?

27. When it is obvious that death rates, mental and physical sickness rates, suicide and family breakdown rates are all much higher amongst the unemployed than they are amongst the employed, why not fight unemployment as we will, instead of simply saying that it's 'disappointing' or 'one of the great mysteries of our time' as Mrs Thatcher does?

28. These people, these Tories dress up the get-rich-quick society as the 'opportunity society'. They continually represent arrogance and aggression as the only proof of strength. They have dedicated every policy to making the very rich richer and the poor poorer. They flaunt a commercial paradise before the young people of this country, but with unemployment and insecurity at a mass level, on the young of this country, they inflict a purgatory on those young people who have been promised so much.

29. With their, with their 40p pensions rise and their concessionary fares cuts and community care cuts, and housing and benefit cuts, they daily, these moralists, breach the commandment that teaches us, 'Honour thy father and thy mother'. That's the morality of this government.

30. I, I look at all that and I ask myself just where do they get their idea of morality? And the British people ask the same question.

31. There's a great grouping in our society that opposes the malice and the meanness of Toryism. There is a huge number which abominates the dual standards and the double-talk sermons. There is in this country, there always has been, there always will be, a moral majority. It is not a narrow, bigoted, self-righteous grouping. It is a broad-minded and compassionate grouping of people. That majority isn't sentimental for it knows that sentiment is very cheap. That majority is realistic too, for it knows that if its morality is going to have practical effect it must be backed by material provision provided in justice.

32. We as democratic socialists make our appeal to that moral majority.

33. It doesn't expect politicians to deliver heaven on earth. It does expect politicians to work to stop hell on earth. That's what the moral majority demands in this country.

34. Part, part of that majority, part of that majority would consider itself well blessed if it had just a roof over its head, if they had a job to go to, if they knew that the colour of their skin inflicted no extra disadvantage on them, they would consider themselves well blessed. If they didn't have to fear electricity or gas bills with all the torturous anxiety of poverty, if they could afford a pair of shoes for the children without being fearful of an economic crisis in the family, they would consider themselves to be well blessed.

35. Of course there are millions who don't live in that condition of penury. And there are many of those – I meet them – who are not themselves impoverished or insecure. But they still say to me: 'We're not badly off, but we can't get our Mam into hospital.' 'We're not

badly off, but with two younger children at home, we just haven't got the room to accept the daughter and the son-in-law, they can't come and live with us.' 'We're not badly off, I'm working, my husband is working, but our twenty-year-old has never had a job and our sixteen-year-old is leaving school this year and doesn't even know where to start looking for a job.' People in security themselves but surrounded by all of the evidence and all of the pressures of insecurity that comes over their own doorsteps.

36. There are millions too who are not even affected at that range by the problems who consider that we need a government that will try to use policies that begin to attend to those material needs and fulfil those moral obligations. They want a government that doesn't preach the pious sermons of Maggie's morality, but practises the policies of provision. They want a government that will back up its morality by policies, by determined effort to operate policies of investment, of production, of growth, of employment. We, indeed only we, will provide that government for Britain.

37. And in doing that, we will be guided by four basic facts of our condition.

38. First, there is no prospect of a sustainable reduction in unemployment in this country unless we can attain stable long-term economic growth.

39. Secondly, there is no possibility of long-term growth and resilient prosperity for the British economy without a major development of British manufacturing industry.

40. Thirdly, the length of our relative economic decline, and the way in which it has deteriorated, been accelerated, been intensified in the last seven years, presents our country with a new set of strategic problems to which there must be a new set of strategic answers.

41. Fourth, none of the major social, commercial, industrial or employment problems that we face is self-correcting. The market will not look after those problems, it can only worsen those problems. If they, if they are to be overcome, systematic, planned action must be taken by government. And it must be taken in concert with all the participants in the economy to construct the framework of the educational, economic, technical and social conditions within which this economy can thrive again.

42. We have to operate on a new agenda and we need new instruments, new policies for that strategic change. We have to combat slump now and simultaneously foster the structural change necessary to stop and to reverse the long-term deficiencies and decline that predate even Mrs Thatcher's rule.

43. On that new agenda is our new two-year programme to combat unemployment and bring unemployment down by a million by generating jobs that need to be done, for people who need to do them, in a country that needs them to be done. Jobs in construction. Jobs in cleansing our environment. Jobs in training people, caring for people.

44. And on that new agenda too there is our five-year medium-term

employment strategy that has the objective of laying the foundations, of steadily expanding investment and employment.

45. And then at the same time the implementation of a ten-year planning horizon that is essential to provide the continuity of development that takes proper account of the change in the pace and the scale of technology, of trade, of employment, so that we are not caught without warning or overwhelmed without [sic] change in the way successive generations have been.

46. For all those reasons it is essential that investment finance is returned to this country and retained in this country. [Applause.] That is why we shall introduce our Capital Repatriation Scheme. If we were to leave it just at that then it is possible that the money would be in Britain but it wouldn't be used for the maximum benefit to our country in any coherent fashion at all.

47. Other countries, indeed our most successful competitor countries, have institutions that provide the necessary coherence in allocating funds for investment and growth. And we need such an institution too. That is why we are establishing the British Investment Bank to give investors the dual advantage of investing in Britain, and getting a rate of return that compares with what they could get elsewhere.

48. Some of those funds will be taken up by companies large and small who have got in existence worthwhile and specific investment ideas. In other cases we need finance to restructure and to modernise, to create and to nurture new industries.

49. It is for that reason that we'll be establishing British Enterprise as a holding company engaged in putting social ownership into practice through taking shares or complete proprietorship of enterprises that are critical to growth and investment in our country.

50. That system of social ownership embraces activities from small co-operatives to the municipal enterprises and right through to the major utility corporations like British Telecom which, in the strategic interests of this country, must come back into social ownership in full. [Applause.]

51. The purpose, the purpose of that practical programme is to produce our way to sustainable recovery, to sponsor new technologies, to strengthen consistent research and development, to promote our export trade and to provide employment.

52. Comrades, I have said it before, I'll say it again, and again, and again, and again, we must literally make our way to recovery, produce our way to recovery, sell our way to recovery in the world. For there is no other way to fully earn the living that we want for ourselves and we want for our children. That's got to be understood. And there's some other factors that's got to be understood too. If we invest in production and provision – and we will. And if we restore and extend social and personal services – and we will. And if we pay better pensions and help the poor and the disabled – and we are going to, then what we've got to make sure of is that the extra demand that we sponsor doesn't all go on the purchase of foreign finished goods, for if that is the case [Applause], for if that were the

case if it were the case that it was actually making jobs, not in Britain but in Japan and in Germany, then the effort will have been kindly but it won't have been very constructive. It would be stimulating but the result wouldn't be very substantial.

53. Second, and equally crucial, if those different policies of growth under a different government of growth were to bring rises in capital costs or in labour costs beyond what could be absorbed by efficiency, beyond what could be tolerated by purchasers, then the chance of significant development and increasing employment would be wiped away.

54. There is in this country now a great reservoir of injustice and impatience that has been built up and is still building in these years of Thatcherism. I know that. You know that.

55. We can empty those reservoirs, those reservoirs of injustice by deliberate and persistent policies and by sticking to our strategy. But if we tried to do it in any other way than persistence and being systematic and sticking to our strategy, if we tried to simply open the flood gates, then the prospect of renewal and recovery would be washed out. That's why we are not going to do that. We cannot. We will not.

56. And our decisions about those things aren't going to be governed by obedience to convention or some fancy idea of political virility. Those decisions are governed by reality, guided constantly by the determination to generate jobs, to re-build industry, to re-establish justice in our country. And those decisions, those policies will operate best and most fruitfully in partnership with trade unionists and with managers who understand that if we were to try to do everything at once we would end by doing nothing at all in the end.

57. That is, that is why our priority for jobs and for growth and for fighting poverty must be strict and straight and it must be sustained.

58. That is, that is how it will be and whilst the speed may vary, because it would be ridiculous to assume that somehow we had inoculated ourselves against the realities of the movement in the market in which we must sell, the world, while that speed may vary, the direction of those policies, of those decisions will unerringly and unreservedly be towards economic recovery and structural change all the time.

59. That is the reason for establishing our new instruments of the British Investment Bank and British Enterprise. That is the reason for our approach to Social Ownership. We need to ensure that the right money is in the right places available to people who want to make, want to invest, and to employ.

60. Like any family or any business or any country, we are going to have to raise money in order to invest in the means of making wealth. Some of the money will come as we cut unemployment. Some of the money will come through the repatriation scheme. And some of it we shall borrow. And what we have to borrow is around about an extra 2 per cent of the total income of this country.

61. Despite the fact that she is the greatest borrower in British history,

Mrs Thatcher is constantly saying that she won't do that, she won't borrow. She won't increase borrowing by that extra 2 per cent of national income in order to fund development. She says she won't do that because she's not prepared to leave the burden of debt to our children. That is very touching. Or at least it would be touching if it wasn't so cruelly obvious that Mrs Thatcher *is* prepared to leave our children with a legacy of decay and decline right through our society.

62. Somehow, somehow she doesn't care that the result of not spending is an increasing unemployment now and a guarantee of future unemployment, future under-employment, future under-investment, future, yes, future under-development in our country.

63. You see, it is one thing to say to your children, since she's so concerned about the children, one thing to say to your children, 'I'll leave you with a house and the remainder of the mortgage to pay after my days.' That's one thing, that's the prudent way, that's the careful way. It is another thing altogether to say to your children, 'Because I wouldn't pay the mortgage I will leave you nowhere to live after my days.' That's the Thatcher option. That is the imprudent, careless way.

64. We socialists, conscious of the fact that we cannot and do not serve just one generation. Conscious that each generation depends upon another. That one generation inherits in the very course of its preparation for the next generation. That there is this continual threat of dependence between the generations of human beings. We, as socialists, we always try to leave this place a little better than when we found it. And that attitude is not confined just to our own country. It is a definition of our view of the world. It's a perception that is more necessary now than it's ever been.

65. For in our One World the dangers know no boundaries. Famine spreads like a contagion. The poisons of pollution spread with the winds and the tides and become more noxious, more dangerous all the time. Terrorism and warfare impose the rule of fear on millions of people across this globe. People of so many countries face the crises of insecurity and inequality and injustice and exploitation.

66. Throughout our world aggression and oppression and starvation kill peace and they kill people and they kill hope and they kill freedom.

67. Afghanistan is still occupied by an invading Empire. Iran and Iraq are still engaged in a merciless war of fanaticism. In Chile Pinochet tramples into his fourteenth year of dictatorship. And the people of Nicaragua are struggling to keep their infant democracy alive against the attacks of terrorists armed and funded by the government of the United States of America. [Sustained applause.] Those people, those people, those people of Nicaragua must look at pictures of the Fourth of July celebrations and wonder what it can be that the United States of America, the great democracy itself born in revolution, finances evil people to murder the innocent of Nicaragua. What makes them do that? [Applause.] They must, they must, they must ask themselves, they must ask themselves, as we ask, how can a President who is so rightly the enemy of terrorism, as any sane

person is, sponsor the terrorism of the Contras in Central America?

68. In friendship and in frankness, in friendship and in frankness we say to the United States, it is wrong to arm the Contra forces, it is wrong to try and squeeze the life out of that poor country of Nicaragua, it is wrong even in your own terms in the USA for it is clear that if Nicaragua ever went into any form of partnership with the Soviet Union, it will have been pushed there by poverty and not pulled there by desire. If Nicaragua, if Nicaragua did become a Russian outpost the reason would lie in the White House and not in the Kremlin. And that is why we say in friendship and in frankness to our fellow democracy in the USA, treating nearby nations as neighbours is one thing, treating those countries as if they were bits of your backyard is another thing altogether.

69. Long ago, long ago, in the United States of America and elsewhere, the human race decided that it was wrong for one person to try to own another person. Long ago, in a revolutionary war of 1776, they decided in America and elsewhere that it was wrong for one country to try to own another country. And what was right in America and between America and Britain in 1776 and what is right about our view of Russia and the Eastern European countries in 1946 is surely right about the USA and Nicaragua in 1986.

70. And just, and just as it is wrong for one country to seek to impose its ownership on another, so it is wrong for one race to impose its domination on another. That is why Apartheid is so wrong. That is why Apartheid must be ended. Apartheid truly is a crime against humanity. And while it remains, none of the people, none of the people of South and Southern Africa will be truly free. No one in the white minority will know real security. No one in the black majority will know anything resembling real liberty. No one in the neighbouring countries will be able to live in real security.

71. That is why we want to hasten the day of change to a democratic South Africa. And the lever which we have long ago chosen for that purpose is strict and strong sanctions against South Africa for now they are the only practical means [Applause], they are the, they are the only practical means of trying to promote an end to Apartheid that is not soaked in the blood of millions.

72. Such sanctions are, of course, resisted by some. Mrs Thatcher, Herr Kohl, President Reagan refused to promote a regime of robust sanctions. The excuse that they offer for refusing to impose the implacable pressures that are necessary against Apartheid is that such pressure, such sanctions, would be 'immoral' because they would inflict upon the poor further wounds of suffering and destitution.

73. I hear the President. I hear the Prime Minister. I hear the Chancellor. And I hear different voices too.

74. I hear louder voices. I hear voices of greater authenticity and greater authority upon the business of the future of the people of South Africa. It is the voice that comes straight from that bitter and bleeding land of South Africa. And it doesn't come from the

high-falutin politicians or people in hotels or air-conditioned suites. That voice that I hear from South Africa comes from the townships and it comes from the homelands, and it comes from the churches, and it comes from the trade unions, it comes from Nelson Mandela in prison, it comes from Archbishop Tutu in his palace.

75. It is the voice, it is the voice that says, in the words of Chief Albert Luthuli, 'shorten the day of bloodshed', impose those sanctions, aid us in our efforts to end Apartheid and oppression. This is the Labour Party. We will form the Labour government. We will answer that call for sanctions for the people of South Africa. We will, we will impose those strict and stringent and comprehensive sanctions. And with the peoples of South Africa we shall overcome. We shall overcome Apartheid with those people, and we shall overcome the instability and the terror of Southern Africa as we go about that. We shall take common action in common cause for common good. That is necessary in so many areas. And that fact is now more obvious to more people than ever before.

76. In this year of 1986, a prophet of that fact, who gave us much more than his prophecies, was killed in his own capital city, out for an evening with his wife. This year we lost my dear comrade and a friend of the world, Olof Palme, a man who gave his intellect to the best possible employment, which is providing practical solutions to the practical problems of humanity. Olof was killed, and the memorial that we have to resurrect to him is to demonstrate that his instruction about the community of interest across the boundaries of the world has not been lost on this generation, and that we work for his objectives in his memory. It is necessary more than ever before.

77. Within two weeks of April of this year, two events, thousands of miles apart, originating from entirely different sources, came together to form an equation in the minds of millions of people in this country and throughout the rest of the world. The bombing of Tripoli and the explosion at Chernobyl demonstrated in the starkest possible way the fragility of our world, the interdependence of its countries and peoples, the need to understand new realities and to provide new responses, for our survival depends upon it ultimately.

78. Those responses include the question of the defence of our country and our system of values.

79. I hold it to be self-evident that it is a first duty of any government to ensure the security of the country over which it governs, especially if they are elected to that government by democracy. That duty does not change in any age and we will discharge that duty fully for this is our country and we defend our country as we always have. And meeting that obligation requires that we defend ourselves effectively by land, sea and air and that we participate properly in the Alliance of which we are full and firm members.

80. We will fulfil that obligation. And that is amongst the most prominent of reasons for implementing a non-nuclear defence strategy. [Applause.] For it is now plainly the case that by pursuing a nuclear-dependent defence policy, the present government is dimi-

nishing the conventional defence of our country.

81. The Ministry of Defence documents – the so-called 'tow path papers' – that were published three weeks ago give the consequences of the Trident programme as being, just for the Navy, let alone the other services, just for the Navy, major reductions in our conventionally armed submarine fleet, a 20 per cent stretch in the life of our surface fleet and a new wave of privatisation in the defence sector, like the indefensible and dangerous sell-off of the Royal Dockyard in Devonport with all the job losses that that's going to involve.

82. Not only, not only does that mean that the government is failing to meet the defence needs of Britain, it also means that because of that increased dependence on nuclear weapons, because of that diminished dependence on conventional arms, the nuclear threshold is lowered. There is no enhanced security for our country in that. There is only increased jeopardy for our country in that. And that is why we say that at this time of choice, yes this time of choice, that the alternatives before the British people are very clear.

83. The one alternative is a Tory policy which, in the very act of building up nuclear armaments at ruinous cost, erodes conventional defence and adds to nuclear danger without enhancing in any way national security for Britain. And the other alternative is our policy – a policy which responds to the realities, ends the nuclear illusions and properly meets the conventional defence needs and duties of our country.

84. They are the real alternatives, although until a short time ago Dr Owen and Mr Steel and parts of the press would have sought to persuade us that there was a third alternative. The so-called 'Euro-Bomb'. Apart from the fact that it is overwhelmingly rejected as an option by the British people, it is an option without substance, the product of a weekend break in Paris that had as its function the patching up of the widening crack in the defence positions of the SDP and the Liberal Party. If it ever was, ever was in any way feasible it would mean more fingers on the nuclear trigger and a great hole torn in the whole idea and treaty arrangements of non-proliferation. It would mean highest jeopardy at lowest security at maximum cost. It wouldn't influence friends. It wouldn't impress potential enemies. It wouldn't buy us a seat at any disarmament conference or give us essential control over the life and death decisions that affect our country. They can call it the Euro-Bomb, they can call it the 'minimum deterrent', 'minimum deterrent' when it could kill 60 or 70 million people, 'minimum deterrent'. They can call it those names as long as they like. But in reality, it wouldn't be increased security, it would be the *entente terminale*. [Applause.] It has, it has, it has nothing to do with protecting our country or our continent and everything to do with the attempt of the Liberal and SDP leaders to conjure an illusion of a policy out of a delusion of grandeur. No wonder they were rejected.

85. Of course, in recent days there have been some other intervening voices from outside Britain. Some of the language has been lurid but

it's been repudiated. It's been made clear that it is not the representative voice of the attitude of the administration. At least, not representative of the American administration, but representative perhaps of the current British administration. The reports are of the Tories asking for a particular element in the United States of America to help combat our defence policies in this democracy.

86. The conclusion is plain. The interventions that we have heard in recent weeks were not so much the product of American anxiety as a result of Tory alarm at the fact that we are defeating them, and that we are going to beat them in the next general election, and they'll try any dirty tricks that they can in order to try and prevent that.

87. The attitude, the attitude of the American administration shows a great deal more common sense and common interest than the Tory attitudes. It arises from the knowledge that if a member of the Alliance of these democracies were to seek to subordinate the policies of a democratically-elected allied government, it would be invalidating the very principles of democracy and sovereignty which NATO exists to defend, and always has existed to defend. [Applause.]

88. And there is another, there is another reason too, another reason for that common sense and common interest. It is that here in Britain and in our territories elsewhere across the world there are installations which are critical to the defence and intelligence needs of the United States of America. From the Early Warning System at Fylingdales to the submarine watching system in Pembrokeshire, from GCHQ to Cyprus, from Hong Kong to Edzell in Scotland, there are essential facilities for the national interests of the United States and the collective interests of the NATO Alliance.

89. We do not propose for one moment, and we never have proposed for one moment, that those facilities should be withdrawn from the Americans, for they are our *allies* and we honour the alliance. But it does demonstrate, it does demonstrate that we play and will continue to play our part in providing security for the American people and no United States government is going to sacrifice that essential link in their security.

90. In all of these matters, in all of these matters, modern men and modern women, whatever their office, whatever their status, whatever their country, whatever their politics, or lack of politics, face the fact that the terrible existence of nuclear weapons puts us in a condition unknown to any previous generation of humankind. We are the first generation in history to have to deal with those weapons. The first generation in history to have to deal not just with the weapons of horror that inflict such dreadful death and suffering during wars. The first generation to have to deal with the existence of weapons of total obliteration. That gives us different challenges, requires different responses.

91. The knowledge mustn't make people panic, hysteria's not the response, but it must mean that people face that fact of the existence of weapons of obliteration and how we control and reduce and abolish them squarely and honestly.

92. I face those questions as the Leader of this party who works to become the democratically-elected Leader of this country. I face those facts too as an adult, as a citizen, and as a father. And I tell you in no casual spirit, no bravado, like, that like most of my fellow citizens, I would, if necessary, fight and die, fight and lay down my life for my country and what it stands for. I would die for my country. But I tell you, I would never let my country die for me. That is the choice that faces everybody. [Applause.]

93. In everything we do, everything we do in this party and every part of it, we refuse to submit to the idea that the present and future are beyond control. We will not bow down to the defeatism that says that our economy is so badly wounded that it is incapable of renewal. We won't succumb to the defeatism that says that the tensions and the dangers and the poisons of the world are so great as to make conflict and contamination inevitable.

94. We look at the weaknesses of our country and we look at the menaces to humankind and we say that inasmuch as these conflicts and dangers are made by human hand so they can be unmade by human man. Just as these horrors are made by human error, so they can be unmade by human effort. That is not a blithe attitude. It isn't lightly put. It isn't evidence of innocence. On the contrary. It is the starkest reality of all, for we either surrender to hopelessness or we stand and fight against it. For us as democratic socialists, there is no real choice. We stand and we fight against hopelessness.

95. It is fundamental to our socialism. It is essential to the case that we put to the people of this country.

96. And it *is* our country. We have nowhere else to go, and we have nowhere else that we *want* to go from this country. That is the investment that we make in it. [Applause.]

97. This, this is our living space. It is the living space that we want to leave secure, prosperous, just, and free to our children.

98. That is the reason why we ask the people of this country to give us democratic power, and it is because we ask for those reasons that they will elect us to that democratic power.

Appendix 4: Speech by the Rt. Hon. Margaret Thatcher MP, Prime Minister, at the 103rd Conservative Annual Party Conference, Bournemouth, Friday 10 October 1986

1. Mr President, before I begin there's just one thing I would like to make clear. The rose I am wearing is the rose of England. [Applause.] It belongs to people of all parties and of none. Mr President, I would like to thank you for your welcome and also like to thank our Chairman, Patrick Lawrence, for his splendid work during the week. He's brought a light touch to the proceedings. We also want to thank Norman Tebbit, our party could not wish for a better Chairman. And we've all been delighted that he's been joined by Margaret.

2. Mr President, this week at Bournemouth, we've had a most responsible conference: the conference of a party which was the last government, is the present government, and will be the next government. And we have heard from ministers a series of forward-looking policies which are shaping the future of our country. And not only from ministers, but from the body of the hall has come speech after speech of advice, encouragement and commitment. We are a party which knows what it stands for and what it seeks to achieve. We are a party which honours the past that we may build for the future.

3. Last week at Blackpool, the Labour Party made the bogus claim that it was 'putting people first'. Putting *people* first? Last week Labour voted to remove the right to a secret ballot before a strike, voted to remove the precious right we gave to trade union members to take their union to a court of law.

4. Putting *people* first? Last week Labour voted for the state to renationalise British Telecom and British Gas, regardless of the millions of people who have been able to own shares for the first time in their lives.

5. Putting *people* first? They voted to stop the existing right to buy council houses, a policy which would kill the hopes and dreams of so many families. Labour may say they put people first, but their conference

voted to put *government* first and that means putting people last.

6. What the Labour Party of today wants is: housing *municipalised*, industry *nationalised*, the police service *politicised*, the judiciary *radicalised*, union membership *tyrannised*, and above all – and most serious of all – our defences *neutralised*. Never!

7. We have two other Oppositions who have recently held their conferences, the Liberals and the SDP. Where they're not divided they're vague, and where they're not vague they're divided. [Laughter.] At the moment they appear to be engaged in a confused squabble about whether or not Polaris should be abandoned or replaced or renewed or re-examined. And if so, when, and how, and possibly why? And if they can't agree on the defence of our country, they can't agree on anything. Where Labour has its Militant Tendency, they have their muddled tendency. I'll have rather more to say about defence later.

8. But just now I want to speak about Conservative policies, policies which spring from deeply-held beliefs.

9. The charge is sometimes made that our policies are only concerned with money and efficiency. And I am the first to acknowledge that morality is not and never has been the monopoly of any one party. Nor do *we* claim that it is. But we *do* claim that it is the foundation of our policies.

10. Why are we Conservatives so opposed to inflation? Only because it puts up prices? *No*, because it destroys the value of people's savings. Because it destroys jobs and with it people's hopes. That's what the fight against inflation is all about.

11. Why have we limited the power of trade unions? Only to improve productivity? *No*, because trade union members want to be protected from intimidation and to go about their daily lives in peace – like everyone else in the land.

12. Why have we allowed people to buy shares in nationalised industries? Only to improve efficiency? *No*. To spread the nation's wealth among as many people as possible.

13. And why are we setting up new kinds of schools in our towns and cities? To create privilege? *No*. To give families in some of our inner cities greater choice in the education of their children. A choice denied them by Labour councils. Enlarging choice is rooted in our Conservative tradition. And without choice, talk of morality is an idle and an empty thing.

14. Mr President, as you've said, the theme of our conference this week is the next move forward. We have achieved a lot in seven short years. But there is still a great deal to be done for our country.

15. The whole industrial world, not just Britain, is seeing change at a speed that our forebears never contemplated, much of it due to new technology. Old industries are declining. New ones are taking their place. Traditional jobs are being taken over by computers. People are choosing to spend their money in new ways. Leisure, pleasure, sport and travel. All these are big business today.

16. It would be foolish to pretend that this transition can be accomplished without problems. But it would be equally foolish to pretend that a

country like Britain, which is so heavily dependent on trade with others, can somehow ignore what is happening in the rest of the world, can behave as if these great events have nothing to do with us, can resist change. Yet that is exactly what Labour proposes to do: they want to put back the clock and set back the country. Back to state direction and control. Back to the old levels of overmanning. Back to the old inefficiency. Back to making life difficult for the very people on whom the future of Britain depends, the wealth creators, the scientists, the engineers, the designers, the managers, the inventors, all those on whom we rely to create the industries and jobs of the future. What supreme folly! It defies all common sense.

17. As do those Labour policies which, far from putting people *first*, would put them *out* of jobs. The prospects of young people would be blighted by Labour's minimum wage policy, because people could not then afford to employ them and give them a start in life. A quarter of a million jobs could be at risk. Many thousands of jobs would go from closing down American nuclear bases. And then Labour want sanctions against South Africa. Tens of thousands of people could lose their jobs in Britain – quite apart from the devastating consequences for black South Africans. [Applause.] And out would go jobs at existing nuclear power stations. Whatever happened to Harold Wilson's 'white heat of technological revolution'? On top of all this, jobs would also suffer as would-be investors in Britain took one look at Labour and decided to set up elsewhere. Labour say they would create jobs. But those policies would destroy jobs.

18. This government has created the climate that's produced a million extra jobs over the past three years. Here in Britain, it is encouraging that more of the population are in work than in Italy, or France, or even Germany. Nevertheless, as you heard yesterday, more has to be done, and is being done. Meanwhile no other country in Europe can rival our present range of help for people to train, and retrain and find jobs. And I would just like to say, Mr President: training is not a palliative for unemployment. Training will play an even larger part in our whole industrial life. For only modern, efficient industry and commerce will produce the jobs our people need.

19. And our opponents would have us believe that all problems can be solved by state intervention. But governments should not run business. Indeed, the weakness of the case for state ownership has become all too apparent. For state planners do not have to suffer the consequences of their mistakes. It's the taxpayers who have to pick up the bill.

20. This government has rolled back the frontiers of the state, and will roll them back still further. And so popular is our policy that it's being taken up all over the world. From France to the Philippines, from Jamaica to Japan, from Malaysia to Mexico, from Sri Lanka to Singapore, privatisation is on the move, and there's even a special oriental version in China.

21. The policies we have pioneered are catching on in country after country. We Conservatives *believe* in popular capitalism – believe in a

property-owning democracy. And it works!

22. In Scotland recently, I was present at the sale of the millionth council house: to a lovely family with two children, who can at last call their home their own. Now let's go for the second million!

23. And what's more, millions have already become shareholders. And soon there will be opportunities for millions more, in British Gas, British Airways, British Airports and Rolls Royce. Who says we've run out of steam? We're in our prime!

24. The great political reform of the last century was to enable more and more people to have a vote. Now the great Tory reform of this century is to enable more and more people to own property. Popular capitalism is nothing less than a crusade to enfranchise the many in the economic life of the nation. We Conservatives are returning power to the people. That is the way to one nation, one people. [Applause.]

25. Mr President, you may have noticed there are many people who just can't bear good news. It's a sort of infection of the spirit and there's a lot of it about. In the eyes of these hand-wringing merchants of gloom and despondency, everything that Britain does is wrong. Any setback, however small, any little difficulty, however local, is seen as incontrovertible proof that the situation is hopeless. Their favourite word is 'crisis'. It's a crisis when the price of oil goes up and a crisis when the price of oil comes down. [Laughter.] It's a crisis if you don't build new roads. It's a crisis when you do. It's a crisis if Nissan does not come here. And it's a crisis when it does. It's being so cheerful as keeps 'em going. [Laughter.]

26. What a rotten time these people must have, running round running everything down. Especially when there's so much to be proud of.

27. Inflation at its lowest level for twenty years. The basic rate of tax at its lowest level for forty years. The number of strikes at their lowest level for fifty years. And the great advances in science and industry, the achievement of millions of our people in creating new enterprises and new jobs, the outstanding performance of the arts and music and entertainment worlds, and the triumphs of our sportsmen and women, they all do Britain proud. And we are mighty proud of them.

28. And then our opponents, having lost the political argument, try another tack. They try to convey the impression that we don't care. So let's take a close look at those who make this charge. They're the ones who supported and maintained Mr Scargill's coal strike for a whole year, hoping to deprive industry, homes and pensioners of power, heat and light. They're the ones who supported the strike in the Health Service which lengthened the waiting time for operations just when we were getting it down. They're the ones who supported the teachers' dispute which disrupted our children's education. And they are those Labour Councillors who constantly accuse the police of provocation when they deal with violent crime and drugs in the worst areas of our inner cities.

29. Mr President, we're not going to take any lessons in caring from people with that sort of record. We care profoundly about the right of people to be protected against crime, hooliganism and the evil of

drugs. The mugger, the rapist, the drug trafficker, the terrorist – all must suffer the full rigour of the law. And that's why this party and this government consistently back the police and the courts of law, in Britain and in Northern Ireland. For without the rule of law, there can be no liberty.

30. And it's *because* we care deeply about the Health Service, that we've launched the biggest hospital building programme in this country's history. Statistics tell only part of the story. But this goverment is devoting more resources of all kinds to the Health Service than any previous government.

31. Over the past year or so, I've visited five hospitals. In the North West, at Barrow-in-Furness, I visited the first new hospital in that district since the creation of the Health Service forty years ago. In the North East, I've seen another splendid new hospital, at North Tyneside, with the most wonderful maternity unit and children's wards. Just north of London I went round St Albans hospital where new wards have been opened and new buildings are under way. I visited the famous Elizabeth Garrett Anderson hospital for women, which this government saved. And the service it provides is very special and greatly appreciated. And then last week I went back to the Royal Sussex County hospital in Brighton, to open the new renal unit. Many of us have cause to be very thankful for that Brighton hospital. [Sustained applause.]

32. But Mr President, in all hospitals everywhere patients were loud in their praise for the treatment they received from doctors and nurses whose devotion and skill we all admire. This government's record on the Health Service is a fine one. We're proud of it and we must see to it that people know how much we've done. Of course there are still problems to be solved. The fact that there's no waiting list in one area doesn't help you if you have to wait for an operation in your area. It doesn't help if there's a new hospital going up somewhere else, but not where you'd really like it. We're tackling these problems. And we shall go on doing so, because our commitment to the National Health Service is second to none. We've made great progress already. The debate we had on Wednesday, with its telling contributions from nurses and doctors in the Health Service, was enormously helpful to us. It's our purpose to work together and to continue steadily to improve the services that are provided in hospital and community alike.

33. This is Conservatives putting care into action.

34. And we care deeply that retired people should never again see their hard-earned savings decimated by runaway inflation. For example, take the pensioner who retired in 1963 with one thousand pounds of savings. Twenty years later, in 1983, it was only worth one hundred and sixty pounds. That is why we will never relent in the battle against inflation. It has to be fought and won every year.

35. And we care passionately about the education of our children. Time and again we hear three basic messages: bring back the three Rs into our schools; bring back relevance into the curriculum; and bring back discipline into our classrooms.

36. The fact is that education at all levels – teachers, training colleges, administrators – has been infiltrated by a permissive philosophy of self-expression. And we are now reaping the consequences which, for some children, have been disastrous.

37. Money by itself won't solve this problem, because money will not raise standards. But by giving parents greater freedom to choose, by allowing head teachers greater control in their schools, by laying down national standards of syllabus and attainment, I am confident that we can really improve the quality of education, improve it not just in the twenty new schools which were announced at this conference but in every school in the land.

38. And we'll back every teacher, head teacher and administrator who shares these ideals.

39. Mr President, we care most of all about our country's security. The defence of the realm transcends all other issues. It is the foremost responsibility of any government and any Prime Minister.

40. For forty years, every government of this country of every political persuasion has understood the need for strong defences; by maintaining and modernising Britain's independent nuclear deterrent, by membership of the NATO Alliance, alliance based on nuclear deterrence, and by accepting, and bearing in full, the obligations which membership brings. All this was common ground.

41. Last week, Mr President, the Labour Party abandoned that ground. In a decision of the utmost gravity, Labour voted to give up Britain's independent nuclear deterrent unilaterally. Labour would also require the United States to remove its nuclear weapons from our soil and to close down its nuclear bases: weapons and bases which are vital, not only for Britain's defence, but for the defence of the entire Atlantic Alliance. Furthermore, Labour would remove Britain altogether from the protection of America's nuclear umbrella, leaving us totally unable to deter a nuclear attack. For you cannot deter with conventional weapons an enemy which has, and could threaten to use, nuclear weapons.

42. Exposed to the threat of nuclear blackmail, there would be no option but surrender.

43. Labour's defence policy – though 'defence' is scarcely the word – is an absolute break with the defence policy of every British government since the Second World War. Let there be no doubt about the gravity of that decision. You can't be a loyal member of NATO while disavowing its fundamental strategy. [Applause.] A Labour Britain would be a neutralist Britain. It would be the greatest gain for the Soviet Union in forty years. And they would have got it without firing a shot.

44. I believe that this total reversal of Labour's policy for the defence of our country will have come as a shock to many of Labour's traditional supporters. It was Labour's Nye Bevan who warned his party against going naked into the conference chamber. It was Labour's Hugh Gaitskell who promised the country to fight and fight and fight again against the unilateral disarmers in his own party. That fight was continued by his successors.

45. Today the fight is over because the present leadership *are* the unilateral disarmers. The Labour Party of Attlee, of Gaitskell, and of Wilson is dead. And no one has more surely killed it than the present leader of the Labour Party.

46. There are some policies which can be reversed. But weapon development and production takes years and years. Moreover by repudiating NATO's nuclear strategy Labour would fatally weaken the Atlantic Alliance and the United States' commitment to Europe's defence caused [sic] by Labour's policies would be irrevocable. Not only present but future generations would be at risk.

47. Of course there are fears about the terrible destructive power of nuclear weapons. But it is the balance of nuclear forces which has preserved peace for forty years in a Europe which twice in the previous thirty years tore itself to pieces, the nuclear balance which has preserved peace not only from nuclear war, but from conventional war in Europe as well. And it has saved the young people of two generations from being called up to fight as their parents and grandparents were.

48. As Prime Minister, I could not remove that protection from the lives of present and future generations. [Applause.]

49. Let every nation know that Conservative government, now and in the future, will keep Britain's obligations to its allies. The freedom of all its citizens and the good name of our country depend upon it.

50. This weekend, President Reagan and Mr Gorbachev are meeting in Reykjavik. Does anyone imagine that Mr Gorbachev would be prepared to talk at all if the West had already disarmed? It is the strength and unity of the West which has brought the Russians to the negotiating table. The policy of Her Majesty's Opposition is a policy that would help our enemies and harm our friends. I believe it totally misjudges the character of the British people.

51. After the Liberal Party Conference, after the SDP Conference, after the Labour Party Conference, there is now only one party in this country with an effective policy for the defence of the realm, and that party is the Conservative Party.

52. Mr President, throughout this conference we have heard of the great achievements of the last seven years. Their very success now makes possible the next moves forward, which have been set out this week. And we shall complete the manifesto for the next election [Pause] within the next eighteen months. [Laughter. Applause.]

53. That manifesto will be a programme for further bold and radical steps in keeping with our most deeply-held beliefs. For we do our best for our country when we are true to our convictions.

54. As we look forward to the next century, we have a vision of the society we wish to see. The vision we all serve.

55. We want to see a Britain where there is an ever-widening spread of ownership, with the independence and dignity it brings, a Britain which takes care of the weak in their time of need. We want to see a Britain where the spirit of enterprise is strong enough to conquer unemployment North and South, a Britain in which the attitude of

'them and us' has disappeared from our lives. We want to see a Britain whose schools are a source of pride and where education brings out the best in every child. A Britain where excellence and effort are valued and honoured. We want to see a Britain where our streets are free from fear, day and night. And above all, we want to see a Britain which is respected and trusted in the world, which values the great benefits of living in a free society, and is determined to defend them.

56. Mr President, our duty is to safeguard our country's interests, and to be reliable friends and allies. The failure of the other parties to measure up to what is needed places an awesome responsibility upon us.

57. I believe that we have an historic duty to discharge that responsibility and to carry into the future all that is best and unique in Britain.

58. I believe that our party is uniquely equipped to do it.

59. I believe the interests of Britain can now only be served by a third Conservative victory.

Notes

1 Introduction
Political Leadership and British Political Culture

1. Because of the very different political and cultural circumstances pertaining, I have excluded Northern Ireland from this study. Many of the issues discussed are common to mainland Britain and the province. Over and above the political situation, however, both the cultural and especially rhetorical conditions of Irish political life set Northern Ireland apart.

2. This popularity often applies to ex-politicians, although their resurrection, or belated popularity, begs the question concerning *potential* popularity. Cases in point are the popularity and influence of ex-leaders such as Wilson, Callaghan, Grimond, and Macmillan and the even less likely figures of influence such as ex-trade union or TUC leaders.

3. Political manifestos always involve myths concerning justice, fairness, compromise and so on, as well as issues of practicality. Also, they never involve reference to individuals.

4. It is interesting to note that protest movements against industrial decline or against a proposed motorway invariably, irrespective of political colour, draw upon the political discursive resource of a threat to the well-being of a community, and portray this latter as sacrosanct.

5. In the context of the discussion of the role of Northern Ireland, the idea of using plastic bullets 'on mainland Britain' is considered anathema, and throws into relief the mythical role the province has come to play in British political culture.

6. If we take as examples the various responses to the IRA, Bobby Sands, the British police, Westminster, Blacks, the SAS, Ian Paisley, Whitehall, trade unions, the nurses, social workers, Enoch Powell, what is significant about them all is that they trigger strong political passions.

7. The population is often referred to in unitarist terms as the silent majority, the vast majority of the British people, all decent people, the nation and so on.

8. This tapping of the idea of a people who wish to go about their business is one of the major rhetorical devices of Margaret Thatcher.

9. For an interesting discussion of this see, *inter alia*, A. Pizzorno, 'On the Rationality of Democratic Choice', in P. Birnbaum and J. Leca (eds), *Individualism* (Oxford: Clarendon Press, 1990).

10. Walk-abouts where security guards are momentarily left behind, chat shows, the revelation of personal likes and dislikes, concerned attention to what someone has to say, are all demonstrations of politicians' continuing relationship to the rest of the population.

11. The apparently mesmerising effect that Margaret Thatcher has

upon interviewers and the implications of this concerning her personality are a very good illustration of this idea of the apparent character traits of politicians.

12. Michael Foot and Shirley Williams are recent examples of figures whose apparent concerned niceness dominated their effectiveness. This idea of concern can, however, work to advantage; Margaret Thatcher, unlike Edward Heath, flattered her MPs by always knowing their names, personal circumstances and so on.

13. Interestingly, one of the most effective instruments affecting the public's knowledge of 'how politics work at the top' was the highly popular television series, 'Yes, Minister'.

14. Williams has argued that the Labour Party sports three possible leadership types, the Pathfinder (for example, Gaitskell), the Problem-solver (for example, Wilson) and the Stabiliser (for example, Attlee). See P. Williams, 'Changing Styles of Labour Leadership', in D. Kavanagh (ed.), *The Politics of the Labour Party* (London: Allen and Unwin, 1982).

15. There seems, however, to be a critical phase where media over-exposure and attacks begin to affect negatively the standing of leaders, second-rank leaders, and sectional leaders within organisations, and to move organisational opinion closer to outside opinion.

16. It is, however, not surprising how quickly political procedure is accepted when people become involved in an organisation like the WVS or a school PTA, and how a respect for procedure, however elaborate, becomes cherished by those who participate.

17. This happens at all levels of political organisations, moreover, with local branches of the Labour or Conservative Parties regarding Walworth Road or Central Office, respectively, as overbearing in their use of central authority.

18. This happened to Neil Kinnock in August 1988 when his popularity declined as that of the Labour Party increased until the party was apparently better liked than its leader.

19. Michel Rocard in France is a very good example of a politician who, unloved by a majority in his party, was nevertheless able to exert an influence upon it via public opinion and become Prime Minister.

20. In the context of our analysis, Neil Kinnock's use of a public occasion, the 1985 Labour Party conference, to undermine the Militant Tendency is a very good illustration of this phenomenon.

21. This idea of former rogues who have become great leaders is surely related to ideas in British culture concerning such figures as Henry V and Thomas à Becket.

22. Part of the problem of properly understanding the nature of political leadership is that it is a generally-held view that debased ideas such as 'charisma' are uncontentious and understood by all, especially by political journalists with access to the mass media.

23. We should perhaps stress the obvious here: that (visual) image plus what politicians *say* are the only really known factors in any assessment by the public of a politician's personality. In spite of the fact that most major politicians are household names, the assumed

'knowing' is a trick. It is the persona and not the person – whether or not the persona is an accurate representation of the person – which is known. We all presume a knowledge of Margaret Thatcher for example; the percentage of the population which has actually seen her, let alone met her, let alone knows her, even superficially, is extremely small.

24. This constraint is undoubtedly one of the reasons for the vociferousness of leadership contestation once it has the opportunity to express itself in a less public arena.

25. Such interventions have always been strictly controlled in the Conservative Party, and, since Neil Kinnock's leadership of the Labour Party, there too.

26. The backdrop for each of the leader's speeches in terms of colour, slogans, visual symbols (and the absence of people walking to and fro behind the speaker) is now designed with the television camera as much as the immediate audience in mind.

27. The conference fringe meeting is a good example of this dual control and enhancement where the leader can be the target for jokes while being simultaneously – especially if he or she is present – offered praise. The conference revues serve a similar function (especially in the Labour Party). These examples are like Saturnalia which, in fact, enhance the status of leaders in the moment they address them humoristically; they highlight the 'humanity' or ordinariness of leaders while marking out their difference. Such diminishing of leadership status ostensibly indicates that the party is aware of the issue of personalism. What is never directly addressed in these asides, fringe meetings and revues, however, is the question of the legitimacy of a particular form of leadership itself and its effect upon the party. It is as if the occurrence of these Saturnalian moments is sufficient indication of the parties' freedom from leadership domination. A second means of resolving this control/ enhancement duality in leadership is the momentary withdrawal by the conference of the solemn status it confers upon itself. This involves, essentially, the 'lightening' of the seriousness of the conference-as-event; jokes, asides, and occasional accidents (with microphones and so on, or the non-appearance of people) all contribute to this. Such humour has the effect of endowing the audience with a non-organisational or 'human' quality. This humoristic element in the conference is, in fact, invariably exploited in leadership discourse.

28. The speeches analysed, included as appendices at the back of the volume, are the verbatim speeches and not the official published ones, which often differ widely from what was actually said. Unless of particular significance, I have omitted from both the appendices and the quotations usual interruptions such as laughter and applause, except where the sense of an utterance (repetition, for example, or its humorous effect) would not be clear. In Margaret Thatcher's 37-minute speech, for example, there were 51 interruptions for applause. For convenience the speeches have been given

paragraph numbers, and these appear in brackets after quotations in the text. Also, for convenience, we shall refer to all the occasions as conferences, even though the Liberal Conference is officially called an Assembly, the SDP conference a Council. Similarly, we shall refer to the 'representatives', 'delegates' and 'council members' and so on as delegates.

2   David Owen and Social Democracy

1. The gang of four were joined by 12 sitting Labour MPs, one Conservative (Christopher Brocklebank-Fowler), and 22 peers.
2. This idea of sacrifice is reminiscent of John Kennedy's 'Do not ask what your country can do for you, but what you can do for your country' speech.

5   Margaret Thatcher and the Conservative Tradition

1. It is interesting to note that Peter Riddell's authoritative account of the Thatcher years up to the mid-1980s (see bibliography) is typical of the dominant view that the second Conservative term – to end in 1987 – saw Thatcherism drawing to a close.
2. Margaret Tebbit had been severely injured in the Brighton bombing and, during Margaret Thatcher's 1986 speech, sat behind her in a wheelchair.
3. Ironically, perhaps, Chamberlain is the British Prime Minister who resembles Margaret Thatcher more than any other, in terms of attitudes and style.

Bibliography

L. Abse, *Margaret, Daughter of Beatrice* (London: Cape, 1989).

B. Arnold, *Margaret Thatcher. A Study in Power* (London: Hamish Hamilton, 1984).

M. Atkinson, *Our Masters' Voices* (London: Methuen, 1984).

A. Ball, *British Political Parties* (London: Macmillan, 1981).

A. Barker, *Public Participation in Britain* (London: Bedford Square Press, 1979).

R. Barker, *Political Ideas in Modern Britain* (London: Methuen, 1978).

P. Bartram, *David Steel. His Life and Politics* (London: W. H. Allen, 1981).

J. Bean, *The Political Culture of Modern Britain* (London: Hamish Hamilton, 1987).

R. Behrens, *The Conservative Party from Heath to Thatcher* (Farnborough: Saxon House, 1980).

D. Bell (ed.), *The Conservative Government 1979–1984* (London: Croom Helm, 1985).

T. Benn, *Arguments for Socialism* (Harmondsworth: Penguin, 1980).

A. Bevan, *In Place of Fear* (London: MacGibbon and Kee, 1961).

P. Birnbaum, and J. Leca (eds), *Individualism* (Oxford: Clarendon Press, 1990).

V. Bogdanor (ed.), *Liberal Party Politics* (Oxford: Clarendon Press, 1983).

R. Boyson, *Centre Forward* (London: Temple Smith, 1978).

I. Bradley, *Breaking the Mould? The Birth and Prospects of the Social Democratic Party* (Oxford: Martin Robertson, 1981).

J. Burrel (ed.), *Democracy and Accountability in the Labour Party* (Nottingham: Spokesman, 1980).

B. Campbell, *The Iron Ladies. Why do Women vote Tory?* (London: Virago, 1987).

J. Clemens, *Polls, Politics and Population* (Aldershot: Gower, 1983).

K. Coates, *Democracy in the Labour Party* (Nottingham: Spokesman, 1977).

M. Cockerell, *Live from Number 10* (London: Faber and Faber, 1988).

Conservative Research Department, *The Campaign Guide 1987* (London: Conservative and Unionist Central Office, 1987).

C. Cook, *A Short History of the Liberal Party* (London: Macmillan, 1989).

P. Cosgrave, *A Tory and her Party* (London: Hutchinson, 1978).

P. Cosgrave, *Thatcher. The First Term* (London: Bodley Head, 1985).

A. Crosland, *Socialism Now and other essays* (London: Jonathan Cape, 1975).

J. Curran (ed.), *The Future of the Left* (Cambridge: Polity, 1984).

A. Cyr, *Liberal Party Politics in Britain* (London: Calder, 1977).

E. Deakins, *What Future for Labour?* (London: Shipman, 1988).

G. Drower, *Neil Kinnock. The Path to Leadership* (London: Weidenfeld and Nicolson, 1984).

H. Drucker, *Doctrine and Ethos in the Labour Party* (London: Allen and Unwin, 1979).

P. Dunleavy, *British Democracy at the Crossroads* (London: Allen and Unwin, 1985).

N. Fisher, *The Tory Leaders. Their Struggle for Power* (London: Weidenfeld and Nicolson, 1977).

T. Forester, *The Labour Party and the Working Class* (London: Heinemann, 1976).

A. Freeman, *The Benn Heresy* (London: Pluto, 1982).

D. Green, *The New Right* (Brighton: Wheatsheaf, 1987).

S. Hall and M. Jacques, *The Politics of Thatcherism* (London: Lawrence and Wishart, 1983).

K. Harris, *David Owen. Personally Speaking with Kenneth Harris* (London: Weidenfeld and Nicolson, 1987).

R. Harris, *The Making of Neil Kinnock* (London: Faber, 1984).

S. Haseler, *The Tragedy of Labour* (Oxford: Blackwell, 1980).

H. Himmelweit *et al.*, *How Voters Decide* (New York: Academic Press, 1981).

M. Holmes, *The First Thatcher Government 1979–1983* (Brighton: Wheatsheaf, 1985).

S. Ingle, *The British Party System* (Oxford: Blackwell, 1989).

K. H. Jamieson, *Eloquence in an Electronic Age* (New York and Oxford: Oxford University Press, 1988).

H. Jenkins, *Rank and File* (London: Croom Helm, 1980).

D. Kavanagh and P. Morris, *Consensus Politics from Attlee to Thatcher* (Oxford: Blackwell, 1988).

W. Kennet, *The Rebirth of Britain* (London: Weidenfeld and Nicolson, 1982).

D. King, *The New Right: Politics, Markets and Citizenship* (London: Macmillan, 1987).

D. Kogan and M. Kogan, *The Battle for the Labour Party* (London: Kogan Page, 1982).

Z. Layton-Henry (ed.), *Conservative Party Politics* (London: Macmillan, 1980).

Z. Layton-Henry (ed.), *Conservative Politics in Western Europe* (London: Macmillan, 1982).

M. Leapman, *Kinnock* (London: Unwin Hyman, 1987).

R. Lewis, *Margaret Thatcher: A Personal and Political Biography* (London: Routledge & Kegan Paul, 1983).

D. Lloyd Thomas, *In Defence of Liberalism* (Oxford: Blackwell, 1988).

D. Marquand, *The Case for Coalition* (The Liberal Publication Department, 1981).

A. Marwick, *Class: Image and Reality in Britain, France and the USA since 1930* (London: Collins, 1980).

A. Marwick, *The Explosion of British Society 1914–1970* (London: Pan Books, 1971).

L. Minkin, *The Labour Party Conference* (Manchester: Manchester University Press, 1978 (and 1980)).

K. Morgan, *Labour People. Hardie to Kinnock* (Oxford: Oxford University Press, 1987).

P. Murray, *Margaret Thatcher* (London: W. H. Allen, 1980).

R. Nisbet, *Conservatism: Dream and Reality* (Milton Keynes: Open University Press, 1986).

E. Nordlinger, *The Working-Class Tories* (London: MacGibbon and Kee, 1967).

P. Norton and A. Aughey, *Conservatives and Conservatism* (London: Temple Smith, 1981).

N. Nugent and R. King, *The British Right* (Farnborough: Saxon House, 1977).

N. O'Sullivan, *Conservatism* (London: Dent and Sons, 1976).

D. Owen, *Face the Future* (London: Cape, 1981).

D. Owen, *A Future that Will Work* (Harmondsworth: Penguin, 1984).

W. Paterson and A. Thomas (eds), *The Future of Social Democracy in Europe* (Oxford: Clarendon Press, 1986).

J. Enoch Powell, *Still to Decide* (London: Batsford, 1972).

R. Punnett, *British Government and Politics (5th ed.)* (Aldershot: Gower, 1987).

R. D. Putnam, *The Beliefs of Politicians* (New Haven and London: Yale University Press, 1973).

P. Riddell, *The Thatcher Government* (Oxford: Blackwell, 1985).

R. Rose, *Do Parties Persist or Disappear?* (Strathclyde: CSPP No. 134, 1984).

J. Ross, *Thatcher and Friends* (London: Pluto, 1983).

J. Saville, *The Labour Movement in Britain* (London: Faber, 1988).

R. Scruton, *The Meaning of Conservatism (2nd ed.)* (London: Macmillan, 1984).

M. Shapiro (ed.), *Language and Politics* (Oxford: Blackwell, 1984).

E. Shaw, *Discipline and Discord in the Labour Party* (Manchester: Manchester University Press, 1988).

R. Skidelsky (ed.), *Thatcherism* (London: Chatto and Windus, 1988).

M. Thatcher, *In Defence of Freedom* (London: Aurum Press, 1986).

M. Thatcher, *Let Our Children Grow Tall. Selected Speeches 1975–1979* (London: Centre for Policy Studies, 1977).

N. Tracy, *The Origins of the SDP* (London: Croom Helm, 1983).

R. Tyler, *Campaign. The Selling of the Prime Minister* (London: Grafton, 1987).

H. Wainwright, *Labour, A Tale of Two Parties* (London: Hogarth Press, 1987).

West European Politics, *Party Politics in Western Europe* (London: Cass, 1984).

P. Whitley, *The Labour Party in Crisis* (London: Methuen, 1983).

Index

admiration, 3, 5
affection, 3, 7
Afghanistan, 141
allegiance, 2, 3, 6, 7, 20, 23, 56, 58,
    89, 90, 99, 132, 133, 195
Alliance, 14, 18, 23, 24, 35, 38, 39,
    40, 45, 47, 48, 56, 58, 60, 61, 62,
    65, 66, 69, 70, 71, 72, 75, 76, 78,
    79, 80, 81, 82, 83, 84, 86, 87, 92,
    95, 97, 98, 112, 131, 145, 160,
    161, 177, 182, 186, 187, 188, 192,
    195
'Any Questions', 8, 43
apartheid, 55, 96, 141
apoliticism, 2
Archbishop Tutu, 142
Archer, Jeffrey, 131
Armada, 81
Ashdown, Paddy, 11, 63
attitudes, 3, 10, 14, 96, 247
Attlee, Clement, 10, 178, 182, 245
audience, 23, 30–43, 53, 54, 60, 64,
    65, 67, 68, 70, 71, 73, 75, 76, 78,
    81, 86, 87, 88, 89, 90, 91, 97, 99,
    118, 129, 130, 138, 144, 157, 179,
    185, 191, 246
Australia, 2

Barrow-in-Furness, 180
Beckett, Thomas à, 245
Benn, Tony, 7, 15, 102, 108, 190
Bevan, Nye, 7, 182
Biffen, John, 93
Birnbaum, P., 244
Black (Blacks), 84, 86, 107, 244
Black rioters, 5
Blake, William, 113
Blunkett, David, 7
BMA (British Medical Association),
    166
Boer War, 42
Brandt, Willy, 106
Brighton, 179, 181, 247
British Airports, 172

British Airways, 172
British Coal, 115
British Enterprise holding
    company, 137
British Gas, 172
British Investment Bank, 137
British Leyland, 150
British Telecom, 151, 152
Brocklebank-Fowler, Christopher,
    247
Brown, George, 9
bureaucracy, 7, 153
'business culture', 152
businesspeople, 4
by-elections, 8, 23, 69, 70, 98

Cabinet, 7, 8, 43, 86, 150
Callaghan, Jim, 109, 244
Cape Town, 96
capital repatriation scheme, 137
'Cathy Come Home', 95
Ceaucescu, Nikolai, 149
Chamberlain, Neville, 176, 247
Chancellor of the exchequer, 26,
    92, 154
charisma, 10, 19, 245
Chernobyl, 73, 143, 144
children, 5, 36, 55, 82, 86, 117, 118,
    119, 121, 128, 135, 138, 162, 165,
    167, 180, 184
China, 172
Churchill, Winston, 7, 156
Churchillian, 145
Clarke, Kenneth, 43
class, 3, 50, 52, 54, 118, 134, 135
Commonwealth, 84, 150
community (communities), 4, 5, 6,
    7, 8, 10, 29, 36, 46, 50, 57, 59, 63,
    65, 66, 72, 124, 136, 244
Conservative Central Office, 154,
    245
Conservative Party (Conservatives,
    Conservatism, Tory, Tories,
    Tory Party), 1, 13, 15, 16, 19, 24,